INSIGHT GUIDES

BAHAMAS

Directed and Designed by Hans Höfer
Edited by Sara Whittier
Photography by Ping Amranand and others
Updated by Grey Gundaker

APA
PUBLICATIONS

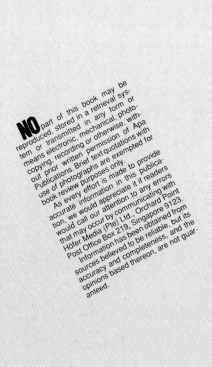
BAHAMAS

Third Edition
© **1990 APA PUBLICATIONS (HK) LTD**
All Rights Reserved
Printed in Singapore by Höfer Press Pte. Ltd

ABOUT THIS BOOK

Slung like a chain of pearls upon a turquoise sea, the Bahama Islands are made for dreaming. Somnolent and sun-drenched in a sparkling sea, the Bahamas possess an irresistable allure and a tapestry of many cultures.

This is the stuff of Insight Guides, a unique series of travel books published by Apa Publications of Singapore. Founded by **Hans Höfer**, Apa publishes a unique kind of guide book that gives an in-depth survey of the culture and history of each subject destination. Based on a formula Höfer developed in his first book, *Insight Guide: Bali*, published in 1970, this series not only emphasizes outstanding writing and great photography but also clear, objective journalism. Höfer, a native of West Germany, was trained in the Bauhaus tradition which combines the disciplines of printing, book design and photography.

A Talented Team

For *Insight Guide: Bahamas*, Höfer designated as project editor **Sara Whittier**, an editor and writer with experience at the U.S. publisher Simon & Schuster, to edit the book and to orchestrate the efforts of writers and photographers she engaged for the project. She has written for and edited the travel periodical *Chevron USA* and edited a guide to U.S. national parks.

Also at the top of Höfer's list was **Ping Amranand**, a gifted photographer who captured the brilliant colors of the Bahamian seas and scenery and the varied faces of the Bahamians. Amranand has published his photography in several publications in Asia and America. Amranand and his assistant, **Andrew Ammerman** traveled to a dozen islands and shot over 4,500 pictures for the book.

Gail Saunders, a noted Bahamian historian, wrote the difficult and important chapters on New Providence Island and the town of Nassau—the place that has been the hub of the Bahamas for over 300 years. Saunders was born in Nassau, educated in England and at the University of the West Indies. She has published a number of books including *Bahamian Loyalists And Their Slaves* and (with Donald Cartwright) *Historic Nassau*. She is the Director of the Department of Archives in Nassau.

Jonathan Ramsay of Nassau made available dozens of antique maps and prints from his personal collection and his Nassau shop, Balmain Antiques, to illustrate *Bahamas*. These were expertly photographed by Nassau photographer **Antoine Ferrier**. Ramsay is technical advisor to the Nassau Public Library on the restoration of artifacts, Vice President of Eurodutch Trust Co. Ltd. (Bahamas) and the author of a regular column in *The Nassau Guardian*. He wrote the feature "Hooked on Fishing."

Peter Barratt wrote the chapters on Grand Bahama and the city of Freeport. An architect, he has lived in Grand Bahama for 22 years, was the town planner of Freeport for 14 years, and designed the Grand Bahama Museum and Lucayan National Park. He has written a full-length history on *Grand Bahama*.

The other writers of the "Places" chapters included **Fred Sturrup,** Anthony Forbes, Donald Gerace and Rod Attrill. Sturrup, a veteran journalist in the Bahamas, is Director of Advertising and Marketing for *The Nassau Guardian*. He wrote the chapters on several key Family Islands: Eleuthera, Harbour Island, Spanish Wells, the Abacos and the Exumas.

Anthony Forbes wrote the chapter on Andros. Born in Deep Creek, South Andros, he was educated at Queen's College in Nassau and has been covering the Bahamian political scene for *The Tribune* since 1975.

Dr. Donald Gerace wrote about the island of San Salvador. In 1971 he set up a field station for the College of the Finger Lakes which has become a mecca for marine biolo-

Whittier

Amranand

Saunders

Ammerman

gists and archaeologists who conduct research on the island.

Rod Attrill, a naturalist, wrote the chapter on the remote Southern Islands—Inagua, Mayaguana, Acklins, Crooked Island and the nearby cays. He was Executive Director of the Bahamas National Trust, editor of the periodical *Bahamas Naturalist* for several years, and a teacher of ecology and natural science at the College of the Bahamas.

Dr. Timothy McCartney, a clinical psychologist, wrote "The Bahamians," about the complex racial and social makeup of the country. In "Obeah, Superstition and Folklore," he introduces the reader to the Bahamas' time-honored link with the occult and the colorful Junkanoo parade.

Support Staff

Writer-photographer **Deborah Williams** from upstate New York, has been scuba-diving in the Bahamas for nine years. She wrote the sections on "The Underwater Bahamas" and "Luxurious Lifestyles."

The Travel Tips was prepared with great diligence and care by writer-filmmaker **Holly Henke**. She has worked for independent film producers and for the University of California Press.

M.A.V.B. Whittier, an art historian who specializes in the world of the 15th and 16th centuries, wrote the box feature on Columbus for the history section.

Bahamas owes its spectacular photography not only to Ping Amranand, but to several photographers with a long association with the Bahamas, especially **Stanley Toogood**, **Stephen Frink** and **Bob Krist**. Toogood provided photos of the Duke and Duchess of Windsor for this volume.

Frink, a Florida-based photographer, was the photographer for "The Underwater Bahamas" chapter. He is vice president and a contributing photographer to The Waterhouse, Inc., in Key Largo, Florida, a photo agency.

Krist, who has traveled extensively in the Bahamas, provided invaluable pictures of the islands Inagua and San Salvador.

Kathy Pursel, a California-based photographer, shot pictures of Long Island and Cat Island. Also contributing photos were **Susan Pierres** and **Maxine Cass**, both of whom have published work in other *Insight Guides*. The London agency Tony Stone Worldwide also contributed photos.

June Maura, president of the Bahamas Historical Society, made available for reproduction prints and photographs from the society's collection. Bahamian artist R. Brent Malone permitted one of his colorful Junkanoo-inspired paintings to appear in the book. Amos Ferguson and his wife Bea consented to be photographed, along with one of Mr. Ferguson's distinctive paintings.

Many thanks are also due to the Bahamas News Bureau, which provided many photographs. Basil Smith, Eileen Fielder and Patricia Kenney of the news bureau provided invaluable advice and gave assistance in travel arrangements.

Clement Bethel, Paul Albury, Frances Armbrister and James Traillhill deserve great appreciation for their insights and information.

Thanks also go to: the officials and employees of the Bahamas Ministry of Tourism, *The Tribune*, Bimini Big Game Fishing Club, Cable Beach Hotel, Chalk's International Airlines, Conch Inn, Fernandez Bay Village Resort, Grand Hotel, Lyford Cay Club, Nassau Beach Hotel, Peace-N-Plenty Hotel, Silver Sands Hotel, Small Hope Bay Lodge, Stella Maris Inn and Treasure Cay Beach Hotel.

The cartography team at Nelles Verlag GmbH, Munich, drew the maps.

-Apa Publications

Gerace

Barratt

Sturrup

Forbes

HISTORY AND HERITAGE

TRAVEL TIPS

WELCOME TO THE BAHAMAS

Look from your door, and tell me now
The colour of the sea.
Where can I buy that wondrous dye
And take it home with me?

— *Bliss Carman*

Bliss Carman is not the name of a rock group, but of a 19th-century poet who visited the Bahamas and memorialized it in enthusiastic verse. But the Beatles did vacation here, as have Richard Nixon, Winston Churchill, and many other, less celebrated, souls. In the 17th Century the Spanish called the archipelago a "receptacle for all rogues", but the first visitor – Christopher Columbus – wrote that "there came from the land the scent of flowers or trees, so delicious and sweet, that it was the most delightful thing in the world." The Bahamas is a nation that can seem as simple as "that wondrous dye", but that in reality is as complex, thorny and full of life as the many coral reefs that lie beneath its shallow sea.

The country's history (which began as the Lucayan Indians, pursued by the bloodthirsty Caribs, migrated north from the Greater Antilles, then burst into worldwide prominence with a sailor's cry, *"Tierra, tierra!"* from the *Pinta* in 1492) is a good place to begin. Forming a wide chain between the south coast of Florida and Cap-Haitien, Haiti, the Bahama islands lie at the crossroads of what for several centuries was one of the hubs of the world. Piracy, slavery, revolution, religion, smuggling and independence have all made their marks. And they have brought to the Bahamas an immensely diverse population.

Expatriates, descendants of freed Africans, of slaves and of plantation owners, and over 3 million visitors per year share the Bahamas. Some call the country "confused", but in this guide's People section you will find an attempt to make some sense of it.

Finally, of course, there are the sights themselves — the "undiscovered" coves everyone knows about, and the ones nobody does; blue holes; sunken ships; homes with limestone walls or wide verandahs or tin roofs; bright Junkanoo masks; pink stucco schools and white churches. The Places and Features sections will introduce you to these sights and sounds — in some depth or with a tantalizing glimpse — and whet your appetite to explore.

So take to heart the words of Columbus when, following his first voyage, he wrote to "Your Highnesses [who] have sent me to explore both the sea and the land." Entranced by the many marvels and wondrous things, he concluded "even the singing of little birds is such that a man could never wish to leave this place."

INSVLÆ AMERICANÆ
IN OCEANO SEPTENTRIONALI,
cum Terris adiacentibus.

FLORIDA.

NOVÆ HISPANIÆ PARS.

Golfo De Mexico.

YVCATAN.

CVBA.

HONDVRAS.

NICARAGVA.

MAR DEL ZVR.

Ampl.mo Prud.mo Doct.mo Viro
D. ALBERTO CONRADI VANDER BVRCH,
I.C. Reip. Amstelredamensis Senatori, Collegii
Scabinorum Præsidi, Societatis Indicæ, quæ
ad Occidentem militat aßeßori, et nuper
ad Magnum Moscoviæ Ducem Legato,
Tabulam hanc inscribit Guilielmus Blaeuw.

THE PEACEFUL LUCAYANS

It is customary to speak of Columbus as the discoverer of the New World, though this of course is not true. When Columbus and his crew struck land on Oct. 12th, 1492, one of the first things they found was that there were already plenty of human beings living there. The Lucayans, the tribe of New World Indians who inhabited most of what we now call the Bahamas, were no newcomers to the area either. They had been in the Bahamas for somewhat longer than 500 years, and it is one of the great shames of European history that they would only last out another 25.

The Lucayans were, by the few accounts that exist from the time, a peaceful, graceful, docile people. They went about naked or with only a small cotton cloth hanging from their waists, they adorned themselves with paint and earrings, and they lived in huts covered with palm fronds. They introduced to the Western world the hammock. Believing that broad foreheads were a sign of beauty, they practiced the ritual flattening of them.

Having only rudimentary tools, they lived primarily off the sea. They were skillful fishermen and expertly paddled the long and dangerous distances between islands in large ocean going canoes.

Their diet was much like that of the modern Bahamian in so far as the sea was concerned – several local fish and a great deal of conch, still the mainstay of Bahamian cuisine. They also made bread from the roots of local plants and practiced some primitive agriculture.

Where the Lucayans came from is open to dispute, as are the origins of most of the tribes that spread out across the Caribbean in early modern history. The most often mentioned hypothesis is that the Lucayans originated on the northern coast of South America, the Spanish Main, but fled north farther and farther before the deadly attacks of the cannibalistic Caribs. Though the Lucayans possessed spears, bows and arrows, they were not warriors and not adept at using them for defense. Down to the time of Columbus' voyage, the Caribs continued to launch small devastating forays against the peaceful Lucayans.

But whatever damage the Lucayans may have suffered at the hands of the Caribs was paltry compared to what lay ahead that long-ago October. When the Spanish arrived, the innocent Lucayans greeted them as gods, perhaps mistaking their complicated clothing and light skin for some figure from their mythology. They offered the Spanish all kinds of gifts, and Columbus reported that "They are so ingenuous and free with all they have that no one would believe it who has not seen it. Of anything they possess, if it be asked of them, they will never say, 'No.' On the contrary, they invite you to share it and show as much love as if their hearts went with it." Yet the Spanish in their hurried exploration had no time to dawdle – the small, mostly barren island was not what they had come for.

In fact, it was not for several years that the fate of the Lucayans was sealed, and primarily by the accident of being too close to the island of Hispaniola, which comprises present-day Haiti and the Dominican Republic.

Cruelly Enslaved: The Spanish, in their crazed search for gold, had established mines on that large island (much to the disappointment of the Spanish, there was no gold at all in the Bahamas). Quickly, they worked the native Taino tribe of the island to exhaustion, and, panicking as their labor force dropped dead at a remarkable rate, hit upon the idea of transporting Lucayans to take the Tainos' place.

Whether the Lucayans understood what was happening is not certain. Some resisted rather than permit themselves to be led away to the boats. A great many died on the sea crossing; their bodies must have floated on the water like a macabre guide to the route to Hispaniola. Many others perished from European diseases against which they had no protection, the rest died from homesickness and overwork in the mines. Within 25 years, the Lucayans–once perhaps 40,000 strong–were gone.

But their disappearance, though horrible, is but a small piece of the Spanish genocide in the New World. No one has any idea how many perished through similar circumstances from South America to Florida – the number is certainly in the millions – but few tribes were decimated as severely as the Bahamas' first residents.

By the early 1500s, the Spanish were searching in vain for additional Lucayans to enslave, and the Bahamas was left depopulated and neglected by its cruel and casual conquerors.

Preceding pages: hibiscus; a friendly Bahamian; cay in the Exumas; Bimini harbor; palmy twilight in George Town, Exuma; dock at Tarpum Bay, Eleuthera; a come-hither look on Green Turtle Cay; and the Caribbean circa 1660. Left, Lucayan hunters.

Engraved for Middleton's
Complete System of Geography

The first Interview of Christopher Columbus
with the Natives of America.

A New World: Discovery And Exploration

It is one of the most widely quoted facts that Columbus' discovery of the New World was an accident. When he spotted the island of San Salvador on a late evening of Oct. 12, 1492, he expected to find the East Indies, for he had come looking for a shorter route to the riches of China and the Far East. His none-too-minor error came from having had the right idea but the wrong dimensions. He knew, as did many of the intelligent men of his time, that the earth was round, but, unfortunately, he vastly underestimated how large it was. With our twenty-twenty hindsight, we can easily see that the shortest way to China from Spain is not by way of San Salvador.

But if history proceeds by mistakes, only a whopping big one like this could have had such an immense impact on the next five centuries.

A stubborn man, when Columbus found a tribe of nearly-naked Lucayans paddling out to him in their oversized canoes, he did not give up. He had simply found, by his reckoning, a barrier island—China was just around the corner.

Perhaps this explains the Spanish behavior on that first voyage to an utterly unknown world. Barely had the Lucayans had time to proffer gifts when Columbus and his weary crew weighed anchor again and set off on their search for the Chinese trade routes. They thought they were so close that in a matter of days they would succeed.

But it was not to be. The intrepid mariner and his crew bounced around the Northern Caribbean, touching on Rum Cay and Long Island which he named, respectively, Santa Maria de la Concepcion and Fernandina, after his royal patron. After only 15 days in the islands, the three ships swung down to Cuba, then to Hispaniola. Here the *Santa Maria* hit a reef and sunk. Several crew members were put ashore until they could be picked up on a future voyage. What went through their minds as they sat on a lonely volcanic island three thousand miles from home we'll never know, for when Columbus returned with a larger flotilla in September 1493, they were dead.

It seems very strange to us, looking back with our 20th Century eyes that the Spanish had so little sense of the immensity of what they had found, that they so pragmatically set about the

business of continuing the search for China, as if missing the significance of their discovery. Even taking into account how much of the world was a mystery to the Europeans of their day, it seems remarkable. But one explanation is that the Spanish were on a mission whose sole purpose was supposed to be economic. And the only economic purpose that might have made them halt in the Bahamas was gold—gold to trade, gold to carry away and gold to steal. But the Bahamas, being a mostly barren coral chain, has no gold at all. Sensible men of business, the Spanish kept on sailing. They would only

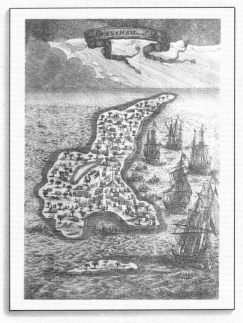

return to enslave the Lucayans and carry them off to Hispaniola, and only because they had found some gold there, even if little compared to the riches awaiting them in Central and South America. Yet this casual attempt, this sideshow in the race to exploit the New World, would wipe out several tribes from the face of the earth.

The Spanish attitude toward conquest—more like a sack than a political occupation—is extremely important to the history of the Bahamas, for once the islands were emptied of Amerindians, there was simply no reason to go there. While the exploration and despoliation of Mexico and Central America continued at a furious pace, the Spaniards completely forgot the islands they had first found.

Columbus gave trinkets to the Lucayans, as noted in an 18th Century engraving (left). San Salvador, where Europe met the New World, as depicted in *Descriptions d'Universe*, 1686 (right).

ADMIRAL OF THE OCEAN SEAS

Christopher Columbus set out to look for China with three small ships with a total crew of 90 and about 20 more "friends of the King" and their servants. There were no priests and no women on this voyage. There was a *Converso*, a Spanish Jew converted to Christianity, who was versed in Hebrew, Chaldean and Arabic to act as translator for people they might meet.

Colon, as he was known in Spain, had spent six years trying to get backing from King Ferdinand and Queen Isabella for his "enterprise of the Indies." By April 1492 they had granted Colon two armed caravels for two years "to go to certain parts of the Ocean Sea on some errands required of our service." By allying with the Pinzón family of Palos, Columbus saw that three boats were prepared. Daily rations per man were one pound biscuit, two thirds of a pound of meat and two liters of wine. They also carried cannon shot, stone and lead, also used for ballast, and trading items of beads, mirrors, little bells, pins and needles, and bonnets.

Martin Pinzón and his son Arias Perez Pinzón commanded the *Pinta* and the *Niña*, Colon the flagship *Santa Maria*. Calculating that he was at the latitude of Cipangu (Japan) and Cathy (China), Columbus sailed west using a compass for direction.

Tierra, Tierra: Ferdinand and Isabella had offered a bonus of 10,000 maravedis to the first person to sight land. When, after four weeks at sea, birds were sighted, the watch for land intensified. Finally, "Tierra, tierra!" rang out, and the New World was discovered by the Old. The sailor who first saw land was a simple man from Palos.

All three ships arrived at Guanahani (named by Columbus San Salvador) on Oct. 12, 1492. Imagine the natives watching these pale strangers come ashore in skiffs, then wondering as they dipped a feather in black juice to make marks. The natives wondered at the clothing and the "tails." These proved to be swords. The Spanish did not prevent the innocent Lucayans from grasping the swords. They recoiled with bleeding hands. The Spaniards gave gifts, and took possession of seven men.

The Lucayans complained that these visitors were no better than "Caniba," a fierce cannibalistic tribe to the south. "Caniba" meant Khan to Columbus, and when told that gold might be found in "Cubanacan" (Cuba-middle) he thought he heard "Kublai Khan." He ended up sending men to the interior of Cuba.

Martin Pinzón then took off in the *Pinta* in a frantic search for gold. The *Santa Maria*, meanwhile, ran aground on a reef on Christmas Day and sunk. The Indians used their mahogany canoes to rescue the crew and provisions. Columbus left 39 men in the Dominican Republic in a fort with provisions, and with assurances of their protection by chief Guacamagari.

The end of 1492 saw Columbus established on the *Niña*, preparing to sail east. He encountered Pinzón in the *Pinta*, admonished him for abusing natives and violating the rules for searching for gold, but spared his life.

The two caravels were separated by storms, but eventually Columbus landed at the Azores for repairs, at Lisbon to send word to Isabella and Ferdinand, and finally at Palos just a day before Pinzón. At the grand reception in Barcelona, natives with gold bracelets and parrots on their shoulders marched with the new "Admiral of the Ocean Seas." In this moment of honor, as he accepted a title and a cash reward of 335,000 maravedis, Columbus also claimed the 10,000 maravedi prize for the first man to sight land. The sailor who had first shouted "Tierra, tierra!" from the crow's nest left for Morocco, discouraged.

As a result, for more than a hundred years after the Spanish bumped into them, the Bahamas would remain deserted. During these years they would have no substantial history at all as they waited, patient and passive in the warming Caribbean sun.

Treasure Hunters: No one came, that is, except for the occasional ocean voyager, most of whom knew enough already to live in terror of the tricky currents, hidden shoals and shifting winds of the islands, a combination that would claim thousands of ships in the years to come.

The most colorful of the visitors to these waters was the peripatetic Ponce de Leon, that improbable figure of 16th Century Spanish history, who sailed through the islands in search of the fabled "fountain of youth." Like an extra in the wrong play, he wandered onto the

sighs of relief when the Bahamas was finally behind them and the open ocean lay ahead. Except, of course, for the dozens who didn't make it, and who, to this day, make the Bahamas a mecca for treasure hunters with visions of Spanish doubloons dancing in their heads.

Where were the British in all this, those eventual masters for three hundred years of the peaceful islands? Nowhere to be seen, for Spain was far ahead of England in formulating a policy toward the New World. English interest would only come about a hundred years later through the accident of the Puritan religious revolution. Those English who did visit the islands did so for private reasons, on slave-trading or privateering runs. English settlement in the New World didn't begin in earnest until the early 17th Century.

scene in 1513, explored several of the smaller islands including San Salvador, found the Gulf Stream, that fast-moving northern warm current, and cruised up the coast of Florida before bouncing back down to the Bahamas again. No fountain, no eternal youth.

Besides Ponce de Leon, other Spanish captains seem to have made a specialty of passing the islands by, their galleons laden with treasures on the way back to Spain. Certainly the treacherous reefs did little to increase their appetite for the islands, and they must have heaved many

"There is no better people in the world," wrote Columbus of the Lucayans who welcomed him (left). A 19th Century romantic interpretation of Columbus (above).

Strange as it may sound, until Charles I granted the islands to his Attorney General in 1629 — islands which he didn't really have to grant — as a throw-away with the Carolinas, the islands didn't belong to any one. Plenty of nationalities sailed through them — Spanish of course, British, French and Dutch — but none with an eye to conquest. And even after the English claimed the Bahamas, which they were to do on two more occasions before the idea caught on, they showed a remarkable lack of interest in pursuing and investigating the claim. Compared to the aggressive behavior of commercial England in India and elsewhere, the next hundred years stand as a monument to neglect, a neglect that determines a good portion of their history under the proprietary lords.

1629 1929
TO COMMEMORATE THE
GRANT OF THESE ISLANDS
BY HIS MAJESTY
KING CHARLES THE FIRST
TO SIR ROBERT HEATH
ATTORNEY GENERAL
OF ENGLAND ON THE
30ᵗʰ DAY OF OCTOBER
1629

PIRATES AND LORD PROPRIETORS

As time passed and the Caribbean grew more crowded, Britain finally woke up to the importance of the Bahamas, at least in a small way. In 1629, Charles I granted proprietary rights to all the land from the Carolinas to the Bahamas to his Attorney General, Sir Robert Heath. Proprietary rights seem to have counted for very little. Technically, they entitled Heath and his heirs to be tenants on the islands, with the Crown having a right to a healthy share of whatever Heath could produce there, which, in 1629, must not have been very much.

But it is one thing to claim a 600-mile-wide island group as yours and another thing to prove it. France, a mere four years later, gathered several of the already granted islands in a grant to a favorite of the King—with an equal lack of concrete results. And Charles I, caught in the growing seriousness of the Puritan revolt, must have thought very infrequently about his still-born claim to the islands. In fact, in 1649, he would lose his head, and Robert Heath, titular head of a good chunk of the New World, would flee to exile in France.

The same religious war that was to cost Charles I his head was to net the Bahamas its first permanent settlement. The basic religious dispute of the early 1600s in England was between the Anglican Church, founded by Henry VIII, which the King of England headed, and the Puritan Congregations, who acknowledged no higher power than the bible and God. While this may seem in retrospect extremely general grounds for a revolution, the various political divisions that resulted not only split England apart, but sent Puritans fleeing to colonize the New World from Plymouth Rock to Bermuda.

In Bermuda, meanwhile, the religious intolerance of the old world was already infecting the new. In the early 1600s Bermuda too split between supporters of the established church and Puritans. Matters came to a head, and it became clear to many Puritans that the time had come again to move on.

For the purpose of finding a suitable new home in the wide-open New World, the Puritans outfitted and sent off two ships. One disappeared without a trace and the other came back without success.

Unfazed, William Sayle, a Puritan former-governor of Bermuda, collected a party of brave settlers. After much fanfare, fund-raising and declarations of principle—including the guarantee of religious freedom and a proclamation of the intent to form a representative assembly in their new home, the Eleutherian Adventurers set out. Had their government succeeded, its assembly would have been by far the oldest in the New World.

Some 70 in all, mostly farmers and fishermen and many experienced in the travails of the New World undertook the journey; they had at least some idea of what they were up against

and what they were hoping to find. Not unlike the Puritans who landed at Plymouth Rock, Sayle's Eleutherian Adventurers dreamed of founding a perfect community in the eyes of God.

But the sea, that harsh backdrop to Bahamian history, was particularly cruel to the men and women aboard the *William*. Their main vessel struck a reef off the north coast of Eleuthera. One man was killed and all supplies lost as the boat sank. One can only imagine how they felt as their precious ocean-going boat and all their stores went down before their eyes. They were suddenly alone.

The settlers were not complete amateurs and they managed for the next few months to get by on the fish and fruit that the island threw

Beginning in 1629, the British laid claim to the Bahamas (left). Anthony Lord Ashley (right), was the most powerful and prominent of the six proprietors appointed in 1670.

their way. Still it was a desperate lot, and they must have prayed often for deliverance from their predicament. To this day there is a cave on North Eleuthera where the Adventurers are said to have gathered for prayer.

Sayle was both practical and religious, however, and he knew that death was just a matter of time if no effort were made to get new provisions. In the small boat that remained to the Adventurers, called a shallop, he and eight other men set out across the open seas for Jamestown, Virginia and their fellow Puritans. Miraculously, they arrived, and word of their distress prompted the residents to dispatch several boatloads of food and provisions.

But relief was only temporary, as the Puritans learned the lesson that Europeans would be learning over and over through the centuries: farming and the Bahamas don't mix. In contrast to the lush volcanic islands to the south, the Bahamas is made up of thin topsoil on a coral foundation, a dreadful base on which to try to develop agriculture. Try as they might to get their farming projects under way, they could not get the poor land to produce enough to subsist on.

After two years, little progress was made and many Puritans, religious dispute or not, began to ship back to Bermuda. Life was intolerably harsh in Eleuthera, which comes from the Greek word for "freedom"—freedom, alas, was not filling their stomachs. Other Puritans continued to come to their aid. Those of Massachusetts raised a large sum and dispatched it to the Bahamas. In gratitude, the Bahamian Puritans shipped back a great quantity of native wood, the money from which would be used in the construction of Harvard College.

Despite the solidarity, the experiment was continuing to fail. By 1657, even William Sayle had returned to Bermuda. Still, even if the dream was gone, the colony kept growing, attracting everyone from new Puritans to freed slaves in search of a home.

Sayle was not done with Bahamian history. During one of his tireless voyages on behalf of the colony, he sought refuge from a fierce storm in a particularly fine harbor. The island, which residents named in his honor, is today far better known as New Providence. Its main city is of course Nassau, the economic and political capital of the Bahamas.

Island Lords: At the same time that the Puritan Adventurers were fighting their battle against the unyielding elements, Charles II, restored to the British throne, was again granting proprietary rights to the Bahamas, this time to several powerful lords. Whether he forgot or chose to ignore the government of the Puritans is not clear.

These lords, cognizant of the value of their new possessions, moved quickly to appoint a governor to run the settlement that was beginning to grow in Nassau. The fine harbor and the slightly more productive soil was attracting a small number of settlers, including Bermudan Puritans apparently uneasy at the prospect of the battle for survival in Eleuthera. From this date on, Nassau became the focus of Bahamian history, assuming the central economic, cultural and political role, until Eleuthera and its tiny band of settlers was dwarfed into insignificance.

The governor the proprietary lords chose was Hugh Wentworth, who died on the way to his post from Barbados. With this none-too-reassuring start began the long and harried struggle of the British to find some way to rule the Bahamas. Whereas Eleuthera was started from high-minded principles of religious freedom,

Nassau seems to have been started with a complete lack of principle at all. While there were certainly some farmers and solid merchants in Nassau, the island from the very beginning was the home of the bad boys in town, shiftless and seedy residents who squabbled with each other, cheated the proprietary lords of their fair cut, and exiled, badgered and wore down one governor after another.

New Providence continued to grow throughout the 17th Century, despite a manifest lack of respect for law and government. And the low **A stone tower outside Nassau was said to have been used as a lookout by the notorious Blackbeard (above). Anne Bonny (right), another pirate, was a woman but no lady.**

road was apparently the best road, for Nassau quickly outstripped all the other islands together in importance and prosperity.

What exactly did the residents of Nassau and the other islands do for a living? What causes their disapprobation three centuries later?

There was farming of course, which seems to have provided only the most pious and diligent with anything resembling a livelihood. Time and again land would be abandoned and settlers would flee for home or to join the throngs of low-life in Nassau. For most, ways of earning a living were decidedly less honest.

The primary one, hard as it is to believe, was the salvaging of wrecked ships. Thousands of ships of all sizes went down in the tricky Bahamian waters, which through the 19th Century were ill-charted, subject to vicious wind and cur-

rents, and without adequate lighthouses. Time and again the word would pass around that this boat or that had run into a reef and the locals would set out to see what could be salvaged.

The laws governing this salvage operation, which would be known by the uncomforting name of "wrecking," provided for the collection, first and foremost, of survivors. Needless to say, the order was not always treated with the respect it deserved. In the rough world of the Caribbean wreckers, it can be assumed that not a few sailors were allowed to perish while coins, biscuits and rigging were saved. Stories have even come down of wreckers deliberately misplacing shore lights to lure hapless boats onto the rocks.

Rogues and Ruffians: Wrecking, when the boat is not yet in trouble, goes under the stiffer name of piracy, and Nassau more and more claimed its share of these ruffians. Much of the Caribbean at the time was like a pirate nation, with the black Jolly Roger flying over countless ships and whole towns succumbing to pirate anarchy. Much of the time this was true of Nassau, where the governor served at the pleasure of the town's rougher elements. Often the governor and the pirates seem to have hit it off well, and more than one governor went home a rich man as a result.

The pirates are the most colorful figures ever to step on the Bahamian stage, and if they did not last in force for very long, their mark is comparable to the cowboy in the American West. Many pirates — Edward Teach, a.k.a. Blackbeard, Mary Read and Anne Bonny (notorious women pirates) — were incomparably cruel and executions, murders, wholesale slaughters of captured crews and general heinous acts of mischief did occur. No doubt though, the average life of the pirate resembled that of any other seaman. Much of what we know of their life comes not from their own accounts, of which they left few, but from the talented romantic musings of Daniel Defoe, the author of *Robinson Crusoe,* a man whose imagination often got the better of his knowledge. In any case, the myth of the Caribbean pirate endures.

Piracy against the vessels of a hostile nation was, believe it or not, perfectly legal. Privateering, as it was called, was another major industry for Nassauvians. The several wars of this period — the War of the Spanish Succession, the War of Jenkins Ear — provided ample opportunity for the ambitious pirate to turn privateer and do himself and his country a favor by sacking gold-laden Spanish galleons on their way back to Spain.

All this wrecking and privateering predictably tried the patience of the Spaniards; they tried to recover their own wrecks, for privateering cost them a great deal of money. In reprisal, they sacked Nassau on four occasions in 25 years, burning it to the ground and causing its inhabitants — pirate and merchant alike — to flee.

But Nassau was just too good a thing to leave alone, and the town after each attack would fill again with its share of criminals, marginal men and solid citizens. Clearly something had to be done. The Lord Proprietors must have felt they weren't getting their fair share of the action, decent citizens were unable to walk the streets in safety, and the Spanish could waltz in at will.

What happened was the arrival of Woodes Rogers as the Royal Govenor of a Colony now under the direct control of the Crown.

RULE BRITANNIA!

The problems of governing the Bahamas must not have weighed too heavily on the King's ministers in the early 18th Century—England's possessions far outstripped its ability to govern them—but sooner or later the Crown had to come up with a solution. The solution was to make the Bahamas into a royal colony. A royal colony meant a royal governor, and a royal governor meant guns and forts.

The man selected to transform the Bahamas into a sedate seat for empire was Woodes Rogers, a salty veteran of innumerable European naval wars. To him the Bahamas owes

But the pirates were only one problem, the pesky Spaniards another. Rogers set about improving New Providence Island's still rudimentary fortifications, and the next time the Spanish sailed in, as part of yet another European war in 1720, a steady volley of cannon-balls convinced them they were not welcome. For the first time the Bahamas had actually repulsed an attack.

In the domestic arts, Rogers was, alas, far less successful. He poured all his own money into farming schemes that the unforgiving New Providence soil would have none of, and when

Gov.ᵗ Rogers & family

a great debt, so great that his own description of his tenure has become the motto of the nation: *Expulsis Piratis—Restituta Commercia* ("He expelled the pirates and restored commerce").

Naturally, when Rogers first arrived in 1718, the pirates were none too eager to be expelled. Rumors had reached the islands that the government meant business this time, and Rogers was renowned for his military skills, but after all Nassau was Nassau. Wisely, Rogers first offered pardons to the pirates, not least because he needed help in defending the islands against the Spaniards. When only *some* pirates accepted his offer, he sweetened the deal with a good bit of public hanging. The remaining pirates either fled or quickly turned law-abiding.

he was recalled to England, he was unceremoniously clapped into debtor's prison.

Besides cleaning up the pirates, Rogers also left one other lasting contribution. In 1729, he convoked an assembly of Bahamians. From that date on, the Assembly rarely missed a session, making it one of the longest continually meeting assemblies in the New World.

The contribution of the Assembly through the years was a decidedly mixed one. It quickly became the repository of local political power, often acting with more self-interest than wisdom. The Assembly began in opposition to the

Woodes Rogers, who expelled the pirates from Nassau, is seen above in a scene of domestic tranquility, and at right as sculpted in a fighting pose.

governor, and so it continued nearly to Independence in 1973. On issue after issue through the centuries, the Assembly, which controlled the colony's finances, took the low road against the idealistic hopes of the Crown's royal governors. On subjects from representation of American Loyalists to the abolition of slavery, the Assembly consistently represented only the narrow interests of powerful Nassauvians.

So it is that an apparently democratic legislature fast became one of the more difficult factors in Bahamian life, wearing out governor after governor, withstanding Crown reforms and 20th Century liberals with its scrappy ability to survive. Only the rising forces of nationalism centuries later would dethrone the oligarchy Woodes Rogers first summoned into being.

For the next forty years after Rogers' depar-

ture, until events on the American mainland would flush the Bahamas with new vigor, the islands muddled along with a mixture of subsistence agriculture, over-aggressive wrecking, a fair bit of piracy and privateering, turtle-trapping, whale-hunting, and salt-farming — a mocking name for the only kind of farming that ever succeeded in the Bahamas, the evaporation of water from shallow ponds and the collection of the salt left over.

The 1760s saw the town of Nassau rally a bit under the direction of Governor William Shirley. A former governor of Massachusetts, Shirley brought a dose of Yankee order and ingenuity to ramshackle Nassau, ordering the town surveyed, swamps filled and straight new streets laid out.

But big events were brewing as the 1770s rolled around, and when the Thirteen Colonies declared open rebellion against Britain, the effect on the Bahamas was immediate and profound.

American Invasion: It is important to realize the degree of interrelatedness between the British Atlantic possessions. The original proprietary grant lumped the Bahamas with the Carolinas; the relationship was more than nominal. Trade with America was vital, relations casual, families interconnected. Nassauvians and Bostonians fought the same enemies of the British Crown. All that changed with the Thirteen Colonies' rebellion.

Did the Bahamians, with all their American links, feel any desire to join the rebellion? The answer is probably no, but there was considerable sympathy for the cause among some Bahamians. We know this, paradoxically, because the fledgling Continental Navy, attacked the Bahamas in 1776.

The action in which the Americans easily overran the hapless British defense of Fort Montague and proceeded to occupy the capital city was one of the first U.S. naval actions ever. What the marines were seeking was not more sympathizers, but the gunpowder the British had hidden away in Fort Nassau. The incompetent British Governor Browne did only one thing right during the attack — he got the gunpowder safely away — and when the Americans arrived at Fort Nassau they found little of military value left.

But the Americans stayed for a couple of weeks anyway, after issuing a generous proclamation assuring the Bahamians of their safety. In fact, they enjoyed themselves, and when they left, taking the pusillanimous Governor Browne with them, there seems to have been genuine regret on all sides.

The Americans came once more, in 1778, sneaking into Nassau Harbor at night. When the residents awoke in the morning, they found the American flag flying over Fort Nassau and the cannons trained on the town.

If the Americans and the Bahamians were at bottom more friendly than otherwise, the Spanish enjoyed no such feelings of camaraderie. Alert to Britain's problems in the north, they attacked Nassau in 1782 and conquered it easily — not surprising, considering they brought more sailors than the island had residents. The Spanish were kinder when bent on occupation than when they were just out for revenge, and many islanders stayed on under their rule.

For almost a year the Bahamas was under a foreign flag, the only interruption in its long allegiance to Britain.

It was a loyalist American named Andrew Deveaux who more or less single-handedly recaptured the Bahamas for England. He set sail in 1783 with 200 men and more valor than good sense. His plan to recover the island was almost childishly clever. Knowing the Spanish soldiers on the island far outnumbered his men, he picked a point offshore to ferry his troops from. The Spanish of course watched, and they saw long boat after long boat laden with men make the ferry run between Deveaux's ship and land. They must have imagined a veritable hoard was about to attack. What they did not know was that the same men who were being ferried in were lying down in the bottom of the boat and being ferried back out again, only to stand up for the return trip! Outsmarted and probably none too eager to lose their lives on an island they were finding unhospitable anyway, the Spanish surrendered and set sail for Cuba.

But the final irony is that Andrew Deveaux's daring and romantic raid was unnecessary. The British had already recovered the islands by the Treaty of Versailles of 1783, by which the Thirteen Colonies gained their freedom. The British had traded Florida for the Bahamas, so Deveaux's attack need never have taken place.

Planters Vs. Conchs: The next 10 years were formative ones for the Bahamas as American Loyalists, terrified at the prospect of remaining in the independent colonies and subjected to persecutions like tar-and-feathering, fled the mainland. Many went to Nova Scotia, others to Florida (and then fled again when the peninsula was handed over to the Spanish). Many others came to the Bahamas.

The old Bahamians were a practical people, doing business with whomever they could, wrecking and farming when they had to. The Loyalists, by and large the Colonies' most distinguished residents, gentlemen farmers and prosperous merchants, didn't see things that way. Within months, they and the old residents, whom they disparagingly called "conchs" after the lowly mollusk, were at each other's throats. The Loyalists wanted a say in how things were run, they wanted representation and they wanted land grants from the Crown. The old Bahamians wanted mostly to leave things alone—life was hard enough.

Despite local opposition, the Loyalists managed to profoundly alter the economy during their short stay. Coming with hundreds of slaves, they built plantations reminiscent of the American south and successfully planted acres of cotton. The Bahamian soil actually became worth something.

Their energy and devotion to the hardworking principles of agriculture might have taught the Bahamians a lesson, except that soon the cotton began to fail. Within a decade, most of the plantations were disasters, victims of cotton bugs and erosion caused by overplanting and deforestation. Loyalist settlers began to look elsewhere, trying out island after island or moving back to the hated United States.

The Loyalists left an important legacy to the Bahamas. They changed the racial composition of the islands, increasing the number of blacks and accentuating a system of discrimination and inequality. Many whites and blacks today bear the names of well-known Loyalist families. At the same time, the Loyalists left their architecture and their concern for public and civic buildings. Lastly, those who did stay continued to make a major contribution to the country, many joining the old establishment as prosperous and powerful Nassauvians.

Slavery as an institution was doomed in the British Empire. In 1772, strong English agitation outlawed its practice in the home country. In 1807 the slave trade was prohibited throughout all British possessions and on British ships. The British navy began to free slaves on wrecked or captured ships. Many of these same slaves became freemen and found a home in the Bahamas in settlements like Adelaide and Carmichael on New Providence Island, and on several Out Islands. In 1834, slaves throughout the British Empire were emancipated. In the Bahamas, they were subject to a period of apprenticeship before total freedom was obtained. In practice the freeing of the slaves went smoothly throughout the islands - despite the Assembly's grudging opposition - in marked contrast to the situation the United States was soon to experience.

The day of emancipation came and went without incident, despite rumors of rebellion and slave riots. It is worth wondering why the Bahamas had so much less trouble than the United States adjusting to a system of freedom. One reason can be found in the fact that Bahamian slave holders had less to lose. The locus of power was already in the offices in Nassau, where slaves were mostly household domestics. Out on the plantations the system had already collapsed. For many failed planters, freedom was doubtless cheaper than even the minimal care of other human beings. Thus the racial battles of Haiti, Jamaica or the United States were avoided and the Bahamas made a smooth transition to a world where all its residents were free.

Free though they were, black and mulatto Bahamians still had a long and difficult road before they would have either political power or equal rights. And progress on this front would have to wait nearly another century.

A fervent British Loyalist from South Carolina, Colonel Andrew Deveaux (right) became a Bahamian hero.

THE ROYAL VICTORIA HOTEL, AS SEEN FROM PARLIAMENT STREET.

SCENES IN SUN-LANDS.

GENERAL IMPRESSIONS OF NASSAU.

NOT the least attractive feature of Nassau is the Royal Victoria Hotel. This imposing establishment is situated in a charming pleasaunce "bosomed high in tufted trees." The lawn, sacred to croquet and to those who revel in dolce far niente, is a sweeping carpet of the greenest grass, fringed with ribbon-borders of flowers that glow in color-glory beneath the amorous rays of the glittering sunlight. In the centre of this "bit of Eden" stands a superb specimen of the forest king, whose branches, spreading far and wide, afford a cool and refreshing retreat for coquettish nursemaids; children whose toilets are veritable poems in lace and muslin; invalids whose sole occupation would seem to be in the reading of word-painted novels, and for the delectation of the stereotyped "whispering lovers." A balcony of gigantic mesh has been constructed in one of the forks, approachable by a wooden staircase, and in the wide world there is not a more delightful coign of vantage wherein to enjoy a favorite author, a cooling beverage, or a reverie. The western semi-detached portion of the hotel was formerly the King's College School, in connection with the King's College, London. The piazzas are mainly utilized by invalids, who, unable to undergo the fatigues of out-of-door exercise, move about here languidly enjoying the charming scenery and the refreshing breezes. On the summit a roomy glazed cupola, with a gallery, affords a bird's-eye view of the entire of New Providence. To lean over one of those balconies and gaze at the glories of the tropical vegetation below, at the gayly attired groups gossiping 'neath the trees, at

TYPES OF THE NATIVE REGIMENT.

the well-appointed equipages as they flash to and fro, at the gambols of gleesome children, or to extend the glance and take in the blue belt of the broad Atlantic, the City of Nassau and harbor and adjacent islands, the eager will find a series of tableaux, unique, refreshing, satisfying.

A STREET IN NASSAU.

To the lovers of the picturesque, of vivid contrasts and bizarre effects, a street in Nassau is "a thing of beauty," and, as a consequence, "a joy for ever." The natives in their quaint costumes, the open bazaars, the delicious store-poems in color, the houses of every hue of the rainbow, so trying to the aching eyeballs of those not to the manner born; the curiously shaped vehicles, the strangely constructed buildings, the tropical vegetation, the neat, yet clumsy, attempts at the recent and modern, as witness the solitary street-lamp in our illustration, tend to form a coup d'œil, a veritable treasure-trove, to the appreciative artist. At every corner lounges a group in attitudes worthy of the lazzaroni, some but scantily attired, others in bright particular effulgence—all picturesque. The women, after the fashion of the women of Spain, carrying baskets upon their heads laden with country produce for the market, not unlike a gigantic lobster-salad, lounging lazily along or tarrying beneath the friendly shade of the banyan for the interchange of mutual courtesies; the men talking, strangers and pine-apples and cocoa-nuts, under their yellow-leaded hats; the drivers of numberless vehicles creeping slowly by the way, glad of any excuse for a pull-up; children squatting in corners munching sugar-cane; and above, the blue sky—blue as that of Italy; below, the yellow-white roadway; on all sides, rainbow-tinted buildings. A

VIEW ON BAY STREET, THE PRINCIPAL BUSINESS THOROUGHFARE.

SCENES IN SUN-LANDS.—INCIDENTS OF A TRIP FROM NEW YORK TO NASSAU AND HAVANA.—SKETCHES OF NASSAU, NEW PROVIDENCE.
FROM PHOTOGRAPHS BY J. F. COONLEY AND SKETCHES BY WALTER YEAGER.

FORT MONTAGUE AND BATHING-PLACE.

THE QUEEN'S STAIRCASE.   THE GREAT SILK-COTTON-TREE.

THE LOOKOUT AT FORT CHARLOTTE.   A COCOA PALM-GROVE.

SCENES IN SUN-LANDS.—INCIDENTS OF A TRIP FROM NEW YORK TO NASSAU.—STREET SCENES IN THE TOWN OF NASSAU, NEW PROVIDENCE.

FROM PHOTOGRAPHS BY J. P. COONLEY AND SKETCHES BY WALTER YEAGER.—SEE PAGE 235.

Boom and Bust: The Late 19th Century

The beginning of the 19th Century marked the end of the romantic period in Bahamian history. The days of sneak invasions under cover of night, of pirates bearing down on unarmed merchants swearing to take them all to hell, of castaways on sun-drenched isles, began to fade away. The world of the Caribbean by the 19th Century had grown considerably smaller and grubbier. The colonial system had its firmest hold, explorers had nothing left to explore, and the merchants and farmers of the Bahamas did their level best to make money and maintain respectability.

great enthusiasm on the part of the Bahamians —had taken its toll on the wreckers' living. More and more old wreckers retired to the parlor to tell the tales of their heydays.

Certain kinds of agriculture and fishing began to make their marks as the transport of materials between the Bahamas and the mainland grew more reliable. Various fruits, such as pineapples and oranges, were in demand, and for brief periods many merchants could reap considerable profits from their crops. But again and again it was only a matter of time before the United States responded to domestic pres-

It is a salient fact of Bahamian history that the Bahamas has consistently benefited from the misfortunes of others. Wars in Europe guaranteed privateering spoils in the straits, and a ship impaled on a reef was a windfall for the islanders. This pattern was repeated in the 19th Century, when the only real economic stimulus the Bahamian economy would have was the sanguinary tragedy of the American Civil War. From 1861 to 1865, the Bahamas enjoyed a boom that would not be matched for 60 years.

With the exception of the Civil War period, the Bahamians eked out a living much as they had always done. Wrecking was still a profitable enterprise, though not nearly as much as it once had been. Better maps and the gradual construction by the British of lighthouses—with no

sure and imposed ruinous tariffs on these imports, freezing the burgeoning industry in its tracks.

Briefly, sisal, a hemp used in making rope, was a coveted item, until it was found that other countries had the soil to make a better quality fiber. The industry collapsed.

One bright note throughout was the sponging industry, which at times was the country's largest money earner. Sponges, which grow naturally on the sea bottom, could easily be col-

Preceding pages: in 1872 a visitor to the Bahamas dispatched reports to this New York newspaper. Unloading cotton circa 1865 (above), and the Royal Victoria Hotel's lobby in 1868 (right).

lected and brought to market. Many thousands of Bahamians made their living this way.

Boom Times: Into this picture came the unexpected boon of the American Civil War. It is, of course, ironic that the Bahamas, by now a predominately black country, should work so hard to support the South, but it is not an unusual irony for the time. The British leaned toward the South, and the Bahamas, as they did in so many areas, followed suit. The economics of the situation predominated, as always with Bahamian shipping.

The Bahamas' good luck came about because President Lincoln believed the South could be blockaded and eventually starved into submission.

At first the idea was regarded as laughably

gling paradise was the Royal Victoria Hotel, which still stands in partial ruins in Nassau. This tremendously opulent structure was put up at great cost and fast became the business center of the smuggling trade. Everyone from sea captains to Union spies to cotton buyers would crowd around the impressive hotel to get wind of which ships were leaving and what they would carry. Fast living, gambling and girls were the way of life for the practitioners of the dangerous profession.

But it was a false bountiful summer that Nassau was enjoying. When the War between the States came to an end, so would the Bahamas' prosperity. But the tomorrow-we-die mentality and the boom went on without concern for its inevitable end.

When the end did come, with the peace

FRANK LESLIE'S ILLUSTRATED NEWSPAPER.

185

May 24, 1873.

SCENES IN SUB-LANDS.—INCIDENTS OF A VISIT FROM NEW YORK TO THE BAHAMAS.

unlikely, and when Bahamian boats ran the blockade to nearly all the southern ports, there was little resistance. But as the war wore on, the North began to succeed in sealing off portions of the coast and the Bahamians had to use faster, quieter boats to elude their grasp. The Bahamians reaped incredible fortunes, bringing in food and carrying away cotton.

All this was good news indeed for Nassau. The island experienced an unparalleled building boom, with warehouses, piers, houses and stores springing up along the harbor streets. Out-Islanders crowded to Nassau to get a piece of the enormous earnings that smuggling was fast producing.

The most splendid product of this smug-

signed at Appomattox in the spring of 1865, the effect was quickly felt in the Bahamas. Warehouses, homes, whole streets became ghostly. A tremendous hurricane swept through the next year as if in divine warning. But the message was clear enough, as Nassau found itself with a huge labor force and nothing to do with it, beyond the old standbys of wrecking, sponging and growing citrus fruits. These could never be long-term economic solutions, for wrecking was gradually coming to an end with maps and steamships taking the terror out of ocean travel. Sponging would also soon be gone.

Alone Again: For all the hundreds of years of toil, the post Civil War Bahamas was remarkably close to the one Woodes Rogers left:

a quiet, marginal society with a great deal of manpower controlled by a powerful few. It is instructive to think of how changed England and the United States were from the 1720s, how massive their industrial and agricultural bases had become. But in the Bahamas, the sea was – and would remain until tourism – the only certain way to get one's food.

As the century wore on, many Bahamians became immigrant laborers, moving to the United States, especially to Florida, to undertake work in the citrus industry and the building boom that the Bahamas had never been able to sustain for long. Migrant immigration persisted right through to World War Two, and only came to an end with the tourist boom of recent years. The Bahamian emigration to the more promising world of Florida was

especially marked in the Out Islands, and the loss of population was significant.

If the Bahamians were far poorer than the English, they were no less proud or patriotic. The outbreak of World War One, in 1914, though half a world away, brought a resounding response from all levels of Bahamian society. Notions of anti-colonialism like the ones that developed after World War Two did not exist in those days, and if the mother nation were imperiled, it was thought every citizen's duty to defend her. Hundreds of Bahamians, black and white, volunteered for Canadian and British West Indies forces, which were sent to Europe and fought bravely. Many Bahamians gave their lives in the battles on that faraway continent. Those who remained at home raised copious amounts of money and sent the proceeds off to England. Armistice Day was a triumph for the Bahamians as well as the rest of the Empire.

Such spirit is all the more remarkable considering that the Bahamians had no real contact with the German or Austrian enemy. The closest the Bahamas came was the sighting of a single German warship, which was dutifully chased by a British cruiser with the happy capture of one longboat.

Sun-Drenched Holidays: The concept of the tourist is an old one in the Western Hemisphere, but it really only gained its modern meaning as the 19th Century came to a close. By this time, the habit of rich people departing for warmer climates was well established. The Europeans had their Riviera and countless Italian and German watering holes, and the Americans began to think more and more of Florida. The result was a great amount of publicity about the healthful effects of vacationing in warm climates. Because of this perception, now widespread, a building boom began in Florida. All this washed off on the Bahamas, for from the Civil War on there was a small but consistent trickle of Americans coming to spend the winter in a balmier clime. Intermittent attempts were made to establish a regular steam boat service. Most notably, Henry Flagler, who did so much for Florida's tourist industry, built a new hotel in Nassau and pioneered the Miami-Nassau steamship service, but both failed. Though he had thought on too grandiose a scale, the consistent winter invasion gave many Bahamians pause for thought. How could their year-round warm climate, so routine to them, be made appealing to Americans?

If many Bahamians thought in these terms, nothing much was done on a co-ordinated level. World War One caused a steep drop-off in visitors, and the volatile nature of the business of entertaining foreigners was no doubt reaffirmed.

Much time would have to pass, the whole notion of leisure time for the working and middle classes would have to become entrenched, the cult of swimming and tanning would have to be sold to American tourists before the Bahamas could hope to siphon off any but the richest and most leisured of Florida's visitors. But, for all that, with a little patience, the Bahamas was slowly finding its way to the most successful industry it had ever known.

Blockade runners rested in Nassau Harbour between runs (left). Uniform of the British West India regiment (right), was unique among British military costumes.

RUMRUNNERS AND BOOTLEGGERS

The Bahamas may not have known the good news that the Eighteenth Amendment to the United States Constitution would mean for them, but they soon found out. To look for a comparable piece of luck, one would have to go back to the Civil War, when the Bahamas became the major entrepôt for the southern United States. But while the profits from the Civil War were enormous, those from Prohibition may well have been higher.

It did not take long for the well-oiled Bahamian fleets to spring into action. The United States had no preparation for defending its coasts from smugglers, and soon Nassau was a great open liquor market, with thousands of galleons changing hands, destined for the great "Rum Row" off New Jersey's coast or the hidden coves of Florida. The government, or more exactly the Assembly which controlled taxes, made a hefty profit on the duty for each galleon and local captains and seamen found themselves in the midst of a hugely profitable business. It sure made more money than harvesting sponges.

Slowly, the U.S. Coast Guard became more equal to the task of policing the endless American coastline and increasingly smugglers were caught and jailed, but it was impossible to stop the torrent rushing up from the Bahamas. Vast numbers of locals participated; it was nearly a national industry.

The local economy grew fat on the profits, with new hotels and harbor improvements being built with the assistance of the flush treasury. A gambling club—the islands' first—was opened, and gangsters and society dandies down for the winter rolled craps side by side. The Bahamas was becoming the mythic gangster paradise, romantic isolated islands full of money and violence.

But paradise couldn't last forever, and when repeal came in 1933, the Bahamas, as always, was caught short. Overnight the elaborate clubs, elegant hotels and expensive stores emptied, streets filled with loafing, idle men.

The Depression, that tremendous economic shock to the world economy, overlapped the end of the Prohibition era, catching the Bahamas out of one job and unable to find another. What little foreign money that continued trickling in came mostly from rich tourists, those few who had escaped disaster. The Bahamas was poor again.

By this time, the oligarchy of powerful merchants and lawyers known as the "Bay Street Boys" was firmly entrenched in power in Nassau. They controlled the Assembly, which was openly hostile to the King's Governor and which disbursed all treasury funds. Many ills have been laid at the feet of the Bay Street Boys, perhaps more than they deserve.

In any event, this oligarchical political arrangement prospered, keeping the far more numerous blacks nearly totally out of power and controlling a remarkable amount of the islands' economic activity. It is difficult to know how the history of the Bahamas might have been different if it had been allowed to move with that of other West Indian countries instead

of remaining subject to an all-white power elite.

In any event, greater events overshadowed the economic woes of the Bahamas by 1940. War had broken out in Europe and the Bahamas once again donated large amounts of money and raised an impressive number of volunteers. But this time the war would truly be international in naval scope, and as a result the Bahamas gained both military and tourist business.

A Royal Presence: Into this decidedly small scene steps the larger-than-life figure of the

The Bahamas gave a royal welcome to the Duke and Duchess of Windsor (above). Cases and barrels of whiskey on the Nassau quai, destined for Prohibition America (right).

Duke of Windsor, the former king of England who had given up his throne to marry a divorcee. Why a man who had once ruled millions was assigned to a small colony of some tens of thousands is not certain. Given the reputation of the Bahamas at the time and the degree to which official England harassed the former King, it is the theory of more than one historian of the time that it was a kind of punishment.

Whatever the motive, the Duke's arrival immediately put the Bahamas back in the spotlight. But the Duke was a serious, able man, intent on righting the economic miseries of the country and countering the extremely backward policies of the Bay Street Boys.

Reforms in agriculture remained elusive, as they always had, but a piece of wartime good luck still serves the Bahamas well to this day.

the hill," to the area of almost entirely black townships away from the harbor. There several men were killed in clashes, the police station and other official buildings were burned, and bar rooms were looted. It took several days for the riots to quiet down, and black wages were quickly raised by the terrified government.

The airbase that was eventually built however, went on after the war and modernization to become Nassau International Airport, opened with great ceremony in 1959.

Harry Oakes: If the war wasn't excitement enough, violence of a more direct kind woke the Bahamas in 1942. Sir Harry Oakes, a Canadian-born gold magnate and one of the richest men in the British Empire was found brutally murdered in his bed one morning. One of the Bahamas' most distinguished philan-

The British and American high command chose a deserted section of the western part of New Providence to construct an enormous pilot training center. Here, in clear weather and far from the enemy, thousands of pilots were instructed before departing for far-off bases.

Despite the Duke's good efforts, the building of the airbase was the cause of a major riot, the closest thing to racial strife that the Bahamas has ever known. Black construction workers on the airbase project were offered a wage which was in accord with army regulations on payment to locals but unconscionably low. Avenging years of poverty and racism, they rose up and set off to sack Bay Street, the longtime seat of entrenched white power. The police were only able to force them back "over

thropists, the constructor of her only pre-war airport and a personal friend of the Duke of Windsor, Sir Harry's murder sent shock waves around the world. No one could imagine who would have done such a horrible deed, though everyone in society and out was suspected in the frenetic hunt. Eventually, Sir Harry's son-in-law was arrested and tried, but found innocent. No one knows, to this day, who Sir Harry's murderer was – he may still be living in the Bahamas. But Sir Harry is important for more reasons that just his horrible death, for his move to the Bahamas was one of the early signs that a new industry lay within reach of these sunny islands – taking care of the exhausted Americans whom the post-war boom would enrich.

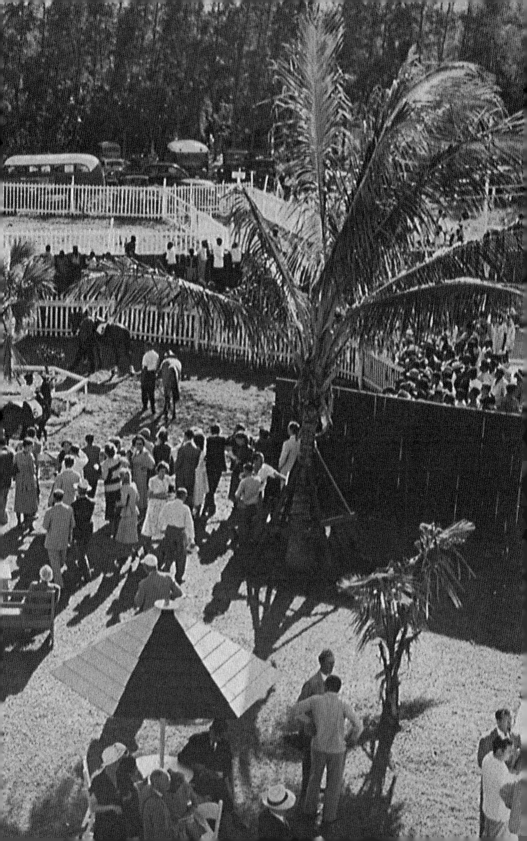

THE ROAD TO INDEPENDENCE

In the aftermath of World War Two, one can imagine the pundits of the Bahamas, collected to ponder what to do with the nation's ever-lackluster economy. Besides small industries like salt-farming, there was the export of workers to the United States to do blue-collar jobs and the possibility of a revival of the fledgling tourist industry. Soon stricter American immigration rules and improved home economic conditions would make the export of workers obsolete, so the way to the future for the Bahamas was clearly through tourism, if such a thing could be made to work on a large scale.

The Bahamas before World War Two was certainly not unknown to tourists. Some rich Americans and Canadians came on winter retreats to the warm islands. Many owned houses or stayed at the few luxury, old-style hotels like the Royal Victoria. But this was clearly an embryo industry, and a highly unstable one at that.

It took a man of unusual ability to find the Bahamas a full-time job, and that man was the controversial Sir Stafford Sands, who began in the 1950s to put together a Development Board to concentrate on the Bahamas' perennial economic problems and finally to do something about them. The Board decided to sell the Bahamas as a vacation spot to North America. Tremendous advertising, the opening of new hotels with Development Board assistance, and the development of year-round tourism put the Bahamas on the map.

The jet engine shortened flight time to the Bahamas, Nassau harbor was dredged to provide docking to even the largest ships in the expanding Caribbean cruise market, and the Bahamas was on its way.

Who reaped the profits from the new economy of tourism—profits that included the vacation dollars of more than 1 million people a year by 1970? Certainly in grand measure it was every Bahamian, for hotels and shops provide nearly all the employment in the Bahamas today. Yet the truly huge fortunes were limited to the insiders in government and industry.

Sir Stafford and his friends did not only rely on the goodwill of American tourists on pleasure vacations—they set up a tax haven in the Bahamas that few companies can resist. A

web of secrecy laws comparable to Switzerland's, no corporate income taxes and the government's constant hand in assisting in construction and the launching of new ventures has made banking and allied businesses the country's most important source of income after tourism. Banking too provides a huge number of jobs for local residents—the government enforces employment laws that restrict the number of non-Bahamians and require special work permits for foreigners on the islands. Through these laws and the healthy banking industry, a whole new professional middle-class bustles in the

once languid islands.

Thus, while a few men have grown extremely rich, many have become at least reasonably well-off. It certainly took a great deal of foresight to make tourism and banking the twin industries of the second half of the 20th Century in islands that before had only known the use of their own natural resources to buttress their economy.

Party Politics: Just at the time of the huge success of Bahamian tourism, the end was nearing for the Bay Street Boys. The affluent, mostly white power brokers who had run the Bahamas for most of the 20th Century began to come under public scrutiny in the late 1950s and early 1960s with the rise of party politics in the country.

Preceding pages: Nassau's toney little racetrack, Hobby Horse Hall, in 1948. At left, the opening of legislature in 1962, under the eyes of Queen Victoria statue, at right.

Before the formation of the Progressive Liberal Party (PLP), Bahamians of African descent had little say in the government. There were some black representatives in the Assembly, and some wealthy black businessmen, but with the rising tide of nationalism in the third world, it was clear that the division of a now profitable pie would change.

This was clear to almost everyone but the Bay Street Boys, who coalesced with other establishment groups to form the United Bahamian Party (UBP). The battle between the UBP and PLP was a long and bitter one. A great step towards black rule was the taxi strike that accompanied the opening of the new international airport, a strike over who would carry passengers to the hotels. What began as a small, not very political issue soon spread to other industries and

miraculous development of the enterprise zone of Freeport, but the PLP had larger forces working on its side. The black Bahamas had only to see what was going on in the 1960s in the United States, to look at the imbalance of wealth in their own land, to see that there was power in solidarity. Now, Lynden Pindling, who was leader of the opposition PLP party, began to play a significant role. He and his party leaders practiced a form of disobedience in the Assembly, refusing to obey the Speaker's dictates and generally reminding everyone that they were a force to be reckoned with.

Finally the PLP boycotted proceedings, forcing another election in 1967. This election, with the largest number of voters ever enfranchised, ended in a near-tie, but when two independent parties dramatically threw in their seats with the

caused a nationwide show of black labor muscle. Understandably, these labor groups saw themselves in alliance with the PLP rather than the establishment UBP.

It was now clear to even the Bay Street Boys that times were changing in the post-world war colonial world, and with the assistance of the British government, a new, more democratic constitution was drawn up in London in 1963. It diluted white Assembly power, and turned the legislature into a more representative body. The UBP, led by Roland Symonette, with Stafford Sands as Minister of Finance, began to rule under this new constitution, after the UBP beat back the PLP in nationwide elections. They certainly brought times of prosperity and growth to the country, not least in the

PLP, Lynden Pindling's party triumphed over the UBP and took power. There it has stayed ever since. Blacks had at last achieved real political power in their own Bahamas.

It is worth reflecting on this truly remarkable chain of events. In contrast to country after country, the black majority had peacefully and democratically taken control of the instruments of government. Without outside negotiation and without violence, a new generation of majority rulers now ran the government.

Not less remarkable is the realization that all

Assemblyman Arthur Hanna, expelled from the House of Assembly in April 1965 (above). The same month, Pindling defiantly threw the Speaker's Mace (right) out the window.

these events took little more than ten years. Through the early 1960s the general idea had been that blacks would benefit from a prosperous economy run by whites. (The distinction between black and white is tricky in the Bahamas where the vast majority are to some degree of mixed ancestry.) Even in day to day affairs, the black majority at that time had quite simply accepted the inferior post to which they were kept. There was little discussion of the realistic possibility that things would soon change; the assumption, among other rationalizations, was that American tourists and bankers would not feel confident dealing with a black government. After Pindling's rise to power, this fear of white flight was proven untrue. Investments and tourism were high on Pindling's list of priorities, and the fears of

But as the 1970s began, it was not clear whether the Bahamas wanted independence. As the party of the black Bahamian, the PLP naturally urged it, while the UBP, now allied with other disenchanted elements of the PLP and several splinter parties and calling itself the Free National Movement (FNM), argued that the Bahamas had more to lose than gain by an immediate try for independence.

To understand how a country could be reluctant to be free, one must realize the extent and duration of the Bahamas' ties to England. Everything from her language to her laws are English. There was an enormous community of expatriate English living in the Bahamas and many others who traced their origins directly to that country. Many felt that with things going so well for the Bahamas and the cost of be-

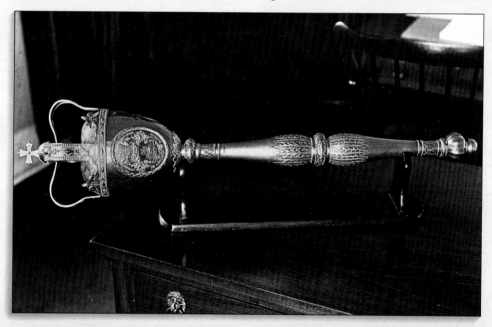

whites were quickly allayed.

Towards Independence: A new constitution was put together in London, turning over responsibility for internal matters and many other areas of colonial authority to the Bahamas. By this time, the British Empire was largely dissolved. The British had lost their desire to govern millions of foreign peoples; they no longer had the economic or military might, and many less advanced nations than the Bahamas had already gone full-tilt toward independence. It was probably the entrenched pro-British powers in the Bahamas, who kept England from ridding itself of the colony sooner. England made it clear that it was out of the colonial game and the Bahamas could have independence whenever it desired.

ing in the Commonwealth so low, independence could be achieved later, when the country was more stable.

But the issue was decided by the general elections of September, 1972, when Lynden Pindling's government party thrashed the FNM. Accepting the inevitable, the FNM gracefully cooperated in negotiating the terms of the nation's first independent constitution, as excitement increased and independence became more and more of an immediate reality. An independent Bahamas was now a certainty and the date had only to be set. The people of the Bahamas, some overjoyed, some indifferent, a fair number terrified, waited for the day when Lynden Pindling's government would rule a sovereign nation.

A NEW NATION

On July 10, 1973, after 250 years as a colony and possession of Britain, the new nation of the Bahamas was born. For the British the moment was one more in the long retreat from imperial power, but for the young Bahamian people it was the fulfillment of a long and steady march toward self-governance.

It was a thrilling sight for thousands of Bahamians who assembled at Fort Charlotte, awaiting the hour when the British flag would be lowered for the last time. At the stroke of midnight the new flag of the Bahamas was raised, to fly over the nation for the first time. A new day had begun.

In truth, the Bahamas had shown that it was ready for independence. All the systems of government were long in place, trained ministers prepared, national and domestic strategy stable and well thought out. To lead the Bahamas, there was the familiar figure of Lynden Pindling, a charismatic, energetic man and the only prime minister the independent nation of the Bahamas has known so far. Whatever the political opinions - and the Bahamas is full of dissenters and gadflies - there was a certain comforting familiarity in the presence of the man who had brought himself and his party so far. To this day, his PLP party continues in power, while the opposition FNM doggedly tries to capture the majority that has for so long eluded it.

Pindling is without doubt his own best secret weapon. His government has endured scandals and controversies but continues to find support from most Bahamians. To the average Bahamian, he is a figure worthy of admiration, the man who took them into nationhood. Other politicians may be better at this or that, but to most Bahamians Pindling is the leader of the nation almost by custom.

The road from 1973 to the present has mostly been more of the same. The economic policies set in place by Symonette and Sands have been fine-tuned but continue fairly well in place. Tourism, banking and luxury homes for foreigners are still important to the economy. Pindling's government allayed the flight

Lynden Pindling and Prince Charles (left) represented the new order and the old at independence ceremony. The Honorable Sir Clifford Darling, Speaker of the House of Assembly (right).

of white capital following independence and as a result the Bahamas has not had to significantly alter its banking policy.

Pursuing the Dollar

On the tourist front, the Bahamas has sometimes taken a battering from other Caribbean nations waking up to the example of this early bloomer, and the country has the constant task of making itself the place tourists choose to go. Many more southern Caribbean nations have

increased their appeal to Americans since the Sixties and this has had its effect. Florida itself, with lower airfares and a highly developed industry, has been a tough competitor. But the Bahamas is experienced and professional in dealing with these problems, and with each new development holds its own. The opening of resorts at Cable Beach and the licensing of a casino on the island of New Providence itself (there have long been casinos on Paradise Island and Freeport) is just one example of this will to maintain a Bahamian market share and to adapt to the tastes of American and Canadian tourists.

Gradually, the goverment is fixing its attention on the less developed Family Islands with the dual goals of speeding their growth as tourist destinations and arresting the steady migration of Bahamians to Nassau in search of work. With thousands of Bahamians directly dependent on tourism and tens of thousands more indirectly dependent on it, tourism is no casual matter for the government but a number one economic priority.

To help keep valuable foreign exchange from slipping out of the country to pay for imported food, the government doggedly attempts to encourage farming, especially in the Family Islands. Fish farming has been started on several islands, and prices guaranteed for Bahamian-grown fruits and vegetables, with the goal of one day making the country largely self sufficient in food production.

and the Bahamas is naturally a perfect base of operations for smugglers. It is near the U.S., the inevitable market. It consists of hundreds of islands and cays, many uninhabitable and most unpatrollable. There are experienced pilots and sailors drawn in by the tremendous profits.

Perhaps the only way out is some parallel to the repeal of Prohibition, but such a course is extremely unlikely on the part of the U.S. Government. Cooperate as the Bahamians will with U.S. drug enforcement authorities, the battle so far grows no easier.

In the World's Spotlight

If the Pindling government faces consider-

Unofficial Industry

One great influence on the Bahamas that has a curious counterpart in the history of the country is the illegal smuggling of narcotics. Like the rumrunners during Prohibition, the narcotics smugglers have had a major effect on the country. Money resulting from smuggling has changed the face of many islands, and the economic results of such a sudden influx of dollars has been profound. No one has a clear idea of the amount of drugs or money involved. Naturally, in contrast to Prohibition, the government and leaders of the country are aghast at the problem and working desperately to find a solution. Yet nature can't be changed,

able internal difficulties and a powerful opposition, on the international level the Bahamas prestige seems to grow and grow. In 1983 Mr. Pindling was knighted Sir Lynden O. Pindling, Knight Commander of the Most Excellent Order of St. Michael and St. George, an order of Queen Elizabeth.

The gathering of all those premiers and prime ministers in Nassau in October 1985 for the Commonwealth Heads of Government meeting undoubtedly boosted Bahamian self-

School children at Hope Town's bicentennial celebration (above). Queen Elizabeth flanked by Governor General Sir Gerald Cash and Sir Lynden Pindling at 1985 banquet (right).

48

esteem and the islands' international image.

On a more homely level, the town of Hope Town on Elbow Cay in the Abacos, celebrated its 200th Anniversary in November 1985, with speeches by local dignitaries, songs by school children, flags fluttering, and the oom-pah-pahs of a small marching band. And in 1992, the island of San Salvador will take the spotlight during celebrations of the 500th birthday of the New World.

So the Bahamas marches on into the end of the 20th Century. With a quarter of a million residents spread out on hundreds of islands, but with most gathered on a few, the islands present vistas both of extreme loveliness – the kind of empty beaches that differ only a little from those the pirates used to see – and the

it is more genuine confidence, but in any case the stridency and difficulty that so much of the developing world continues to experience has little counterpart in the Bahamas. Just as its history is consistently different from that of larger island nations like Haiti and Jamaica, so has it avoided difficulties and strains that have made a few islands in the Caribbean politically unstable. It is difficult to pinpoint how the Bahamas, from deepest poverty to the rumblings of majority power, has managed to avoid giving off any sense of strain, but it is so. Political freedom was not encouraged in past times, but neither was it curtailed. Equality for blacks was not pushed, but neither when independence loomed ahead did blacks or whites react with the violent sentiments that can curse

modern over-crowding of the medium-sized city. If Nassau seems very much in the later part of the 20th Century, other islands seem to have changed far less. And even in Nassau, despite a large population busily engaged in the rat race to make a living, the feeling of cordiality and relaxation is never far from the surface.

Onward Together

The road from today for the Bahamas is both uncertain and inviting. Despite all its problems, the country seems cocky and sure that it is on the right track. Maybe this comes from keeping on a good front for visitors or maybe

former colonies on their way to self-rule.

What has gone on in the Bahamas may be an accident of sorts, but the country has successfully weathered the kinds of difficulties that have beset much greater and more powerful nations.

Whether this pattern will continue is impossible to predict. Equally impossible to foresee is how the tourist economy will fare in the coming decades, or whether the Bahamas will keep its position as one of America's preeminent vacation destinations. Whatever the result, one hopes and even expects that the Bahamas will make it through, as it has done for so long, remembering the nation's motto, "Forward, Upward, Onward, Together."

51

THE BAHAMIANS

The time is 8 o'clock on a weekday morning and on the main thoroughfares of New Providence there are wall-to-wall cars. (It has been estimated that there are almost 45,000 cars for a population on this island of about 180,000.) These cars are not old by any means; in fact, there is a preponderance of new Japanese cars: Crowns, Mazdas, Datsun 300 ZXs, Mercedes Benzes, BMWs, Cadillacs, Lincolns and, yes – Rolls Royces!

On Bay Street at the center of the commercial area, beautiful women strut in elegant clothes as if before an audience of sophisticated Parisians. Bahamian men in three-piece suits, silk monogrammed shirts and alligator or lizard shoes, look furtively at the girls, but hurry along.

There are other Bahamians as well - or perhaps they may not be Bahamians but Haitians or people from other West Indian islands - who have become part of the Bahamian scene, hurrying along to their jobs or perhaps trying to avoid the Immigration Officer.

The Bahamian policemen and policewomen are here too – directing traffic, giving parking tickets or guarding arrested persons awaiting trial in the Magistrate's and Supreme Courts, situated not far from Queen Victoria's statue in Rawson Square.

There is a cacophony of noises - car horns, police whistles, laughter, fruit and vegetable vendors, straw-workers jostling for places in the new market and on the sidewalks. The clomp! clomp! of a horse and carriage blends with the roar of traffic. Tourists on motorbikes, with T-shirts proclaiming "It's Better in the Bahamas" try hard to ride on the left side of the road. From the many cruise ships at Prince George Dock, horns blast and hordes of tourists emerge like ants scurrying from an anthill. Young boys, running from the Police, hustle tourists for coins that they dig up from the sea.

Reggae, soca and American rock music emanate from the stereo systems of cars or young men with stereos strapped on their shoulders. Then there's the spectacle of zombie-like young men trying to either push drugs

or obtain money to buy drugs and the "locks" of the Rastafarian brethren who shout: "Peace and Love, brother – Jah Rastafari!"

Believe it or not, this is a typical scene in the so-called tranquil "island-in-the-sun" - the "isles of perpetual June" - the Bahamas, that haven for the rich and famous, the land of Junkanoo, a tax haven and one of the most complicated, but stable and successful Caribbean nations in the modern world.

Yes, modern Nassau, the capital of the Bahamas on New Providence island, has come full circle from a quaint, sedate "fishing village" to a fast-moving, razz-matazz, American-like city which nevertheless retains a distinctly Bahamian flavor.

The scene just painted, however, does not tell the whole story. The Bahamas are an archipelago with the most beautiful beaches in the world, charmed islands and villages where, in many instances, time appears to have stopped. Bahamians are fortunate in having islands that cater to the needs of the more than 250,000 people that inhabit them and make their living through tourism, banking, light industry and agriculture and fisheries. The more modern cities have an infrastructure of electricity, water, communications and airports that tie them closely to the more "developed" world. The proximity of the United States has placed the average Bahamian in an enviable position where he can boast that no other third world country has access to 13 television channels. In fact, it is estimated Bahamians have more satellite systems per capita than any other nation!

The geographical position of the Bahamas has allowed it to play significant roles in world history as a haven for pirates; a station for slave ships on their way to the Southern Caribbean and South America; an ideal base for gun-runners during the American Civil War; a source of alcohol during Prohibition in the U.S.A.; a hideaway for German submarines during two World Wars and now, unfortunately, a transshipment area for illicit drugs, especially cocaine and marijuana.

These episodes in Bahamian history have brought some negative and dangerous effects, partly outweighed by the economic boost, evidenced by construction, money circulating, cars, luxury items – plus a yearly average of over 3 million tourists in the late '80s, bringing in annual revenues of over *1 billion dollars!*

Preceding pages: clowning after school in Alice Town, Bimini; chic Bahamian Sunday best; and a family reunion brings together several generations. At left: Garet "Tiger" Finlayson, a Nassau entrepreneur.

The First Bahamians: The descendants of the original inhabitants of the Bahamas are no longer around to reap the benefits.

The Lucayan Indians, also known as Arawak, were the original inhabitants of these islands. The Indians called themselves *Lukku-caire*, meaning "island people." This was later adapted by Europeans into the name "Lucayan." Dr. Julian Granberry in an article "The Lucayans," in the 1973 *Bahamas Handbook and Businessman's Annual*, suggests that during the early years of the Christian era, the Arawak peoples of the Guianas, on the northeast coast of South America, began a lengthy migration up through the Antilles. By about 700 AD, they had reached and occupied all the major islands of the Caribbean (but not yet the Bahamas). Unlike the Paleo-Indians and their Meso-Indian descendants, who lived in the Caribbean at an earlier time, the Arawaks both used stone tools and made pottery in astounding variety. There were many styles of Arawak pottery – and it is primarily through the remains of such artifacts that archaeologists locate and describe the Indian cultures of the West Indies.

The earliest known pottery is called "Palmetto Ware." Since it is definitely Arawak in origin, we conclude that the Lucayans were Arawak Indians. Palmetto Ware is found all over the Bahamas.

The Lucayans probably came north to the Bahamas from the Southern Caribbean to escape the cannibalistic Carib Indians. Since the Lucayans were a peaceful, non-violent people, their very survival depended on staying as far as possible from the Caribs. The Lucayans were evidently beautiful people. Two chroniclers, Christopher Columbus in 1492, and Peter Martyr in 1511, described them. Columbus wrote in his journal:

They go about naked as they were born, the women also... everyone appeared to be under thirty years of age, well proportioned and good looking. The hair of some was thick and long like the tail of a horse, in some it was short and brought forward over the eyebrows, some wearing it long and never cutting it. Some, again, are painted, and the hue of their skin is similar in colour to the people of the Canaries - neither black nor white.

Peter Martyr wrote that "it was reputed that the women of the Lucayan Indians are so beautiful that numerous inhabitants of the neighbouring countries, charmed by their beauty, abandon their homes and, for the love of them, settle in their country."

After Columbus' rediscovery of these is-lands, the Lucayans totally disappeared from the Bahamas. Although there were approximately 20,000 to 40,000 Lucayans living in the Bahamas during the time Columbus visited, a slaving expedition in 1511 reported that it found no Lucayans despite having "searched with the greatest diligence." When Ponce de Leon sailed through the Bahamas looking for the "Fountain of Youth" in 1513, he only found a frail old Indian woman living alone on one of the smaller islands north of Grand Bahama. The Lucayans were captured and taken to Hispaniola, Puerto Rico and Cuba to work in the mines. A significant number were also taken to Cubagua, an island off the coast of Venezuela, to dive for pearls. Most of them died of hard work and cruel treatment, or by disease and suicide. It is alleged that when they no longer served any useful purpose, they were cruelly killed.

After Columbus' journey through the Bahamas in 1492, other explorers, mostly Spanish, passed by these islands, but since the land was barren and there were no mineral resources or precious stones, the Bahamas were mostly ignored.

Early Adventurers: It wasn't until around the 1640s that new settlers came to the Bahamas. A group of about 70 people, led by William Sayle, called "The Eleutherian Adventurers" sailed from Bermuda to the Bahamas where they received 300 acres of land plus £100. Thirty-five more acres were given to each family member. With them also came 28 slaves.

During this time, there was great upheaval in England. In 1649, Charles I was beheaded and Prince Charles was made king. As a result, more Puritans set out for the Bahamas, after refusing to take the Oath of Allegiance to the new king. This period in Bahamian history was one of particular hardship. The small population failed to prosper because of devastating hurricanes, the inability of the soil to yield profitably and poor administration of the Colony's affairs.

The period from 1684 to 1717 can be called "The Era of Buccaneers and the Pirates" because during these years no ship or colony was safe. Ships were constantly attacked and plundered, and the Bahama Islands were ripe for corruption with lax government, and many isolated and protected harbors.

In 1684, the Spanish raided New Providence and for two years there were no permanent settlers in the island. The Bahamas got such a bad name in world history that the Spanish labelled the colony a "receptacle for all rogues." It was not until 1718, when a former pirate, Woodes Rogers, gained the support of King George I of England and became the Governor-in-Chief of the Bahama Islands that order was restored. Woodes Rogers offered amnesty for the pirates, solidified the local government and gave a semblance of security to the inhabitants by arming the Forts. However, the Bahamas continued to be a colony in turmoil. Many pirates didn't surrender, and a devastating epidemic reduced the population.

The next significant period was "The Loyalist Period" from 1783 to 1788, when international events played a significant role in the population of the Bahamas and the development of the Bahamian people.

By this time, England was beginning to rule

of Loyalists by the thousands, with their slaves. These Loyalists to the British Crown were no longer prepared to stay in the newly independent colonies. Some came on their own, others received free transportation from the British, and each Loyalist was given 40 acres of land for the family head and 20 acres for every member, free of rents and charges.

In 1789, the total population of the Bahamas was estimated to be 11,200 with 8,000 of these Negroes. By 1831, there were 12,259 Negroes in the Bahamas, outnumbering the white population by three to one. Out of this majority, 2,991 were free; indeed there were some Negroes who owned slaves.

Plantation Slaves: The system of slavery, which became very important economically to

the waves. French power in North America disappeared with the loss of Montréal in 1760 and Caribbean Islands like Dominica, Grenada, St. Vincent and Tobago fell to the British. Despite these, Britain was having problems with her 13 American colonies. In 1775, open hostility broke out and Bahamas was affected by the war for American Independence

The significance of the American War of Independence to the Bahamas was immigration

A Hope Town girl dressed up for Hope Town's bicentennial pageant in the costume of her Loyalist forebears, left. Braids and beads on a Harbour Island Girl, right.

the colonizers, differed somewhat in the Bahamas from Caribbean and U.S. slavery. The poor soil of the Bahamas only allowed small farming to flourish. Plantations were very small, compared to other islands, like Jamaica, for example: the largest plantation had about 380 slaves.

The relationship between master and slave was quite benevolent, since most were trusted "house niggers." But there were incidents of cruelty, poor living conditions, and slave customs were monitored or legislated to prevent uprisings. Masters tried to convert their slaves to Christianity. Many owners engaged in sexual intercourse with their slaves, developing "mixtures." Male slaves were often encouraged (as "studs") to copulate with as many female slaves as possible to ensure an increased population. Strong family ties were discouraged among the slaves as was the sense of mutual responsibility between husband and wife, father and son.

Because of poor Bahamian soil, after emancipation, there was not much demand for forced labor. Hence there was no need for imported labor as there was in most Caribbean countries where Indians (from East India) and Chinese were brought in under contracts of indenture.

On Aug. 1, 1834, the Emancipation Act came into force in all British colonies and the majority of the population of the Bahamas - the Negroes - were free. Emancipation

Yoruba, Mandingo, Nango, Congo, Fullah and Housa.

The first recorded blacks to arrive in the Bahamas came in 1656 and they were all free men. A document found in Registry Book C, pages 166-78 in the Registrar General's Department is believed to be a copy from the 1671 Census and this list gives the first mention of slaves and Negroes in the Bahamas.

After Emancipation: The post-slavery era heralded a growing population with growing problems: colonialism, racism, social class and discrimination. The majority of people were black yet the Bahamas was ruled by a white power structure, similar to the racial divisions in parts of the United States, especially the south.

brought freedom but there were grave problems with regard to former slaves creating a social structure. Then, too, there were Africans in the Bahamas who never functioned as slaves per se. Slave ships intercepted by the British were brought to the Bahamas where the Africans were freed on arrival.

The lack of records makes it difficult to identify the precise ethnic origins of many Bahamians. It is believed that the majority of Bahamian Negroes came from the more northerly parts of West Africa, but no-one has been able to find patterns of living or any strong African traits to point to any definite tribe or race of Africans. Most Bahamian historians claim that tribes who peopled the Bahamas were Ibo,

There were no laws or regulations fixing the status of the black people, but they were subjugated to a position solidly at the bottom of the social structure.

During this period, liberated Africans and ex-slaves lived in specific areas well known for their heritage (family). For example, Grant's Town was one of the areas where a large African population was found. A visitor describes living conditions: "The houses are mostly of wood, some with limestone walls, roofs covered with shingles or thatching of

In Nicholl's Town, Andros, the bride's side (above) and the groom's side (right) check each other out at a typically lavish wedding reception.

60

palmetto leaves."

On the other hand, a few minority Bahamian whites and colonial administrators lived in elegant opulence. Discriminatory attitudes and practices were everywhere - in schools, banks, clubs, hotels and residential areas. Very rarely did black and white have any meaningful social intercourse.

Sir Etienne Dupuch in his book *The Tribune Story* writes: "At the turn of the century, we lived in a complex society. Every man had a place and every man was expected to know his place. There were three main groups - the coloured people at the bottom, the Bahamian white, largely descendants of Loyalists who left the United States during the American War of Independence, and the British Official nials, which placed them below Englishmen. Thus for Bahamians black, white and in-between, to become like the British was the single most important prerequisite for attaining self-esteem and status.

This process, therefore, encouraged black Bahamians to place less emphasis on their African heritage. During this post-slavery period and up to the late 1960s, Bahamians, especially blacks, tried to be as British as possible culturally, politically, educationally and legally.

The stifling of the majority of the black population's African heritage, the economic hold by the white oligarchy and the psychological bad image of the Bahamian black, created a seemingly powerless and passive

class. The coloured people were split in groups determined entirely by degree of colour, starting with black at the bottom, through off-black, dark brown, brown, light brown, high yellow and near white." These divisions of color, social class, nationality and race caused insecurity and tension among all groups. Naturally, those who aspired to social advancement, even within their own set limits, got their bearings from the beacon that shone at the top – the deep-rooted British and white-oriented value system. This value hierarchy not only applied to the blacks. Although the British Government Official group accepted some element of the white wealthy Bahamians socially, they were all officially classed as Coloured individual. This passive acceptance of deprivation and discrimination continued up to the early Fifties, except for a riot in 1942 when workers protested differences in wages for foreign whites and local workers. Probably the greatest factor that worked against liberation for the majority were those "mixed" Bahamians who denied their African heritage by finding more "exotic" strains and by living in a style that would project them as "white" or "cultured." The higher educated blacks and these "displaced mixed" were set to infighting and confusion, with the white, ruling class dividing and threatening the majority blacks who were held in an economic bind. This white-black division, the lack of unity among blacks and the basic mistrust among them, perpetuated their condition as third class citizens in a country where they were not only in the majority, but essential to the life and well being of the country.

Colonials: In the past the British Colonial Administrators (the Governor, Colonial Secretary, etc.) were at the top of the socio-economic ladder. These people kept to themselves, led a high class lifestyle and even snubbed local whites.

Local whites were, of course, descendants of foreign whites. But most of them were lower class descendants of pirates, buccaneers and Loyalists. The basic distinction is that these people were born in the Bahamas. In some of the Bahama islands, there are settle-

the person is based on material things and *money*. Today more Bahamian men and women marry and/or have babies across racial lines. Many live somewhere between past and present attitudes.

The minority whites are not now politically viable, but still form the main-stream of Bahamian economic life. Some have ventured into interracial social interaction if it suits their business or otherwise, but old prejudices still exist. Discriminatory barriers have been broken down, with the exception of the last remaining "security" white vestiges – the Yacht Clubs. Other barriers between people are more subtle.

Conch Lifestyle: The term "Conchy Joe" has no official meaning and there are various inter-

ments populated totally by local whites (some on Abaco and, of course, Spanish Wells).

These whites were very sensitive about their heritage and rigidly tried to maintain the "purity" of the race by setting up strict social-racial barriers. These whites were merchants and businessmen and (with the British administrators) were members of ruling class.

The present-day Bahamas, although still basically the same from the racial and socio-economic point of view, has seen some radical changes since Independence in 1973. There are decidedly more middle class and upper class black Bahamians, due primarily to politics and education. A new "political" class appears to be emerging, and the importance of

pretations as to what a Conch Joe is. The local white (a small number) is looked upon as the original Conchy Joe, and indeed call themselves "Conchy Joe." Others believe that "Conchy Joe" is the fairest type, the near-Caucasian featured mixed Bahamian; many live on the islands of Long Island, Eleuthera and Exuma. These Bahamians identify more with the white cultural lifestyle and reject anything suggesting "black."

Anglican formality in George Town, Exuma (above left) and a Long Island man's private devotion (above right). Right, a woman displays a flag and letter of recommendation she received from a British dignitary.

It appears that the majority of Bahamians today would think of "Conchy Joe" as the mixed Bahamian with near-Caucasian features who think, act and live "white." The "Conchy Joe" of the past and present has always been in that "never, never land" of Bahamian social-racial acceptance. Many find themselves rejected by foreign whites, local whites and browns and blacks. Many Conchy Joes survived in the past primarily because of their skin color; their sons and daughters achieved little education because there was so little competition for jobs. All that was necessary was a light skin, straight hair and a job was assured – especially a bank position! Today, the situation has changed. Many Conchy Joes are just not prepared to

The advent of Black Government widens this gap.

At worst, the Conchy Joe lives in fear that the Bahamian black will return his hatred in kind. All in all, the basic stereotype of the Conchy Joe remains the individual sitting in a rocking chair, listening to hillbilly music and talking about "Unca Dodie."

High Yellow: The High Yellow Bahamian is sometimes classified as "red" or a Conchy Joe, except that he is more "colored." These Bahamians are also the result of unions between black and white. In one family, there may be those who look "pure white" and those who are decidedly "colored." This can cause some problems of identification and racial hangups. Sometimes brothers and sisters have

compete educationally or otherwise and are experiencing difficult economic times, even though they tend to help each other more than other Bahamian ethnic groups.

The ultimate goal of the stereotypical Conchy Joe, is to marry a foreign white. (Many Bahamian blacks had/have the same strivings! And some mixed Bahamians that have married white have even adopted a white child to avoid the possibility of having children darker than themselves.)

The present-day Conchy Joe can be found in every social-class, but primarily, the middle class. Many Conchy Joes in the lower socio-economic level have the added pressures of being in the Bahamian minority racial group.

moved into the "white world," rejecting their darker siblings.

Many old, respected Bahamian families are of this type. They once made up the upper class of colored Bahamian society. These families are very proud to acknowledge their white ancestry – "I'm French, you know." "My ancestors came from Sweden." "My name is McCartney. It is not an assumed name taken from some slave master, grandfather was an Irish seaman!"

As the whites and Conchy Joes had their exclusive clubs, these high yellows formed their own. The Gym Tennis Club in Nassau could probably be the counterpart of the Yacht Clubs, except that whites were not only accepted, they were highly desired. Some high yellows explain their "coloring" by "finding" Indian or other exotic strains in their ancestry.

Many of the present-day descendants of the high yellows have gone either white or have been assimilated into the "Conchy Joe" world. Hair straightening, or very close hair cuts to help eliminate the kinks and bleaching creams were once popular with the high yellows. Unfortunately, those black genes still give "pickie" hair and other features that foreigners, especially, can distinguish immediately!

Exotic Browns: Then there is the image and coloration that the foreign world conjures up as being typically Bahamian. These "browns" are not too "whitish" or pale (or Conchy Joe-ish) and not too black. The browns are very middle class. It's the Bahamian professional, that British-trained individual, the typical "black Englishman" (now the "black American"). In the old days, he wished he were more "fair" – like the high yellow.

The "browns" never looked at themselves as Negro, African or black - just "colored" - exotic! There was constant movement upward into the fairer shades. The fairer one got, the better were chances of survival in the Bahamas' highly socio-racial class society.

Today Bahamian browns make up the mainstream of Bahamian life – the professional, politician, artist, musician and the upcoming businessman.

Upwardly Mobile Blacks: The black Bahamian has always been at the bottom of the socio-racial Bahamian hierarchy. He is a descendant of the African slave, the "field hand" and other imported blacks.

There were, however, black Afro-Bahamian families who owned extensive property, took part in politics and were highly respected in the community. Some of these blacks traced their ancestry directly to an African tribe and many Africans who settled in the Bahamas were elite Africans.

The Loyalists brought their most intelligent, strongest and trusted slaves to the Bahamas. The runaway slaves who came to the Bahamas as free men were men of imagination and great courage. The slaves that were intercepted by British ships and brought here were never in bondage. Indeed many of these free Africans were from African royal families.

Slave ships stopped first either at Bermuda or the Bahamas. As a result, slave owners had a choice of healthy, robust and intelligent slaves. All these facts, and the generally good treatment of slaves by Bahamian white and black slave owners, account for the small number of slave uprisings and eventually the peaceful transition from white to black government in the Bahamas.

The present-day Bahamian black has added to his ranks all those Bahamians with African heritage, since the term "black" appears to be mostly accepted today, to describe such people. Indeed many of the high yellows, fair browns and even some "Conchy Joes" are now more "black" than actual black. Natural hairstyles are "in," African customs are being revived, and "black is beautiful" is becoming a reality. Even local whites are indicating their changing attitude by inviting token blacks to their homes for parties. The great strides in social class and color interaction, pressures of white and black expatriates, Haitians, West Indians, Central and South Americans plus the very many foreign wives of black and white Bahamians, further diversify the "pot pourri" of interracial-interpersonal relationships. Mixed marriages, social and racial intercourse, and unlimited job opportunities in all areas are fast becoming commonplace.

Other Minorities: Greeks, Chinese, Syrians and Jews make up less than 1 percent of the Bahamian population. These groups came in the early 1900s (some from Cuba, the U.S. and Hong Kong) and have made valuable contributions to Bahamian life. They still tend to be clannish, and have maintained their language and other cultural customs. Greek women dressed in their traditional black gowns can still be seen walking towards Nassau's Western Esplanade during Epiphany.

These groups are primarily businesspeople (clothing and shoe shops, restaurants, etc.) and professionals (doctors, journalists and lawyers) and have their own local organizations. Many have married into their own ethnic group either from outside the Bahamas or locally. Their relationships with the black community have been limited socially, though there are a few Chinese and Greeks with a "lil touch of the brush."

Among many Bahamians, the goal is not to look at each other as either black, white, Conchy Joe or yellow, but as Bahamian - this would cover a multitude of sins and probably ease some of the tensions that still exist. People find comfort and security in family and heritage; in the Bahamas, these powerful institutions show little sign of waning.

The colorful paintings of Amos Ferguson and the smile of his wife Bea reflect the warmth of Bahamian family life.

LUXURIOUS LIFESTYLES

Oct. 12, 1992 will mark the 500th anniversary of the most famous visitor to the Bahamas — Christopher Columbus. He first set foot on a tiny island to plant the banners of his sovereign. Though he could not have foreseen the future, the banner of royalty was prophetic, for these isles were later to become one of the world's foremost playgrounds for the royal, the rich and the famous.

It all began in 1919 when the 18th Amendment to the U.S. Constitution was adopted, putting Prohibition in full force. In the Bahamas the Roaring Twenties started with rumrunning and bootlegging, and a rapid influx of new wealth.

The private yachts of some of the most powerful industrial tycoons crowded Nassau's harbor. They included the yachts of William K. Vanderbilt, Vincent Astor, J.P. Morgan, and E.F. Hutton, as well as the Whitneys, Armours and Mellons.

Sir Harry Oakes was the man who popularized the millionaires' trek to the Bahamas. He started out as a Maine school teacher but switched to prospecting, and after a 14-year search found in Canada the second richest gold mine in the western hemisphere. He met Harold Christie, a pioneer in land development in the Bahamas, and in 1934, resenting the Canadian tax he had to pay, he transferred his enormous fortune to the Bahamas. He became a baronet (gaining the Sir title) in 1939 after giving large sums to charity.

Another well-known industrialist who lived in the Bahamas prior to World War Two was Joseph Lynch, a partner in the brokerage firm of Merrill, Lynch, Pierce, Fenner & Smith. He lived on Hog Island, now Paradise Island. Lynch sold his lands to Dr. Axel Wenner-Gren, the late Swedish industrialist and real estate tycoon.

The advent of World War Two brought wealthy refugees from Europe and Britain who flocked to the sunny and peaceful isles. What stamped the Bahamas with the ultimate seal of approval and guaranteed worldwide media attention was the arrival of the ex-King of England and his American bride, the Duke and Duchess of Windsor.

After the Duke's abdication to marry Wallis Simpson, the Duke and Duchess lived a life of

Preceding pages: colonial splendor characterizes the Lyford Cay Club House. Left, cuisine with panache for well-heeled guests at the Bimini Big Game Fishing Club.

luxury at their Paris mansion and their estate on the Riviera. When the Nazis marched into France the couple fled to neutral Portugal. They became the victims of a plot hatched by German and Portuguese diplomatic officials to lure the Duke into the German orbit, by kidnapping, if necessary. Prime Minister Winston Churchill learned of the kidnapping plot and determined to send the Duke as far from the war zone as possible. The Duke was ordered to the post of Governor and Commander-in-Chief of the Bahamas Islands, a tiny speck of the empire.

Colonial Splendor: The news that a man born and trained to be King of England was coming to rule a remote outpost was greeted with great astonishment and excitement. No one could remember when royalty had ever set foot in the colony although it was recalled that Prince Albert Victor, the second son of Queen Victoria, had once landed here.

Everyone realized that the ex-King would certainly draw American money to Nassau. Even as the Duke and Duchess were sailing toward the islands, tourists (most unusual for August) and journalists were already awaiting the royal couple.

As the great grandson of Queen Victoria who had liberated the slaves, the Duke was invested with near-divine status in the eyes of many of the black people. The story of how he gave up his throne for love had passed into Bahamian folk legend — and into the lyrics of songster Blake Higgs which always drove the Duke into fits of laughter:

It was Love, Love alone
Cause King Edward to leave the throne.
It was Love, Love alone
Cause King Edward to leave the throne
We know that Edward was good and great
But it was Love that cause him to abdicate.

The Duke and Duchess brought not only constant media attention to themselves and their wartime home but also a style, an elegance, a certain chic that had not been seen before in Government House.

It was Sir Harry Oakes, considered the most important man in the Bahamas, who lent his house, Westbourne, to the Windsors while they were waiting for Government House to be refurbished. Oakes owned almost a third of the island and was the largest private employer. He had built an airfield, a golf course, bus lines and hotels and he loved to operate a bulldozer on his lands.

It was also Sir Harry who unwittingly brought unwanted worldwide attention to the

Bahamas after his murder during a night of wild thunder and lightning on July 7, 1943. The world press tagged it "the Crime of the Century." There was an influx of American journalists and crime reporters and writers including the famed Erle Stanley Gardner.

The murder has remained unsolved to this day though Oakes' son-in-law, Count Alfred Fouquereaux de Marigny, was originally charged with the crime. He was acquitted after trial but deported as an undesirable.

It was a particularly brutal murder. Sir Harry had been beaten and burned and his body was covered with feathers from a pillow. Harold Christie, who eventually became Sir Harold, had spent the night in the house and there were reports that he had been threatened. The murder and the resulting publicity had

their last visit to the colony staying with their friends, Lord and Lady Dudley who lived at Greycliff, a lovely colonial mansion next to Government House—now an inn and elegant restaurant. They were received with all honor by the Governor, the New Zealander Sir Ralph Grey.

Royal Visitors: Although the British king who gave up his crown for "the woman I love" was the only member of British royalty to actually live on these isles, it has been a popular vacation spot for a number of various royal families.

Queen Elizabeth II was the first reigning monarch to visit the Bahamas. A national holiday was declared when her yacht, *HMY Britannia,* dropped anchor in Bahamian waters for a three-day official visit in February, 1966. A highlight of her visit was the banquet served in

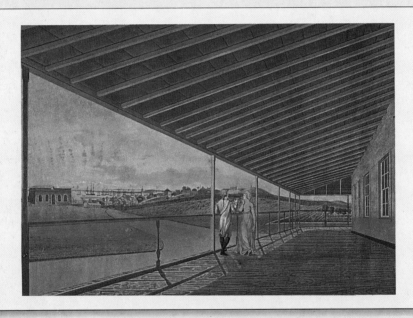

caused a great deal of anxiety for the Duke and Duchess and may have contributed to the Duke's decision not to finish his full five-year term. He resigned in the spring of 1945, a few months before the term officially ended. The Duke of Windsor formally ceased to be Governor of the Bahamas on April 30 and he and his wife left the Bahamas on May 3.

They returned over the years, staying for a few weeks most winters. They tried to keep these trips as quiet and unpublicized as possible and rarely went near Government House. They enjoyed the company of such old friends as the Vernays, the Sigrists, the Killams, Arthur Davis, Austin Levy, Rosita Forbes, Lady Oakes and Lord Beaverbrook.

In April, 1968, the Duke and Duchess paid

the Government House ballroom.

Other members of the British Royal Family who have been entertained at Government House include: Prince Philip, Prince Charles, Princess Anne and Capt. Mark Phillips, Princess Margaret, the late Princess Alice, the Duke and the Duchess of Kent, Princess Alexandra and the Hon. Angus Ogilvy.

Nassau has many permanent reminders of visits undertaken by the British Royal Family. There is a plaque at the Central Bank of The Bahamas noting its opening dedication by

British Colonel John Irving etched this elegant Bahamian scene in 1802 (above). Ever in the social spotlight, the Duke and Duchess of Windsor enjoy an evening out in Nassau (right).

70

Queen Elizabeth II. Another plaque notes the laying of the bank cornerstone by Prince Charles. Princess Anne unveiled a monument in the gardens of the former Royal Victoria Hotel. The monument was a salute to the 250th year of Parliamentary democracy in the Bahamas. Princess Margaret earned herself the nickname as the "Calypso Princess" because of her love for music and dancing.

Nassau's largest dock was named the Prince George Wharf after a Royal Navy visit that featured a Bahamas tour by Prince George, later the Duke of Kent. He returned in 1935 for a honeymoon with his Greek bride, the Princess Marina. Their honeymoon was filled with sunny days, fishing trips and social events. The royal couple also met U.S. President Franklin D. Roosevelt who was fishing in Bahamian waters.

Greek and other Balkan Kings have for many years favored the Bahamas as a holiday and honeymoon retreat. Bulgaria's King Simeon II honeymooned with his Queen Margarita at the Emerald Beach Hotel in 1962.

Other royalty have graced the Bahamian "Playground of Kings." The octogenarian King Olav V of Norway, an expert sailor was the guest of the Robert H. Symonettes for three weeks in 1981. For his 80th birthday King Olav V was presented a gold trophy for winning the Duke of Edinburgh Series in Nassau. The King's son, Crown Prince Harald has also competed in Bahamian sailing events.

Romania's King Michael and Queen Anne added a touch of royal glamor to the Hellenic Ball in 1984 at the Crown Ballroom of Paradise Towers. The royal couple was accompanied by their daughters, the Princesses Margarita, Maria and Sophie.

Among the most famous royal visitors in recent years were Princess Diana and Prince Charles. But Princess Diana unwittingly garnered most of the publicity when she was photographed with telescopic lenses in a bikini. She was visibly pregnant and the photo was published in a London newspaper. Buckingham Palace was outraged and the photo was deemed an inexcusable violation of privacy. For the remainder of the royal holiday on Windermere Island, press activities were severely restricted.

Windermere Island, which is connected by bridge to Eleuthera, became a holiday mecca for Prince Charles through his late great-uncle, Earl Mountbatten of Burma. Lord Mountbatten visited Windermere Island on an annual basis and introduced the Prince of Wales to this resort. Titled visitors who have spent holiday time on Windermere Island include the Duke and Duchess of Abercorn, the Viscount and Viscountess William Astor, Lady Anne Orr-Lewis, the Marquess of Milford Haven and the Viscountess Harriet de Rosiere.

Another titled fan of Bahamian holidays was the Baroness von Trapp whose life was portrayed in the prize-winning film, *The Sound of Music.*

Beyond Posh: With such a strong strain of royal history in the Bahamas it is appropriate that Wyndham Hotels has chosen "Royal Bahamian" as the name of one of the Bahamas' most elegant hotels. Formerly the Balmoral Beach Club, this plush hotel reopened late in 1985 after a $7 million restoration. The Royal Bahamian reflects the physical grandeur of what was once the Bahamas' most prestigious resort hideaway.

The old Balmoral Beach Club was the creation of British developer Sir Oliver Simmonds who began work on its construction almost immediately following World War Two. For years he had been aware that the very wealthy, very

powerful, world leaders, royalty and the most famous stage, screen, opera, ballet and concert stars, were constantly searching for closed little corners of the world where they could find peace and privacy along with the best accommodations. To further enhance the prestige of his new property, Simmonds spent a full year spreading the word that his Balmoral Beach Club was so ultraexclusive that it would operate as a private club and would be restricted to members only and their approved guests.

As a result, Simmonds found himself besieged with requests for membership and reservations from all corners of the world. They gravitated to the club for its elegance and fanatical commitment to privacy, which went so far as to rule out records of many celebrity visits.

"The Balmoral was always one long continuing secret," said Valencia Saunders, a former Balmoral employee and now a restaurant manager at the Cable Beach Hotel. "The guests came for privacy and service and we gave them both. But you couldn't help wondering on occasion what intricacies brought a Prince from Spain or a multi-millionaire from Italy to seek the seclusion of the Balmoral."

Simmonds opted for semi-retirement after 16 years of success, and the private club became a public hotel in 1967. However, it could (and frequently did) reserve the right to accept only the type of clientele it had catered to in the past. There were some notable exceptions. When the Beatles were being mobbed from New York to Hong Kong and

years at the Balmoral. He now manages the Ambassador Beach Hotel.

Other post-war developments in New Providence and some of the Family Islands served as a magnet for the wealthy and notable. Dr. Wenner-Gren sold his Hog Island property to A&P heir, Huntington Hartford, who brought up much of the remaining property from individual owners. Hog Island was renamed Paradise Island and Hartford embarked on an extensive development program designed to attract the jet set. Dr. Wenner-Gren's guesthouse by the shore of the man-made Paradise Lake was converted into the now famous Cafe Martinique and the Ocean Club, which used to be Dr. Wenner-Gren's winter home, became a luxury resort. The late Shah of Iran stayed at the Ocean Club while he was in residence on

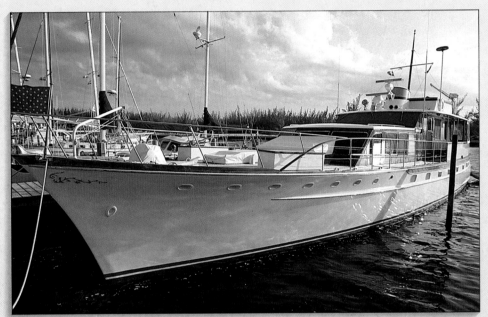

could find no escape from the effects of their fame, they were accepted by the Balmoral.

The Beatles were awed by the fact that they could walk the byways of the compound, sun at the poolside, walk through the dining room and roam the beaches of Balmoral Island, seemingly unrecognized. On return visits to the island, the Duke and Duchess of Windsor enjoyed the privacy and pleasures of Balmoral. Richard Nixon was known for arriving unexpectedly during his tenure as president, often dropping in by boat.

"He knew he had perfect privacy once he got onto the property and that coming by boat he circumvented news of his arrival so that he could enjoy that privacy," remembered Tommy Thompson, who rose to maitre d' during his 16

Paradise Island. One of the island's most famous and certainly the most elusive guests in recent years was the late Howard Hughes who took over the entire ninth floor of Britannia Towers from 1970 to 1972.

Highly Exclusive: Lyford Cay, actually a peninsula on New Providence, is another Bahamian haven for international socialites, royalty, the titled, and financiers. The club was founded in the 1950s by multimillionaire Canadian developer E.P. Taylor. He set out to create a top-notch club resort which operates more like

Since the Thirties luxurious yachts have sailed the world's wealthy around the Bahamas (above). Poolside posh, ready for the best of them at the Lyford Cay Club (right).

a community. Behind the pink walls and guarded gates is a lush 1,200-acre-(500-hectare) residential resort. It is geared toward golf and tennis, yachting and deep sea fishing. More than 225 private houses are set on winding sea canals, along white sand beaches and around an 18-hole golf course.

There are a diverse mix of nationalities here — British, French, Swiss, Greek, Brazilian, Spanish, Canadian, German and Americans. One thing that has remained constant is the privacy and security the club continues to offer. "It is the only really private place left in the world today," declares Baroness Meriel de Posson, a long-time Lyford member who returns year after year from London. The club maintains its own fire and security staff headed by Security and Fire Director Arthur Hailey

U.S. President Lyndon Johnson's daughter, Lucy, spent her honeymoon.

Eleuthera is another popular gathering spot for the wealthy and powerful movers and shakers. The Windermere Island Club continues to be favored by royalty and financial barons. There is the nearby Winding Bay Beach Resort, the one-time estate of the late Arthur Vining Davis, boss of Alcoa. The Cotton Bay Club has welcomed guests such as Henry Luce and Pan Am's founder Juan Trippe.

The Bimini Islands are still known as the "Big Game Fishing Capital of the World." They first gained attention in the 1930s through the visits of novelist and big game fisherman Ernest Hemingway as well as Howard Hughes and Zane Grey. Hemingway headquartered in Lady Helen Duncombe's Compleat Angler Hotel and

(author of such best-sellers as *Airport* and *Hotel*), a permanent resident of Lyford Cay.

Other residents include Greek shipping magnate Stavros Niarchos who usually has his 380-foot (116-meter) yacht brought to the Bahamas as an auxiliary to Villa Niarchos. Other residents include Sean Connery, American TV personality Gary Moore, Princess Annmari Bismarck, Sir Harold Christie, Wendy Vanderbilt Lehman, Count and Countess de-Rovenel, Lord Martonmere, a former governor of Bermuda, and Canadian actress Rosanna Seaborn whose house includes Roman baths.

Not far from Lyford Cay is a waterfront mansion called Capricorn now owned by international singing star Julio Iglesias. It was once the home of Sir Francis Peek and was where

was the first person in memory to land a bluefin tuna on rod and reel. The hotel's popular bar today houses a priceless collection of Hemingway memorabilia.

Hemingway's property on Bimini was given to him by Mike Lerner, the philanthropist who shared Hemingway's passion for big-game fishing and hunting. Lerner's elegant home, "The Anchorage," is now the hotel and restaurant of Bimini Blue Water Limited's complex. One of the cottages is famous as Marlin Cottage, Hemingway's hideaway. The late Congressman Adam Clayton Powell also made Bimini his second home.

Another elusive Bahamas resident is financier Robert Vesco. Sought by the U.S. government in connection with a multi-million-dollar investment fraud case, his off-and-on presence supports the islands' reputation as a place where the most sought after and most public figures can achieve a measure of privacy and secrecy.

Tracking 007: Vesco conjures up images of real cloak and dagger intrigue—the centerpiece of the James Bond mythology. Ian Fleming liked the Bahamas so much that he set some of his most glamorous James Bond novels here. He allowed 007 to amuse himself playing baccarat in the gambling rooms of Nassau's posh casinos.

The setting for *Dr. No,* the first Bond film, was inspired by Fleming's visit to Inagua. He found this Bahamian isle as strange as it is beautiful. He realized that this island, with its lake "only a couple of feet deep and the color of a corpse," would make a fitting home for Dr. No.

Besides Sean Connery, the other star of

Thunderball was the Bahamas itself; the screenplay was designed to take full advantage of the islands' natural assets. This film revealed to the world the Bahamas' fabulous underwater world. Bond (Sean Connery) and Domino (Claudine Auger) meet underwater and swim through coral gardens among brilliantly colored tropical fish. Later they engage in the first underwater love scene and swim to a perfect beach where tall palms grow from a crescent of sugary sand.

At the time that *Thunderball* was made in 1965 Paradise Island was still called Hog Island and you got there by boat (there's a bridge now). There were only a handful of estates scattered across the island. One of its biggest attractions was the glittering Cafe Martinique.

Filmmakers promised a hefty contribution to a favored charity and convinced the local gentry to allow themselves to be filmed enjoying their favorite haunt with their customary refreshments — a bucket of Beluga caviar and several cases of Dom Perignon. The result was a splendid affair which was captured on film as Nassau's finest citizens stepped from their motor launches dressed in black tie and sipped champagne in the tropical night.

Although Connery moved from island to island in *Never Say Never Again,* the Bahamas once again figure in this film as Bond travels to Nassau. He walks through the famous straw market and along a tropical street lined with colonial buildings in Bahamian pink. Later, Bond stands at an outdoor bar over the water as an ocean liner steams toward the Nassau dock. Clearly, James Bond has become one of the Bahamas most visible and elegant visitors.

Island Kingdoms: In a nation that numbers at least 700 islands there are enough isles for wealthy Bahamians and the expatriate community who seek the ultimate escape to set up their own island kingdoms. For some, the islands are a weekend refuge from the bustle of Nassau. For others the islands are their winter or year-round home.

"Most people who own their own islands are very wealthy people who look to the island as their own little kingdom," explained a Bahamian whose family owns an island. "The island idea makes it possible for someone to set up everything exactly as he wants it. The police hardly ever appear and to a limited degree one is the law on his island.

"The trip down to the island is somewhat like Fantasy Island. We fly down on an old seaplane from Nassau and when we arrive we are met by the caretaker and taken up to the main house. As soon as you step on the island there is a feeling of incredible peace. The sounds are the sounds of waves, sea gulls and other birds. There are no intrusions. You just don't have to have anything on the island you don't want. It is really a rare privilege to be on the island and know that it is yours."

Some of the private islands aren't developed at all and the owners use them as private campgrounds. Other are elaborately developed with a number of houses including guesthouses and boat houses. Owners use their isles as a base to enjoy beaches and remote fishing and diving spots. For those who are seeking the ultimate in privacy a personal island offers the perfect solution.

English teatime on the terrace remains the custom at the Windermere Club on Eleuthera (left), while hot tubs bring California chic to other enclaves (right).

PLACES

Around these 700 islands, tiny cays and nameless rocks, the many-shaded sea sometimes seems to rise around the land like a billowing quilt. The sea has been a source of isolation, of sustenance in hard times, and a bearer of fortune to the Bahamas, and for many visitors the sea is the siren that calls them here — to sail, to swim, to dive among coral encrusted wrecks. Spanish explorers called the sea here *bajamar,* or shallow sea, yet to know this sea is to know only the approach to the Bahamas, the beginning.

On Inagua flamingos posture and preen unseen. On Cat Island, at the end of an overgrown road, an old plantation lies in ruins, covered with vines. These are islands of secrets — and of brash realities — of tangled gardens and manicured lawns, of satellite dishes and weathered sloops.

On the streets of Freeport and in the high-rise resorts, a visitor can feel as close to middle America as the 30-minute flight from Miami to Bimini. A step beyond the well-known destinations can take you worlds away, to a land of unexpected colors and characters — the flaming red blooms of a poinciana tree against a bright yellow house, *warri* players on a shady porch, a young woman in a dark business suit hurrying down a narrow road to work.

Although the distances between the islands are not large, travel between the less populous one must often be leisurely — on infrequently scheduled flights or by boat. It is at this gentle pace that they are best enjoyed.

A seaplane rumbles, roars and takes off; the tide laps against a dock; a diver's splash breaks the skin of the water; sailboats return home to the harbor in the last of the light. From the mud flats of Andros to the fish-laden waters off the Berry Islands, it is a country to be felt, seen and heard, and — in some quiet moment between high tide and the turning back out to sea — discovered.

The following chapters have been divided into three sections: New Providence Island, Grand Bahama Island, and the Family Islands. Though small in size, New Providence Island is the hub of the Bahamas and site of the capital. Easy to reach, with many large hotels and other facilities, New Providence attracts more visitors than any other Bahamian island, followed by Grand Bahama Island and its city, Freeport. The rest of the islands — the Family Islands — are like the family jewels of the Bahamas, each one unique. We've covered the major Family Islands and a number of those that are almost "undiscovered."

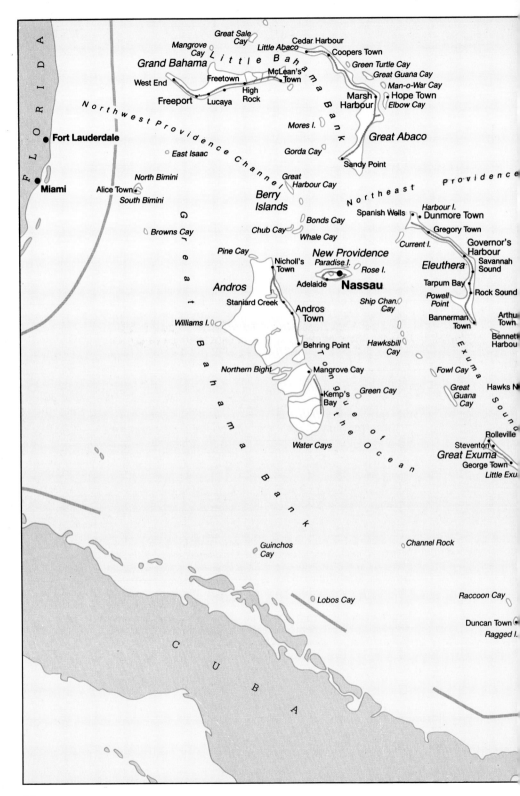

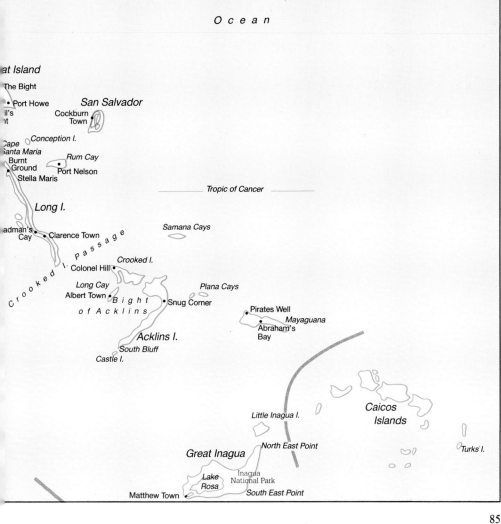

The Bahamas

70 km

Channel

A t l a n t i c

O c e a n

at Island

The Bight

Port Howe   *San Salvador*

il's
t   Cockburn
           Town

Cape   *Conception I.*
Santa Maria
  Burnt   *Rum Cay*
  Ground   Port Nelson
  Stella Maris

Long I.

                              Tropic of Cancer

adman's   Clarence Town   *Samana Cays*
  Cay

                    P a s s a g e

                  Crooked I.
            Colonel Hill

  Long Cay   *Plana Cays*
  Albert Town *B i g h t*
    o f A c k l i n s Snug Corner

C r o o k e d   I.   Pirates Well
                                                Mayaguana
                                        Abraham's
                                        Bay

          Acklins I.
            South Bluff
      Castle I.

                                                            Caicos
                                                            Islands

                              Little Inagua I.

                          North East Point   *Turks I.*

          Great Inagua

            Lake   Inagua
            Rosa   National Park
  Matthew Town   South East Point

85

NEW PROVIDENCE ISLAND

For centuries New Providence Island has been the hub of the Bahamas, where "everyone" went, "everything" happened, and the town and port of Nassau reigned in bustling splendor at the center of it all. Reclining seductively on the north end of New Providence Island, Nassau is the island's Victorian mistress, idyllic paradise, financial center, worldly capital — a coquette with many masks.

Located on a large, sheltered harbor, Nassau has swung many times from boom town to backwater and back again. But she has always been an enticing lure for both Bahamians and foreigners seeking easy riches or just an honest day's work.

Young people from the Family Islands have traditionally come to Nassau to "make it" when employment prospects on their own islands are non-existent or grim, and to be born on New Providence Island implies an automatic sophistication. (You might hear an old-timer boast, "I don't know those other islands. I'm a Nassau boy.")

Proud Bahamians call their country the "Switzerland of the West," and with justification. The Bahamas' strict bank secrecy laws, huge Eurodollar market and nearly 400 banks licensed to operate within or from the Bahamas make its capital a magnet for foreign currency. Magnetic, too, is the appeal of diamond watches, pearls and seductive perfumes in the windows of Bay Street shops. Nassau is an enticing figure, half dressed in old, half in new, where cool verandahs, limestone walls and jalousies cracked open to catch an afternoon breeze compete for space with traffic circles and offices.

If the sights and sounds of Nassau grow too heady, or too tiring, just a short drive down the right road will take you away from it all — to the rest of New Providence Island. From the old settlements of Adelaide and Fox Hill, to the posh seclusion of Lyford Cay and Mount Pleasant, you will find another fascinating world. Old money, new money, foreign money and money eked out to "get by" combine to give New Providence a generous helping of Bahamian tradition, improvisation and pizzazz.

And then, there are the warm days and bright nights of Paradise Island. Formerly called Hog Island, she is an upstart can-can girl compared to elegant Nassau — and attracts more tourists than any other island in the Bahamas. East of Miami, west of the French Riviera, her hotel towers and gambling casino are the natural habitat of shieks, financial wizards, grandmothers and bikini-clad beauties.

So let the chapter on Nassau be your guide to a fascinating walk about the old town — the government buildings, bustling Bay Street, dozens of historic homes. Then the New Providence chapter will introduce you to the island beyond — ancient forts, old African settlements, quiet beaches, elegant homes. And when you're through, the sparkling white bridge over the harbor will take you to Paradise Island, where you will take up the intriguing story of the men and dreams who made this tiny island across Nassau Harbour what it is today. Put on your walking shoes and sunhat, and enjoy!

NASSAU

For many people Nassau is the Bahamas. Located on the island of New Providence, since early times it has been the commercial hub of the archipelago. Once a quiet, sleepy sort of place, Nassau is now a rapidly expanding city, where the pace is sometimes hectic and traffic often crowds the narrow streets.

The city is one of contrasts. Downtown Nassau still retains much of its colonial architectural heritage and charm. While downtown Nassau developed into a quaint and architecturally attractive colonial town, containing the major commercial outlets, and reserved for the white elite, Grant's Town, or "Over-the-Hill," had much poorer and more humble buildings. Its settlers lacked the necessary capital to develop it properly, and it grew without supervision. Today it is an area where streets are seething with life. Small wooden ramshackle shops abound though concrete buildings are becoming more common.

Originally known as Charlestown, but renamed in honor of the Prince of Orange — Nassau, who became William III of England, in 1695 Nassau comprised about 160 houses, one church and two public houses. The buildings, constructed mainly of wood with thatched roofs of palmetto leaves, huddled around the large, sheltered harbor which was to make Nassau both the most suitable seat of government and a haven for pirates and privateers.

After about 1670, privateers and pirates increasingly used Nassau as a base from which to plunder and destroy French and Spanish ships. The town suffered from several attacks of retaliation by the Spanish and French in the early 18th Century, and the attack on the town in 1703 by a combined Spanish and French fleet frightened most of the inhabitants away. Those who remained, "lived scatteringly in little huts, ready upon any assault to secure themselves in the woods," wrote a contemporary who visited Nassau in the early 1700s.

Woodes Rogers, the first Royal Governor of the Bahamas (1718-1721 and 1729-1732), arrived in Nassau to find the town in a dilapidated state and immediately set every available man, including pirates, to work to clean and rebuild Nassau "so that

Preceding pages: Nassau Harbour; street on Green Turtle Cay; Sunday in George Town, Exuma; view from Nassau water tower; Nassau buggy; Nassau policeman; and the Paradise Island lighthouse.

it began to have the appearance of a civilised place." When, during Rogers' second term of office, the House of Assembly convened for the first time, the twelve Acts passed included one to "lay out the town of Nassau."

Further expansion occurred in the 1740s when Fort Nassau was extensively renovated and Fort Montagu built. During William Shirley's governorship (1758-1768) Nassau was expanded and developed. He initiated a new survey of the town and reclaimed much mosquito-breeding swamp land, so that the town could expand eastwards. Among the many streets, lanes and paths laid out then was Shirley Street, which still honors the name of the governor who created it.

During his brother Thomas Shirley's governorship, the town faced bankruptcy and poverty. In 1783 a man named Schoepe, a German traveler in the Bahamas, described Nassau as having one tolerably regular street which ran next to the water.

Perhaps the greatest impact on the architecture of the town, until the building boom of the 1860s, was made by the Loyalists. Fleeing from the newly independent United States of America, those colonists loyal to King Goerge III soon transformed the shabby little port "into a town as well built as any ... and one which promised to become distinguished for its beauty." In four years the Loyalists and their slaves more than doubled the population of the Bahamas, and they brought with them the architectural style of the southern United States and their own variations of Georgian architecture.

Construction in the town was accelerated in the mid-19th Century, prompted by the sudden flow of money brought by the American Civil War when Nassau became the headquarters for the colorful blockade runners. In the late 19th Century, the town relied on the development of local industries, especially sponge, pineapple and sisal, but her spirits rose again — stimulated by profits from the transshipment of liquor (otherwise known as bootlegging) to the United States during Prohibition (1919-1933). By the early 1950s, tourism was established as the Bahamas' main industry. Parallel with the phenomenal growth of the tourist industry came Nassau's entry into worldwide banking and business. These developments — as tax

Below, the town and port of Nassau, as drawn for the Illustrated London News.

haven and resort hideaway — caused rapid expansion of the city of Nassau.

Old Town: Perhaps the most interesting streets and buildings in the city are in the old town which in 1788 was bordered on the east by East Street, the west by West Street, the north by Bay Street, and the south by West Hill and East Hill Streets. If this seems complicated, remember that **Bay Street,** or the Strand, as it was called, was the oldest street and bounded the town along the harbor. It is still the main street through Nassau. Facing Bay Street, in the center of the old city, between what is now Bank Lane and Parliament Street, are the **Public Buildings**. Built between 1805 and 1813, the three buildings originally housed the Post Office, Legislative Council, Court Room (center building), the Colonial Secretary's Office and Treasury (eastern building), and the House of Assembly, Surveyor General's Office and Provost Marshal's Office (western). They then overlooked the harbor, and the sea came right up to Bay Street immediately in front of them. Loyalist influence is evident here, for the Public Buildings were based on Governor Tyron's Palace in New Bern, an early capital of North Carolina.

The middle structure now houses the Senate Chamber, the Supreme Court and the Government Publications Office. The eastern building contains an office of the Ministry of Tourism while the western building still houses the House of Assembly. It was from an upstairs window of this latter building that the then opposition leader Lynden Pindling, now Prime Minister, threw the mace out in protest at the Government Boundaries of the Constituencies. As he walked over to the Speaker's table and took the mace up, he said, "This mace is the symbol of authority of this House and the authority belongs to the people, and the people are outside." He then hurled it through the window. Mr. Pindling and the Progressive Liberal Party Members then left the house. This day in 1965 was destined to go down in political history as "Black Tuesday."

Immediately south of the Public Buildings is the more modern **Supreme Court Building**, which is adjacent to the unusually shaped **Nassau Public Library**. Built as a prison between 1798 and 1800, it was converted to house the Nassau Public Library in 1873. Its exterior has recently been renovated and repainted. Inside this quaint building can be found one of the

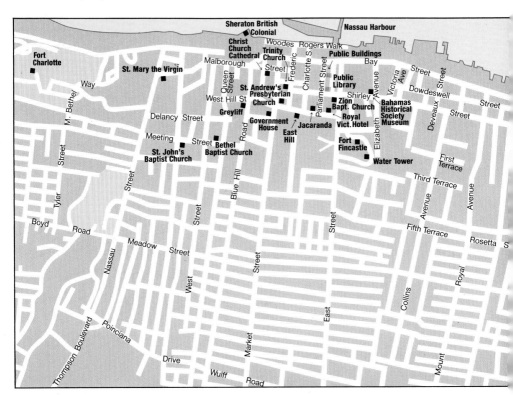

94

best collections of books on Bahamiana. It also houses a collection of prints, maps and old photographs which have been recently restored. There is also a fine newspaper collection, and a stamp collection. The library has a small collection of Arawak artifacts including a Lucayan skull, stone celts and a stone duho (or Indian ceremonial stool).

Smugglers, Spies, Royalty: Just across Shirley Street from the library are the grounds of the **Royal Victoria Hotel**, which was built between 1859 and 1861 to accommodate winter visitors. The main building, now vacant, can be best seen from East Hill and East Streets. Horace Greeley called it "the largest and most commodious hotel ever built in the tropics," and the three-story structure with its lofty encircling verandahs lived up to the praise. Floor-to-ceiling windows assured natural air conditioning for the luxurious bedrooms. It had separate Gentlemen's and Ladies' Parlors, a Hair-Dressing Salon, a Billiard Room, a Bar, a Dining Room in which servants outnumbered the guests, and a botanical garden. The centerpiece of this garden was a kapok tree so enormous a bandstand reached by a flight of stairs was erected in its branches. With the American Civil War, the Royal Victoria became overnight a hive of activity for buyers of cotton, dealers in munitions, Confederate officers, Yankee spies and newspaper correspondents. According to legend, the man who inspired the character Rhett Butler of *Gone With The Wind,* frequented the hotel bar and lounges. Blockade-runners lived there like sultans, and at the hotel's Blockade Runners' Ball, 300 guests consumed 350 magnums of champagne. Later, the Royal Victoria was used for more sedate social gatherings. Queen Victoria's consort, Prince Albert, and Neville and Austen Chamberlain were feted there. Winston Churchill also dined at the Royal Victoria. The hotel hung on tenaciously through the Depression, but the century-old hostelry could not keep up with the demands of post-war tourists, and closed in 1971. The present owner, the government, plans to convert portions of the Royal Victoria into a museum

Walking south on Parliament Street, one passes the **Green Shutters**, a lively and popular restaurant, with a pub-like atmosphere. The actual structure is believed to date back to 1865. Next door, on the southwest corner of Parliament Street, is

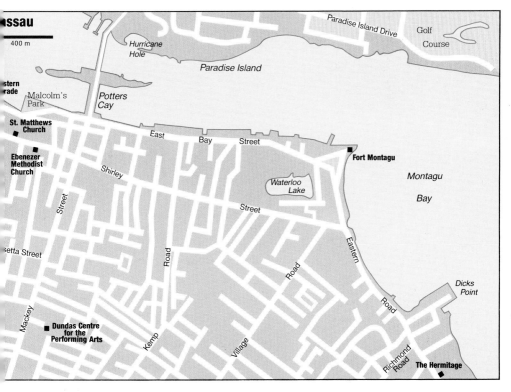

Jacaranda, built in the 1840s by the then Chief Justice Sir George Anderson who included in its structure a load of ballast stones at the corners. The house has a low pitched shingled roof, wide latticed verandahs, and the south side is covered with the traditional jalousies.

Opposite Jacaranda is the **Post Office Building** which houses various government ministries. Just west of the Post Office is **East Hill**, another 19th Century mansion. Built between 1840 and 1860 on a 5½-acre site, East Hill is built in the Georgian colonial style of handcut limestone blocks. Rooms open onto louvered wooden verandahs on the north and south sides, and doors and windows have wooden louvered outer shutters which allow for ventilation. Behind the house is the original stone kitchen which has two ancient fireplaces with an open hearth and dome-shaped ovens. Until recently the residence served as a club and restaurant but in 1986 was renovated to house offices.

To the west of Jacaranda is **Glenwood**, one of the oldest houses in Nassau. Its expansive grounds contain the grave of a former Chief Justice, Thomas Walker, a friend of Woodes Rogers. Opposite this property is **St. Andrew's Court**, formerly called Bank House. This fine old house which today houses law offices, was once owned and occupied by Alfred E. Mosely, Editor of the *Nassau Guardian* from 1887 to 1904. Continuing west, you pass the clean, white, fresh-looking **St. Andrew's Presbyterian Church** (The Kirk), built in 1810, but added on to at various periods. In 1864 the sanctuary was enlarged and the modern transept, portico and bell tower were built, and extensive renovations were made in the early 1950s. Leaving the Kirk one passes over Gregory Arch, named after John Gregory, Governor of the Bahamas from 1849 to 1854. On top of the hill known as Mount Fitzwilliam is **Government House**, the residence of the Governor-General, the Queen's representative in the Bahamas. Commanding an extensive view of the island, it is a pink and white neo-Classical mansion built in 1801. On the front steps one passes a statue of Christopher Columbus, modelled in London and imported by the then Governor, Sir James Carmichael Smyth, who presented it to the colony.

Sir James Carmichael Smyth, who became Governor of the Bahamas on May 8, 1829, worked diligently during his governorship to ameliorate slave conditions and

A peaceful moment before lunchtime at Greycliff, left. Columbus poised before Government House, right.

to abolish corporal punishment for female slaves. He met with fierce opposition in the House of Assembly which he was forced to dissolve twice. Ironically, more cases of cruelty were evident under his administration than at any other time.

Immediately across the road from Government House's western gate on the picturesque West Hill Street is **Greycliff**, partly hidden behind a high, handcut limestone block wall. This house is elegance itself, and is now one of the leading restaurants in Nassau. The graceful main doorway is supported by pillars; the house has an airy porch at the front and back, the rails and lattice work showing considerable craftsmanship. It is believed that the house, which was once French's Hotel, housed the West Indian Garrison which protected the city in the 18th and 19th centuries. An old kitchen, set off from the main house, contains a fireplace where the cooking was done.

Leaving Greycliff you immediately pass a plaque set in the "cliff" claiming that the oldest church in Nassau was on that site. Continuing west along West Hill Street, one passes several interesting old houses, including **Postern Gate**, **Ranora House** and **Sunningridge** situated at the top of Queen Street. This magnificent house's main entrance is part way up the steps leading to West Hill Street. On the corner of West Street and West Hill Street is **Villa Doyle** which was a partially restored palatial named after resident William Henry Doyle who was Chief Justice of the Supreme Court in the 1860s and 1870s. Opposite stands **St. Francis Roman Catholic Church**, built between 1885 and 1886, the first Catholic church in the Bahamas.

Turning north on West Street and descending the hill, we pass some fine old buildings and the **Greek Orthodox Church** which was built in the 1930s to accommodate the small Greek community which, until the late 1930s, was mainly employed in the sponge industry.

Turning east on Marlborough Street, one passes the quaint **Queen Street**, which still has an air of the past. No. 16 Queen Street is said to be 200 years old, and No. 28, with its ornate lattice work and traditional dormer windows, probably dates back to the mid-19th Century. **Devonshire House,** or No. 11 Queen Street, was built about 1840 and is an outstanding example of early British colonial architecture. It stands opposite a large modern office complex which was once occupied by Joseph

"The Kirk," St. Andrew's Presbyterian Church.

E. Dupuch. Mr. Dupuch, grand uncle of the well-known and controversial editor of Nassau's *The Tribune,* Sir Etienne Dupuch, was an architect, and was responsible for building the Kirk Hall on Princess Street, and the Masonic Temple on Bay Street.

Farther south on Queen Street is No. 30 which reflects Victoria and Colonial-style architecture. The bottom story of this two-story house is constructed of cut squared stone, while the top floor is of wood. It has the typical verandahs of bygone years which shade the northeast, east and south sides of the building. It may be as old as 170 years.

Next to Queen Street off Marlborough Street is Nassau Court at the foot of which stands an historic building, formerly the Town Chapel of the Methodist Church. It later became the Boys' Central School, the Government High School (established 1925), the Ministry of Works and until recently the Ministry of Tourism. It now houses the Ministry of Economic Affairs.

Cumberland Street runs parallel to Nassau Court. In the middle of this wide road stands **Hillside Manor**, once a rambling residence. Farther south is **The Deanery**, the residence of the Dean of Christ Church Cathedral, and one of the oldest residences in Nassau. Completed about 1803, this three-storied building is built of stone and chamferred quoins. Verandahs of three tiers were originally built on the north, east and west sides of the house. The fittings of the house, such as doors, dadas and cornices, some of which have been removed, were typical of the Queen Anne period. The original kitchen still stands to the west of the house. A one-storied building, it has a fireplace and domed brick oven. The northern end of the building is divided by a thick stone wall with narrow loopholes in lieu of windows. Known as the "Slaves' Quarters," this out-building is thought to have housed domestic slaves in the 19th Century.

Re-entering Marlborough Street, we face the **Best Western British Colonial Hotel**, said to be built on the site of Fort Nassau, which was constructed in the 1690s. The original Hotel Colonial was of wood and was destroyed by fire in 1922. The new Colonial Hotel, built in six months, opened for the reception of guests in February 1923. It is designed in the Spanish-American style, imported from South Florida as appropriate for the newly emerging tourist industry.

A portion of the hotel and its attrac-

The Colonial Hotel brought a Palm Beach ambience to Nassau when it was built in 1923.

tive arcade which contains offices and shops is on George Street. At its northern end is one of the oldest buildings in the city. **Vendue House**, a two-story building, most recently occupied by a section of the Bahamas Electricity Corporation, was built in the mid-18th Century as a single story arcaded building where traders sold goods at public auctions. Once known as the Bourse, it was the scene of many sales and auctions of slaves, cattle and imported goods. One of Nassau's best preserved buildings, it is scheduled to re-open as the Emancipation Museum.

Not far from Vendue House on George Street is **Christ Church Cathedral**, built in 1837. Standing on the site of a very early church, the new structure is of plain stone consisting of a nave, a center aisle, two side aisles and a western tower. The main west entrance is through a central square clock tower from which there is an immediate view of the large and beautiful stained-glass window over the altar. Immediately south of Christ Church is **Lex House**, which is thought to be one of the oldest houses in Nassau. It may have housed the Commander of the Spanish Garrison which occupied Nassau between 1782 and 1783. In 1978 an attorney, Roy Henderson, purchas-

ed the property and successfully restored this fine old house. The building now houses a law firm and real estate offices.

Turning north again, you can walk down George Street into Bay Street, the main street of the city. Opposite Market Street is the **Nassau Market**. On the site of the old Public Market, constructed in 1901, and which was destroyed by fire in early 1974, the modern market is located under the Ministry of Tourism's new office buildings. At the lively and bustling local market, Bahamians, mainly women, barter their straw work, tee-shirts, native jewelry, carvings and other assorted knick-knacks. It is a tough life but a lucrative one. The market women depend largely on tourists to buy their wares. Straw-work is the most popular. Most of it, which is made into baskets, hats, mats, table mats and dolls, is made from the top of the thatch palm. Plaiting the silver-top was traditionally carried out in Nassau and in many Out Island settlements, especially the Exumas, Long Island and Cat Island. It was customary, in the black settlements in New Providence and on the Out Islands, for women to weave the silver-top into long bands which were rolled into balls to be sold to agents in Nassau. There, other

Christmas stars brighten Bay Street, while in the background the Colonial Hotel's clock ticks off rush hour.

women made up baskets, hats and mats with the plait. If you walk through the entire market you emerge onto **Woodes Rogers Walk** along the harbor which was once the Market Range, where mail and sponge boats docked, and where conch, fish and vegetables were sold.

The harbor of Nassau, which has been so important to the development of the city, once came up to Bay Street. To cope with increased shipping in the late 1920s, during the era of Prohibition, the harbor was dredged to 25 feet (eight meters) and **Prince George Wharf** was built. The wharf was named after Prince George, Duke of Kent, to commemorate his visit here in 1928. The *HMS Britannia,* Queen Elizabeth II's yacht, the world's largest, has docked here often, most memorably when the Queen came for The (1985) Commonwealth Heads of Government Meeting at the Cable Beach Hotel.

Passengers arriving at New Providence by ship all land at Prince George Wharf. Cruise ships make frequent calls here and plans have been drawn up to add five new piers to the existing seven. Debarking cruise passengers will find inexpensive ferry boats to Paradise Island docked alongside the wharf ($2.00 each way), and a Tourist Information booth just beyond the wharf gates.

Not too far from the Market on Market Street is **Balcony House**. As the shipbuilding industry was active in Nassau in the first half of the 19th Century, houses were often built from shipwrights timbers and included peculiar features like the wooden brackets which support the balcony on Balcony House. The house was built of American soft cedar, probably near the end of the 18th Century. There is a slave kitchen and an ancient staircase which is thought to have come from a ship.

Britain on Bay Street: Re-entering Bay Street by Frederick Street, where the historic **Trinity Methodist Church** is located, we see some fine shops located in old buildings. Nassau is a mecca for collectors of china and crystal, and the shops are well supplied by European manufacturers, including Crieff Perthshire of Scotland, Lalique of Paris and Lladro of Almacera, Spain. Royal Doulton figurines and Wedgwood boxes, ash trays, vases, cups and saucers abound. Visitors can also purchase perfume at bargain prices, and sweaters of velvety lambswool and cashmere.

Also on Bay Street is the **Royal Bank**

Drivers await customers near Bay Street.

of Canada, which is the oldest extant bank in the Bahamas. This branch opened in Nassau in 1908 and moved to the ornate structure it now occupies in 1919. Formerly next door was the Prince George Hotel, a once popular night spot. Across the street is the **Masonic Temple** building, constructed in 1882. Masonic Orders have met in Nassau since its early days.

Farther east on Bay Street is the **Public Square** which has been recently relandscaped. The **Churchill Building**, housing the Prime Minister's Office, the Treasury, the Ministry of Finance and Department of Public Personnel, looks onto a spacious and well manicured square which boasts a bust of Sir Milo Butler, the first Bahamian Governor-General in an independent Bahamas. This bust, which is representative of the modern Bahamas, was sculpted by William Johnson of Little Harbour, Abaco. A statue of the British Queen Victoria, reminiscent of the Bahamas' colonial past, reigns on the opposite side of the square.

Leaving the Public Square in a southerly direction on Parliament Street, you pass a Memorial to Sir George Gamblin, an esteemed legislator (1901-1930), and also the **Cenotaph**, which displays plaques commemorating Bahamians who died in the two World Wars. Opposite the Cenotaph is the **Parliament Hotel**, a quaint three-storied structure dating back to the late 1930s. The Parliament Terrace is a pleasant restaurant which serves lunch and dinner on an outdoor patio. On the western corner of Parliament and Shirley Streets is **Magna Carta Court**, a building recently restored by a Nassau lawyer. The exposed cut stones displayed on this ancient structure are more reminiscent of St. Augustine, Florida, than of Nassau, but it is a fine effort in historic preservation.

The original city of Nassau expanded over the years. During the blockade era (1861-1865) the town grew rapidly as a result of increased wealth. By 1866 the existing boundaries of the town extended east to Victoria Avenue (originally Culmer Street). The Prohibition years brought further prosperity and, in the decades that followed, increasing tourism, foreign investment and banking led to further expansion. By the early 1980s, the city included Mackey Street to the east, Nassau Street to the west, and Meeting Street and School and Sand Lanes to the south. Thus you must travel a bit farther to explore the rest of the town.

Leaving East Street on Shirley Street in

Wood sculpture at the straw market (left) and near Parliament Square (right).

an easterly direction, you pass **Addington House**, the official residence of the Anglican Bishop of Nassau and the Bahamas. Given to the Diocese by Bishop Addington Venables, the second bishop of the Diocese, in 1876, legend has it that the house had been occupied by the Officer-in-Charge of the troops stationed at Fort Fincastle.

Fort Fincastle, situated on Bennet's Hill, to the south of the Bishop's residence, can be approached from Elizabeth Avenue. To reach the fort, pass the Princess Margaret Hospital, named in honor of Princess Margaret's visit in 1955, to the **Queen's Staircase**. These 66 steps lead to the fort and are said to have been cut in the sandstone cliffs by slaves in 1793 to provide access from the town to the fort. Shaped like a paddle-wheel steamer, Fort Fincastle was built by Lord Dunmore overlooking Nassau to guard "all the town and the road eastward where the enemy might probably effect a landing." Nassau, however, was never to be attacked after the construction of the fort in 1793. The fort served as a lighthouse until 1817, and was subsequently used as a signal tower.

Sharing Bennet's Hill with the fort is the **Water Tower**, erected in 1928. Its purpose is to maintain water pressure throughout the city, and it stands 216 feet (66 meters) above sea level, itself being 126 feet high (42 meters). The view of the island from the top of the tower is breathtaking. On special occasions, such as the visit of Queen Elizabeth II, the tower is adorned by a crown of lights, enhancing its beauty.

Descending from the vicinity of the fort, you can pass through the quaint district known as "Fort Fincastle." Opposite Prison Lane on East Street is the **Police Headquarters**. Erected in 1900 on the site of the old Agricultural Gardens, the buildings are a replica of the Old Military Barracks which were demolished at the turn of the century to provide the site for the building of the Colonial Hotel. The old **Guard House** has been renovated and preserves much of its original facade.

On the corner of East and Shirley Streets is **Zion Baptist Church**, built in 1835 shortly after the arrival of Rev. Joseph Burton of the Baptist Missionary Society of Great Britain. The spacious and popular church was destroyed by the 1929 hurricane and rebuilt under the leadership of Rev. Talmadge Sands. The church has been recently renovated and is now capable of holding 500 persons.

Policeman keeps watch at Nassau's water tower.

Returning to Shirley Street and Elizabeth Avenue, you find the headquarters of the **Bahamas Historical Society,** founded in 1959 to stimulate interest in Bahamian history and to collect and preserve historic materials. Inside is a small museum with a variety of artifacts, paintings, photographs and maps. Its prints and paintings include depictions of the infamous pirate, Blackbeard, and sketches of Lucayan Indians. There is a fine shell collection, some Loyalist artifacts which include a large grindstone for making meal flour, and household utensils including a coffee grinder and a chamber pot. The sponge collection gives insight into the different types of sponges, sponging being a Bahamian industry which, from the 1880s, sustained the economy for more than half a century. A few Arawak artifacts are also on display, including pottery sherds, stone celts and stone jewelry from various sites in New Providence. The building was given to the Historical Society by the Queen Victoria Chapter of the Daughters of the Empire who in 1904 planted **Victoria Avenue** with Royal Palms, many of which still tower gracefully over the street, which was once lined by residences of some of the leading citizens of the town.

Turning into Dowdeswell or Middle Street (so named because it is in the middle of Bay and Shirley Streets) you will notice some fine old houses with traditional verandahs, lattice work, dormer windows and gingerbread fretwork. One example is the **Carey Home,** which was constructed towards the end of the 19th Century of Abaco pine. Because the Dowdeswell Street area is subject to flooding during very high tides, the Carey House, like many on the street, is built on a three-foot (one-meter) stone foundation.

At the eastern end of Dowdeswell Street is the **Eastern Parade** and **Malcolm's Park** recreational and fair grounds. The latter was said to rest on reclaimed swampy land filled in by a Mr. Malcolm. The Eastern Parade used to be bounded on the south by several fine residences including **The Corners,** home of the late Cyril Solomon and **The Ark,** home of the late Sir Aubrey Solomon. On the northern side of The Parade was the Pan American Airways Building, now the Traffic Division of the Bahamas Royal Police Force. Pan American Airways operated the first passenger service between Miami and Nassau, the first flight taking place Jan. 2, 1929. The planes, the Commodore flying boat and

the Sikorsky amphibian twin-engine craft, landed in the harbor, and passengers were taken ashore in small boats. Later a ramp was laid so that planes were able to taxi onto the ramp and discharge their passengers directly onto the land.

At the end of the Parade is a part of the old burying ground, an extension of **St. Matthew's Churchyard**. This area contains many ancient tombs including one "In memory of John Wells, Esq., late Editor of the *Bahama Gazette*," the first newspaper to be published in Nassau. **St. Matthews Church**, the foundation stone of which was laid in 1800, is the oldest church building in the Bahamas. Opened for divine service in 1802, the church, once considered at the eastern extremity of the town, has a distinctive tower and steeple. Its architecture is a strange mixture of neo-Classical forms with Gothic proportions. The original stained-glass window was erected in memory of Bishop Venables. It was enlarged by the erection of a vestry room, organ chamber and new chancel, consecrated in December 1887.

Pondites and Potter's Cay: Near to St. Matthews, on Shirley Street, is **Ebenezer Methodist Church**. On the site of an earlier "meeting place" the present church was constructed between 1839 and 1841. Both churches are near to the **Pond** area. People living in this area refer to themselves as "Pondites", and celebrate together annually during Pond Festival Week held week of Easter Sunday. Eminent "Pondites" include the first two Governor-Generals in an independent Bahamas: Sir Milo B. Butler and Sir Gerald Cash. Part of the Butler family still lives in the Pond and operates businesses there. The area was also the site of the first **Gym Tennis Club**, which is now located in Winton in the eastern district. The original Gym Tennis Club, established by Nurse Florence Wood, was a gym club offering exercises for girls. It opened for ladies and men in about 1928. One concrete tennis court was constructed on the "Pond" property of Bob Hanna, whose son-in-law, Ned Isaacs, and daughter, Bertha Isaacs, were to become excellent tennis players and early champions in Nassau and Florida. In the 1930s, '40s and early '50s, there was discrimination against black players, who needed special permission to play on the courts of the hotels such as the New Colonial and the Montagu. The Gym Tennis Club produced some leading players, including

At Potter's Cay, fruit from the Family Islands for sale.

the Minns brothers and Cyril Burrows, and the Isaacs family which dominated the tennis scene for a few decades.

Not far from the "Pond" is the Paradise Island Bridge, and the busy Mackey Street/Paradise Island traffic roundabout. Underneath the bridge, is **Potter's Cay** dock and a teeming market where vendors sell conch, fish, fruit and vegetables. This market was formerly held along the Market Range, closer to the center of town, but today New Providence and Family Island fishing boats tie up here to sell their catches, including the Bahamas' special delight — grouper. Conch is also a Bahamian favorite, and is considered an aphrodisiac. In front of the boats, ladies, and some men, also sell vegetables and fruit, some of it local. There is a Ministry of Agriculture Produce Exchange at the end of the dock, and an outlet which sells chilled fish. Mailboats from the Family Islands tie up at the dock to take and unload freight and passengers. The bulky wooden boats carry everything from chickens to mattresses, stowed aboard and lashed to the sides.

Going south on Mackey Street, you soon come to the **Public Records Office**, **Department of Archives** and **Eastern Public Library**, located in a neo-Georgian-style building constructed in the early 1950s. The Archives, established in 1971, has a rich deposit of historical documents and books, and serves as a major research resource in the Bahamas. Records preserved in the Public Records Office include those of the executive branch of the Government, the Legislative branch and the Judicial branch. There are also photographs from the various Government Ministries and Departments, Family Islands, Schools, Churches, public corporations and private families. Microfilm copies of early original documents held in foreign repositories are also found there. The records held at the Archives are a treasure trove for the historian, the economist, the social and political scientist, the genealogist, the student and the general public alike. The Department of Archives additionally sponsors an annual exhibition during the first week in February. Booklets on these exhibitions are printed annually. Other publications include *A Guide to the Records of The Bahamas, Important Facts to know about the Commonwealth of The Bahamas* and *A Guide to African Settlements in New Providence*. The Library is a popular lending library and is well patronized by local students.

Conch shells cleaned and shined as souvenirs at Potter's Cay.

Next door is the **Salvation Army Headquarters in the Bahamas**. Started in the Bahamas in 1931, the Salvation Army soon built a wooden chapel and made attempts to spread the Christian mission in the Family Islands.

Mackey Street, once residential, is now one of the main thoroughfares running north to south in New Providence. It abounds with small shopping centers, restaurants and various businesses. It also contains the **Ranfurly Home For Children**, a charitable institution which houses orphans, and **The Dundas Centre for The Performing Arts**, a live theater which stages year-round entertainment.

At the western end of the old city on West Street, going south, you can explore **Meeting Street**, which received its name from its two Baptist churches, Bethel Baptist and St. John's Baptist, which met there from the 18th Century. Bethel Baptist Church was founded by a runaway slave, Sambo Scriven, and the land on which the present church sits was purchased in 1801. A dispute in the church led to the formation of St. John's Native Baptist Church, a few hundred yards away in 1832.

Nearby, on Delancey Street is a delightful old residence, **Buena Vista**, which is now one of the finest restaurants in the Bahamas.

Farther north, on Virginia Street, is **Mary's Anglican Church**, first used as a Chapel-of-East to Christ Church. The original church, which was destroyed in the severe hurricane of 1866, was replaced by the present building begun two years later. The Church's graveyard borders **The Western Cemetery**, which contains many ancient tombs. One approach to the cemetery is from Nassau Street which links the interior of the island with West Bay Street.

Nassau Awake: Modern Nassau, although it has lost some fine old buildings, which in some cases are replaced by modern office complexes and parking lots, still retains much of its charm. It is no longer a "quiet, sleepy hollow sort of place" as it was called by the poet Bliss Carman in the last century, but a busy, bustling modern town, known the world over as a fine tourist resort and banking center. For some nostalgic Bahamians, Nassau has changed for the worse. However, in recent years, the drive for preservation and change-of-use of some of the ancient buildings, originally residences, has taken root. Led by such institutions as the Bahamas Chamber of Commerce, the Bahamas National Trust, the Department of Archives and the Ministry of Tourism, efforts have been made to push for preservation and conservation while welcoming progress. Plaques giving historic information on buildings and sites have been erected by the Bahamas' Ministries of Tourism and Works, assisted by the Department of Archives, and walking tours sponsored by the former Ministry have begun. Efforts have been made to train taxi drivers and tour guides and to tutor them in the history of the city and its buildings.

Although not as quiet as Bliss Carman found it when he visited the town in the late 1880s, the city has upheld the dignity of which he wrote in the poem "White Nassau." Still to be seen on streets like Queen's Street are the colorful flowering plants and creepers, so vividly captured in some of the paintings of Winslow Homer. The center of the city, we must remember, is no longer residential. Every morning, thousands of people pour into Nassau to do business. At the end of the working day, the town becomes almost deserted except for police officers and the few tourists who stroll at night. It is then that the mystique and beauty of the historical and charming city of Nassau emerges to the full.

Winston Saunders, Nassau playwright, posed before the Dundas Center for the Performing Arts, left. Tangled gardens of old Royal Victoria Hotel, right.

NEW PROVIDENCE

New Providence, small as it is, 21 miles (34 km) long by seven miles (11 km) wide, is an island full of contrasts. Although its heart is in Nassau, its soul surely lives somewhere on the rest of the island, between the elegant homes and bright bungalows, threadbare sprawl and suburban developement. New Providence is the Bahamas' most populous island, and here, if anywhere, among the old British forts and African settlements, walled estates and inviting beaches, may be found the key to the country's diversity, contradictions and beauty.

The island is mainly flat but has a ridge of low hills along the north coast, which stretches from Nassau as far west as Love Beach. The Blue Hill Range, farther inland, separates New Providence's two lakes and rises to about 120 feet (37 meters). Prospect Ridge is an extension of the range which can be seen in Nassau. The eastern end of the island has a mainly rocky coast while the southern coast is flat, often very swampy, with shallow water along its rocky shore. Western New Providence is known for its pine barren forests (typical of the northern islands of Andros, Grand Bahama and part of Abaco), its potholes and caves. It has two lakes, a natural freshwater inland water hole called Mermaid's Pool, and fine white sandy beaches. Although there are reefs along the western coast, the water is generally favorable for swimming.

The pace of life on New Providence can seem slow outside of Nassau, although in recent years the increase in traffic has made even a leisurely drive on the outskirts somewhat hazardous. Yet excursions by car, motorbike or bicycle are the best ways to see the island. Visitors with more time than money might try the buses as well.

Cookouts, Cannon, Cricket: To the west of Nassau Street, past Nassau, **West Bay Street** winds along the seashore. The aquamarine color of the water is almost indescribable and can be distracting to the casual motorist. The road first passes the **Western Esplanade**, a popular stretch along the waterfront for strollers and

Canon of Fort Charlotte once guarded the harbor.

swimmers. On weekends Bahamians congregate there for the numerous "cookouts" where experienced culinary experts sell cool drinks and Bahamian food - often fried grouper, cracked conch or spicy conch salad.

From the esplanade you can see the western end of **Paradise Island** and its picturesque stone lighthouse. Built between 1816 and 1817 from native-quarried stone, the lighthouse long served as the signpost to the Port of Nassau and warned sailors of the perils of the sea. At first kerosene fueled, it was completely automated by 1958.

To the west, West Bay Street passes **Xavier's College**, a private school operated by the Roman Catholic Diocese, a section of the Road Traffic Department and the Bahamas Girl Guide Headquarters. South, on a hill, is a gunpowder storage unit, and on a hill to the west is **Fort Charlotte**, the largest fortification built by John, Earl of Dunmore, Governor of the Bahamas from 1787 to 1796. Manned with 42 large cannons in its heyday, the fort never fired a shot in anger. It stands today as a historic monument on 100 acres (40 hectares) which Lord Dunmore reserved as public lands. From the fort there is a commanding view of **Nassau Harbour**, **The Guns**, a small battery of cannon, and **Arawak Cay**, a man-made island constructed by the government of the Bahamas in the late 1960s. The cay accommodates the Customs Department, the Public Service Training Center and serves as a base for the reception of fresh water which is brought in by barge from Andros Island.

Strolling the ramparts of Fort Charlotte today, you might see two white uniformed cricket teams playing a match on the field below, or in the distance a cruise ship easing slowly towards the harbor. The main part of the fort, named in honor of the wife of King George III, was completed in 1789 when the memory of American revolutionary soldiers' brief occupation of Nassau was still fresh in everyone's mind. The middle bastion, Fort Stanley, came next, and the western section, called Fort D'Arcy, was added later. Cut out of solid rock with the walls buttressed with cedar, a dry moat surrounded the fort. The moat was spanned

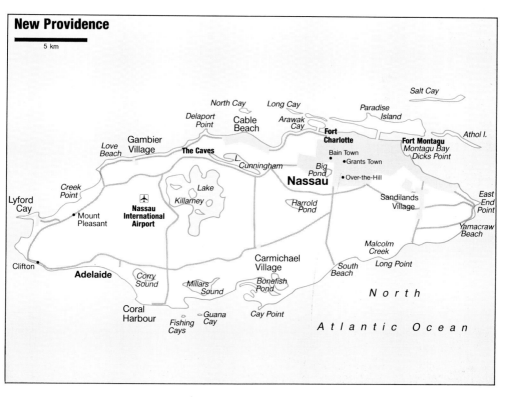

New Providence

5 km

by a wooden bridge on the northern side.

Leaving Fort Charlotte, turn right onto Arawak Cay and follow the signs for **Coral World** to a second human-made island, **Silver Cay**. Coral World is an educational and entertainment park, including an underwater observatory and tower, shark and turtle tanks, and marine garden aquariums. Adjacent to the park, Coral World's hotel offers sea-side villas, each with its own private pool.

Directly across West Bay Street from the entrance to Arawak Cay is Chippingham Avenue, with the entrance to the **Botanical Gardens** on your left and **Ardastra Gardens and Zoo** around the first bend, to your right. Both gardens feature numerous species of tropical plants in beautifully landscaped settings. In addition, Ardastra Gardens Zoo contains over 300 birds, mammals and reptiles – from lions to marching flamingos.

Returning to West Bay Street and continuing west you will soon approach **Saunders Beach**, bordered by large, somnolent casuarina trees. These magnificent trees, which seem like a cross between a pine and a willow, thrive on New Providence although they were imported from Australia. Saunders Beach is a popular bathing place.

On its way west, the road soon glides past the Grove, once a sisal plantation. Developed in the 1920s, the Grove is now an enviable residential suburb of Nassau. Adjacent to it is Highland Park, also a sought-after neighborhood.

Rooms with a View: West Bay Street then passes **Brown's Point** or "Go-Slow-Bend" where motorists can first capture a glimpse of the Bahamian Riviera known as **Cable Beach**. So named because the Bahamas' first cable communication with the outside world was made from there to Florida in 1892, the area began to develop as a resort facility in the 1950s. Throughout the 19th Century, horse racing was the main attraction, and it continued there until 1975. Pineapples were also cultivated until the 1920s when, according to historian Michael Craton, the area "became dotted with the stucco palaces of the American *nouveaux riches*." In 1954 the Emerald Beach Hotel opened, the first hotel in the Bahamas to boast airconditioning.

Blue lagoon of Carnival's Crystal Palace Resort.

A complex of hotels dominates this strip of beach. The Wyndham Ambassador Beach Hotel, built on the site of Westbourne, where Sir Harry Oakes was mysteriously murdered in 1943, is the most easterly. Next to it is the Nassau Beach Hotel, which lies adjacent to the former site of the old Emerald Beach Hotel. In the late 1980s, the Emerald Beach was replaced by a five-tower complex of gleaming glass, Carnival's Crystal Palace Resort and Casino with an adjacent convention center. It includes a huge gambling casino and a complex of shops which sell an assortment of Bahamian and imported goods. About a mile farther west is the **Meridien Royal Bahamian Hotel**, a luxury hostelry on the site of the once famous Balmoral Club and Hotel. This elegant spread, where the cottages have names instead of room numbers, is worth a visit, if only to gaze at the pink colonial hideaway that was once a favorite private retreat of the world's elite – from the Beatles to Richard Nixon. Other hotels and time-sharing villas line the coastlines as well.

Caves and Coves: Leaving Cable Beach behind, you soon arrive at **Delaport Point**, and another strip of inviting beach. Near the point is Delaport Village, formerly a plantation. The road continues hugging the coast, affording lovely views of the sea. Very soon it reaches **The Caves**, which developed naturally out of soft limestone. Above them is an inscription commemorating the arrival of the first member of the British Royal Family to visit the Bahamas, Prince Alfred, Duke of Edinburgh, who landed on New Providence on Dec. 3, 1861. Not far from The Caves is Blake Road, which leads to John F. Kennedy Drive and to the airport. At the intersection of Blake Road and West Bay Street is Conference Corner where John F. Kennedy, Harold Macmillan and John Diefenbaker planted three trees to mark their meeting in 1962.

The road then passes Orange Hill, a small hotel and restaurant overlooking a fine swimming beach which stretches for several hundred yards. The coast becomes rocky near **Gambier Village**, which was settled originally by liberated Africans brought to the Bahamas by the British Royal Navy in 1807. An early settler in Gambier Village was Elizah Morris, an ex-slave who was involved in the Creole Mutiny which occurred in Bahamian waters off the coast of Abaco in 1841. The villagers, who were eventually given a school and a church, lived mainly by farming and used to sell their produce in the Nassau Market. The village also has some small shops.

Farther west along the coast is **Love Beach**, named after a family of that name, now a fine residential area of private homes and a series of apartment complexes. Near Love Beach is Old Fort, originally part of the Charlottesville Estate. An old house remains on the site overlooking one of the best beaches in New Providence. Passing Lightbourn's Creek and the old Waterloo Estate, once owned by William Wylly, a plantation owner and political firebrand in 19th-Century Nassau, we soon approach Lyford Cay.

Exclusive Paradise: Once owned by the Loyalist William Lyford, development of **Lyford Cay** was begun in the early 1950s by H.G. Christie. However, it was a Canadian financier, E.P. Taylor, who turned the wooded area into a rich man's paradise. This exclusive enclave is the home or second home of the rich and famous, among them shipping magnates and American novelists. Outside its security-controlled gates is a small shopping center with several shops, including one with luxurious furnishings and posh bric-a-brac. Inside are tasteful, sometimes elegant homes along well paved streets that meander past manicured gardens and past canals that enable yachtsmen to dock their vessels literally in their backyards. There is also a luxurious Club and Hotel, one of the finest golf courses on the island and numerous tennis courts. The club caters to swimmers, with a large pool, and extensive beachfront, and also promotes scuba diving and waterskiing.

Nearby is a less exclusive suburb, **Mount Pleasant**, where many professional Bahamians have made their homes. Some work at the nearby Divi Bahamas Beach Resort and Country Club. On the edge of the club's golf course are the ruins of an old plantation.

Clifton Plantation: At the extreme western tip of New Providence is **Clifton**, a former plantation, once owned by an Attorney General of the Bahamas, William Wylly, who also owned plantations at Tusculum (near Gambier) and Waterloo (near Lyford Cay). By 1818, Wylly owned 67 slaves who lived on his three plantations. Clifton was the largest. Some ruins can still be seen, although not as extensive as those found in 1891 by a travel writer named J.H. Stark, who reported finding the remains of three large gates and a wide carriage drive leading to a house built on the English plan, and the remains of a coach house and stables for several carriage horses. He also noticed large slave quarters.

Today, Clifton is the site of the main power plant of the Bahamas Electricity Corporation and also serves as a gasoline storage depot. A large brewery has also been constructed there. The rocky coast of **Clifton Point** offers a fantastic view of the ocean - the color of the water a deep blue. In days gone by, Clifton was used as a landing place for passenger ships when the weather was too rough for them to enter the harbor at the Nassau Bay.

Adelaide and Carmichael: Continuing along the coast road, you pass the Divi Bahamas Resort's golf course where the remains of another old plantation can be seen. About two miles (three km) east of

this is **Adelaide** named after William IV's Queen. Situated at South West Bay, Adelaide was founded in 1831 by Governor James Carmichael Smyth. The original inhabitants were liberated Africans, captured from the Portuguese vessel *Rosa*. At that time, slavery had been outlawed in England, so the 157 Africans were automatically free upon landing in Nassau, a British port. They were settled at Adelaide. Supplied with hatchets and hoes for farming, they were encouraged to build their own homes in this new village. Some years later a school was founded there. In the early 1960s, the village contained quite a number of thatched huts typical of dwellings built by the Africans in the 19th Century. Today, although the village is fairly modernized – it has electricity and telephones – it still retains some of its quaintness and has an aura of peacefulness.

Not far from Adelaide is **Coral Harbor**, a mainly residential area which also accommodates the Bahamas' Defence Force Headquarters. It has man-made canals and fine docking facilities.

Several miles inland to the east is

Sparkling clean Adelaide Village.

Carmichael Village, originally known as Headquarters. This was perhaps the earliest Liberated African settlement founded by James Carmichael Smyth. In the 19th Century many of the Carmichael residents worked as domestics and laborers in Nassau. From a very early date in its existence, around 1825, some of the natives of Carmichael formed a settlement near Nassau, Grant's Town, in order to be nearer the Nassau Market. Today, Carmichael is a widely scattered settlement containing many modern residences, subdivisions and farms. Very little of the original village is to be seen.

From Carmichael Village you can follow Gladstone Road to John F. Kennedy Drive, which runs along the shores of **Lake Cunningham**. Continuing along Carmichael Road, turn north on Blue Hill Road to pass the Independence Shopping Center at the intersection of Harold Road and Blue Hill Road.

On the corner of Blue Hill Road and Wulff Road is St. Barnabas Anglican Church. If you go north you reach **Bain Town**, located just west of **Grant's Town**. Originally distinct, the two have merged into one. The original Bain Town was bordered on the east by Blue Hill Road, on the north by South Street, on the south by Poinciana Drive, and on the west by Nassau Street. The area, originally a 140-acre (57-hectare) land grant to one Susannah Weatherspoon, was in the mid-19th Century sold to a black Bahamian businessman, Charles H. Bain. At the turn of the century, most of the houses in the area were made of wood, with porches and thatched roofs. Today, much development has taken place, and while there are still some small wooden houses, now with shingled roofs, there are also some larger modern buildings like Woodcock Primary School.

Over-the-Hill: This area, like Grant's Town to the east, is seething with life. Laid out between 1820 and 1829, it included the area of land bordered on the east by East Street, west by Blue Hill Road, north by Cockburn and Lees streets and south by the Blue Hills. The entire area, which is densely populated, is known as **Over-the-Hill** – a place of sharp contrasts – an area abounding with quaint shops where checkers, dominoes

Adelaide Village Church.

and *warri* (an African game) are still played under shady roadside trees, and where porches, yards and streets are utilized heavily by a bustling and lively population, some of which is migrant from Haiti.

Many prominent people, including Sir Lynden O. Pindling, Prime Minister of the Commonwealth of the Bahamas, hail from East Street, one of the main streets of Over-the-Hill. Begun as a suburb for former slaves and Liberated Africans, Over-the-Hill has always had humble buildings. Its early years boasted a market and many fruit and other trees. Gradually, though, it became more urbanized and today has few open spaces. The people who live there are mostly workers, artisans and shopkeepers, who depend more or less directly on business generated by Nassau. Today, Over-the-Hill comprises not only dwelling houses and small shops, but also is the home of many native restaurants, bars, clubs, large stores and professional offices.

Over-the-Hill is also the home of a variety of churches, including **St. Agnes Anglican Church**, first consecrated on April 8, 1848 on Market and Cockburn streets. Not far from St. Agnes is **Wesley Methodist Church**, established in 1847. The church stands on the site of an earlier one which had a thatched roof. Early Methodist services were held in the homes of various people. Another prominent church in this area is the **Church of God of Prophecy** on East Street. This is the mother church of numerous churches of this denomination that have been established thoughout the Bahamas through proselytizing from its headquarters in Cleveland, Tennessee. Many other churches, including The Church of God and several Baptist churches are also located in Over-the-Hill.

Progress and Preservation: A main artery and the southern boundary of Grant's Town is Wulff Road, which is dotted with various businesses, small shops, eating houses and schools. To the west of Wulff Road is Poinciana Drive which leads to the College of the Bahamas, established in 1974 on the former site of the Government High School. The College provides a two-year program which leads to an Associate Degree in a number of aca-

Checkers contest in Over-the-Hill.

demic and technological subjects. Several degree programs are also offered in conjunction with the universities of the West Indies and Miami, which includes a combined internship and academic program in hotel management.

Much further east, Village Road runs from north to south, connecting the interior with Shirley and East Bay streets. It is mostly residential but boasts a large food store, a bowling alley, a plant nursery, a Squash Raquets Club, a few small shops and **The Retreat**, the headquarters of The Bahamas National Trust. The property, an 11-acre (5-hectare) estate, contains a cottage, part of which dates to the 1860s, and has some of the rarest palms in the world, collected by the late Arthur and Margaret Langlois, former owners of the estate.

Along Montagu Bay: Built in 1742 on a point at the eastern entrance to New Providence's harbor, **Fort Montagu** was built to defend Nassau, and was not very successful at it. It saw action in 1776 when a small force of the American Navy attacked the British in Nassau. Its defenses faltered again in 1782 when the

Spanish captured New Providence and occupied the capital for a year. Today, the fort and the adjacent beach is popular for the sandy shore and large shady trees. Nearby, on Shirley Street, is the derelict Montagu Hotel, built in 1926 to cater to the then fledgling tourist trade.

Turning east onto **East Bay Street**, also called the **Eastern Road**, you soon pass **Blair**, a subdivision, once a large estate. The drive up East Bay Street is most beautiful. On the coastline are many fine homes surrounded by large gardens and lush foliage. Most properties are surrounded by picturesque native stone walls and many flowers. Just past **Dick's Point** is **The Hermitage**, originally built as a country home by Lord Dunmore in the late 18th Century, now the home of the Roman Catholic Bishop of Nassau. Farther east the homes on the road's sea side have smaller gardens, but these are well kept and reminiscent of Bermuda-style houses.

Joshua, Congo, Nango: Shortly after passing High Vista you arrive at Fox Hill Road. Just opposite the intersection with East Bay Street is the former site of Creek

Village, which existed in the 18th Century. Most of the original settlers, who were probably Africans, sold their properties and moved inland after one Samuel Fox, an ex-slave who owned a piece of property in that district. Later, the then Chief Justice of the Bahamas, Robert Sandilands, who bought about 1,200 acres (486 hectares) in the **Fox Hill** area, in 1840 laid out a village and made about a hundred grants of land varying from one to 10 acres. Grants were made to various African individuals who had paid either money or labor to the value of $10. The Africans, who called the settlement **Sandilands Village**, after their benefactor, grew fruits and vegetables which they sold in the Nassau Market. The village women often walked from Fox Hill to Nassau with trays of their wares balanced on their heads.

Sandilands Village was later divided into four towns: Joshua, Congo and Nango towns (once occupied by freed African-born persons), and Burnside Town (settled by people of African descent born in the Bahamas).

Located on the first rise going south on Fox Hill Road is **St. Anne's Anglican Church**, a quaint structure, originally erected in 1740. The present church, built between 1867 and 1870, is adjacent to St. Anne's School, catering to primary and secondary levels and run by the Anglican Diocese.

The Fox Hill/Sandilands area still contains some of its ancient charm as a rural village with heavily wooded areas, small wooden and limestone and dabble wall houses. Containing many churches, small shops, a public library, fire station and a school, it is also the home of the Boys and Girls Industrial schools, the Geriatics Hospital and the Sandilands Rehabilitation Hospital for the mentally ill. At the center of the village is **Freedom Park**, opened in 1967. Emancipation Day (August 1) and Fox Hill Day (the 2nd Tuesday in August) are happily celebrated every year by the residents of Fox Hill and others on the Village Green and in the Park.

Off Bernard Road, one of the main streets in Fox Hill, is **St. Augustine's Monastery** and St. Augustine's College. Developed by Benedictines from Minne-

St. Anne's Church in Fox Hill.

116

sota, the two structures were designed by Monsignor John Hawes (or Father Jerome) known also as the Hermit of Cat Island. The monastery and the college were completed in 1947, perched high on a rocky hill near Fox Hill. Each room opened onto cloisters and had an arched stone roof to match; the floors were cemented and tiled. The long and low structure resembled a fortress. Today the school is co-educational.

At the intersection of Fox Hill Road and Yamacraw Road is H.M. Prison, which was moved from its former East Street site in 1952.

Turning east on Yamacraw Road, you pass Yamacraw Beach Estates to the south and the southern entrance to Nassau East, a subdivision developed in the late 1960s. It adjoins Nassau Village and Winton Meadows, both recently developed areas. To the east is **Yamacraw Beach**, which is open to the public.

Hugging the coastline with its brillant sea views, the road soon curves around McPherson's Bend, named for a resident who was said to park his car there every night to take in the view. Traveling on East Bay Street towards **Winton Heights**, formerly a large plantation called Lookout, the road passes Solomon's Lighthouse, a candy-striped house built by Fane Solomon, a local merchant. At the top of Winton Highway are the remains of an ancient battery built by Lord Dunmore. **Fort Winton**, as it came to be known, has a commanding view of Nassau, the eastern harbor and Rose Island, which runs almost parallel to the eastern end of New Providence.

West of East Bay Street are Camperdown, once a heavily wooded area, now quite developed, and Sans Souci, a popular subdivision. The eastern end of the island is mostly residential.

New Providence, with its many contrasts, has become one of the great resorts of the western world. The cosmopolitan island is an international banking center which locals like to call "The Switzerland of the West." Its modern office buildings, fine subdivisions, historic settlements and quaint neo-colonial architecture somehow blend – the phenomenal growth of tourism and finance has not diminished the charm of the island.

The Bahamas' coat-of-arms, and students in Fox Hill.

PARADISE ISLAND (HOG ISLAND)

Since an angry God drove Adam and Eve out of Eden, mankind has been trying to regain Paradise. Whether it is a Miltonian heaven or a place of refuge, who is not sure that perfection exists – somewhere? The trick is to find it.

When the Swedish industrialist Dr. Axel Wenner-Gren docked his 322-foot (100 meter) yacht in Nassau Harbour in 1939, he had already traveled the world. In two years the *Southern Cross,* which he had bought from Howard Hughes, had carried him over 70,000 exotic miles (130,000 km). According to Dr. Paul Albury, who chronicles the island's history in his book *Paradise Island Story,* while docked in Nassau Harbour, Wenner-Gren saw low-lying Hog Island. Its fringe of ragged shrubs and trees was visible a stone's throw from his decks, and it must have whispered to him, "Paradise!"

The tall, handsome magnate bought the Lynch estate on Hog Island. He dredged old Burnside's pond and renamed it Paradise Lake; he dug canals to link the lake with Nassau Harbour and the open sea. He refurbished the already commodious Lynch estate, built only two years before by Joseph Lynch of Merrill, Lynch and Company. Inspired by the imaginery land in James Hilton's 1933 novel *Lost Horizon,* he christened his refuge Shangri-La.

Then the United States entered World War Two, and Wenner-Gren's companies were blacklisted. In 1935 he had purchased a major interest in Bofors munitions works. This was the Swedish branch of Krupp, and Krupp, of course, supplied weapons and ammunition to the Axis powers. Rumors flew: the *Southern Cross* carried Bofors antiaircraft guns; the canals were hideouts for German submarines. None of these tales were substantiated, but by the end of the war, Wenner-Gren was reputed to be one of the richest men in the world. Though he spent much of the war and later years in Latin America, after the armistice he returned for visits to his Hog Island Shangri-La.

Wenner-Gren's utopian dream found a still more ardent supporter when in 1961, the year he died, he sold his Hog Island holdings to another man of great wealth, Huntington Hartford — the man who got Hog Island's name changed to Paradise.

Today Paradise Island is a modern resort linked to Nassau by an arching concrete bridge over the harbor. The five highrise hotels gleam chalky white, in a landscape of tropical palms, parking areas and speed bumps. At the foot of the bridge is a toll booth; drive in, two dollars and Paradise is yours – OR walk across for only a quarter.

At first Paradise seems to be an island of hotels. This impression is corroborated by statistics. There are well over 1,000 hotels rooms, dozens of restaurants, lounges and bars serving food ranging from French to Bahamian to Polynesian, and more Bahamians employed in maintaining this tourists' paradise than at any other destination.

Most of the buildings like the 12-story **Britannia Towers**, the **Paradise Towers** and the **Sheraton Grand Hotel** – were built between the late '60s and early '80s in the tropical version of the international style that has raised many skylines in Florida and California. The late '80s has also been a time for face-lifting and expansion, with new lobbies, atrium restaurants and bars. Tucked away behind screened fences are over 20 tennis courts. Behind a sleek exterior and a plush

tunnel of asuarina ees, left. A ourist gets way from it ll, right.

chandeliered lobby lurks a casino. Inside the hotels' airconditioned lobbies are plenty of potted palms and tropical rum drinks, and their rear doors open onto commodious swimming pools and the white sand of **Cabbage Beach**. If this is your version of Paradise, look no farther.

Marooned: As early as the 18th Century, Paradise Island, then known as Hog Island, began its career as a pleasuredrome. A map of 1788 shows a few farm huts, two buildings that were likely a shipyard, and a structure called "Banqueting House." If Banqueting House were once the site of idyllic feasting, its tales remain lost in the sand, but in 1834 an American doctor wrote of being taken by the Governor of the Bahamas on a "maroon" at the island's abandoned barracks. There they ate a picnic banquet of salmon, corned beef, pickled oysters, cider and good madeira, in the shade beside a snow-white sandy beach.

When swimming became popular in the 1890s, Hog Island's reputation as a tropical paradise grew. According to Dr. Albury entrepreneurs capitalized on the fledgling tourist trade and offered boat trips to the island leaving Nassau every hour. For one shilling (sterling), Victorian

pleasure-seekers received use of a changing room and bathing suit, a swim in the warm waters and a feast of fruit. "All you can eat" fruit was advertised — as well as oranges guests could pick right off the trees. As competition grew, enterprising proprietors added attractions: sack races, candy-pulls, high-wire walkers and trick-bicycle riders, ventriloquist shows, fireworks and even dancing lessons. The center for much of this activity was Saratoga Beach, renamed in the 1920s **Paradise Beach**. A left turn after crossing the Paradise Island Bridge, and a right down shady Casuarina Drive will take you to this slender crescent of white sand on the northwest end of the island – still a mecca for holiday frolickers.

Although no sign remains of the Victorian bathing houses, circus acts or Twenties dancing pavilions, the exuberant commercial spirit of the place lives on. For an entrance fee anyone can enter Paradise Beach, where a plethora of mechanical toys crowd the sand: sunfish, windsurfing boards, Hobie 14s, paddleboats, snorkeling equipment, jetskis. They rent by the hour or half hour. From offshore rafts, parasailers take off. Their brightly striped parasails fill with air like parachutes,

Early birds on Paradise Beach.

carrying the hearty fliers high as kites while their towboats cut swift curves through the water. The scene on Paradise Beach can resemble a circus – under the casuarina trees instead of a bigtop.

Just next door to Paradise Beach a **Holiday Inn** rises above the casuarina trees, the tallest hotel in the Bahamas. The activity in its huge lobby and on its beach, **Pirates Cove**, rivals that of Paradise Beach.

West of the hubbub of Paradise Beach, the island's narrow western finger extends into a more private realm. Dr. Albury relates that in the early 1900s this area became a second home to a small enclave of wealthy Americans who in 1913 banded together in a group they called the Porcupine Club. By 1930 the club's membership had increased from 11 to 50, and they had moved from their first club-house to a larger one. This is not to suggest that membership requirements grew lax; it was understood that only *multi*-millionaires need apply. Some members arrived in fabulous yachts owned by Mellons, Morgans or Astors. After World War Two many of the original members died off, club enthusiasm waned and many remaining members joined the Lyford Cay Club on New Providence Island. The homes, land and clubhouse were sold, and gradually entered a new era.

Swamis and pop-beads: Visible on Casuarina Drive is the entrance to **Club Méditerranée** (Club Med), part of the international resort chain that popularized the "all-inclusive" vacation hotel where you pay for incidentals "by popping a bead from the string you wear around your neck." It occupies the former Porcupine Club land, and though Club Med has constructed some new accommodations, it also maintains the old houses and cottages relatively unchanged. Club Med employees (*gentils organisateurs* or GOs, as they are called) tell ghost stories about a Porcupine Club member's appearances in her old home, now an oceanfront restaurant and dormitory for employees.

Other enclaves on Paradise Island's western tip can be reached only by boat. The **Yoga Retreat**, founded by Swami Vishnudevananda, author of *The Complete Illustrated Book of Yoga*, occupies four acres donated by one of the swami's grateful students. Chanting, meditation, breathing exercises and vegetarian meals fill the days, which begin with a rising

Isosceles sunfish.

bell at 5:30 a.m. The all-volunteer staff grows produce in the retreat's own gardens, and someone has put up a rustic sign reading "Club Meditation."

Several private homes also occupy the western end, and at the tip is the **lighthouse,** built of limestone quarried nearby. Citizens of Nassau laid its cornerstone in 1816 with great pomp and ceremony. They commemorated the event with speeches, prayers, a phial containing historic information, and a few coins and medals cemented into the bedrock.

On a calm day it is difficult to imagine the many storms the lighthouse and its keepers have endured, particularly the hurricane of 1866 when 60-foot (18-meter) waves surged into Nassau Harbour, their crests level with the lighthouse's gallery. Since there is no road on Paradise Island's western end, the best view of the lighthouse can be enjoyed from a plane or boat.

Venice to Vegas: Today, at the center of the island, the waters of Wenner-Gren's romantic Paradise Lake no longer reflect a rich man's dream. "Buy one gallon; get one free" was the slogan of the Mary Carter Paint Company, an American firm

that determined to put Paradise Island on the map as a major tourist resort. In the late Sixties the paint company built the 1,500-foot (460-meter) **Paradise Island Bridge**, the **Paradise Island Hotel** and a half-acre **Casino**. Subdued lighting, whirring slot machines, clicking chips, the rattle of roulette wheels, plush carpet: the Casino is Monte Carlo minus the foreign accent. **Le Cabaret Theatre**, with its Radio-City-size stage and plumed and spangled chorus girls is as American as apple pie.

The success of this enterprise prompted Mary Carter Paint investors to give up latex and semi-gloss entirely and form Resorts International, Inc. which today owns over 600 acres (2.5 sq km) on Paradise Island. (This is the entire island except the western end and selected parcels sold to builders of hotels and condominiums.) Wenner-Gren's sparkling little Paradise Lake has become waterfront property for several restaurants, the Britannia Towers, tennis courts and landscaped pathways. The aging industrialist standing in his boathouse, greeting guests as they sail up his canal, is but a memory.

That past seems less remote on the

Hurricane Hole.

eastern end of the island. After crossing Paradise Island Bridge you will see to the right a narrow road that leads to **Hurricane Hole**, a haven for luxury yachts. Built in the early Sixties, it was one project of Huntington Hartford, the man who succeeded Wenner-Gren as the island's visionary.

Grandson of the founder of the Great Atlantic and Pacific Tea Company (A&P), Huntington Hartford was born in 1911 to enjoy the wealth of what was for a time the fifth largest corporation in the United States. The popular press portrayed him as an incorrigible playboy who married a cigarette girl, and later an irrepressible art critic and patron who viewed most 20th Century art, particularly abstract-expressionist painting, as a scourge. In 1959, while married to the second of his four wives, he bought a house and two acres on Hog Island. As Dr. Albury relates the story, Hartford became friends with Wenner-Gren, who still spent winters at his estate, Shangri-La. His finances running low, the older man could no longer dredge lakes, build guesthouses or otherwise augment his private paradise. Hartford, however, was rich in cash and artistic fervor. In a celebrated deal that began with an agreement signed on the back of a dinner menu, Hartford bought Wenner-Gren's extensive Hog Island properties for $9.5 million.

Hog Wild: A sybarite and a capitalist, Hartford must have dreamed of finding both pleasure and profit in Hog Island's sunny beaches and sylvan glades. Its name he saw as an impediment. ("Hog is an ugly name — the island should be called Paradise," Wenner-Gren reportedly declared, perhaps inspiring Hartford). So Hartford saw that Hog Island became Paradise Island by decree on May 23, 1962. Then Hartford was ready to indulge his imagination.

After crossing the Paradise Island bridge, a right turn on Paradise Island Drive leads to the heart of Hartford's dreams. The road passes several condominium and time-sharing developments, then glides past a small unobtrusive sign that says **Ocean Club**. A turn up this narrow, shady driveway leads to a pale pink Georgian-style mansion with white verandahs and, likely as not, a limousine purring under the carport. It is not a private mansion but Hartford's Ocean Club hotel, the centerpiece of his many projects. A doorman in livery opens the front door; you

Anticipating the arrival of a limo or Rolls at the Ocean Club.

sweep into the entry hall, across its polished floor, perhaps up the gently curved staircase. If it is dinner hour, on one of the balconies above the inner courtyard a jazz band bops and wails; candles flicker at tables around the pool. Surrounding the hotel, Hartford's elegant **Versailles Gardens** seem fresh from France via Hollywood. From behind a screen of trees you hear the bounce-pop of a leisurely tennis game. In the long narrow swimming pool, which doubles as a reflecting pool, you half expect to see a 1940s starlet swimming a graceful lap. Inspired by Louis XIV's gardens at Versailles, Wenner-Gren initiated the landscaping, and Hartford completed it. Grassy terraces stretch for a quarter mile (0.4 km) in an unbroken vista; shady niches off the terraces shelter bronze statues, not of Venus and Apollo, but of David Livingstone and Franklin Delano Roosevelt, two of Hartford's heroes. There are also statues of Napoleon and Josephine, Hercules, and a 1920 bronze called "Mother and Child." The statue of Gretchen, Mephistopheles and Faust was once owned by Wenner-Gren.

That tennis game you hear in the background may not be as leisurely as you first

suppose. The Ocean Club's guest book includes a pantheon of tennis greats, including John McEnroe, Vitas Gerulaitis, Brian Gottfried and Eddie Dibbs. For many, the Ocean Club's nine Har-Tru courts are *the* place for tennis in the Bahamas, day and night. The Ocean Club annually hosts the Bahamas International Open and the Paradise Island Classic, both of which draw players from the world's top 20.

From the garden's highest terrace one can cross Paradise Island Drive to the **Cloisters**. Brought from a monastery near Lourdes, France, by the American newspaper baron William Randolf Hearst, the pieces of this 14th Century cloister languished in crates in Florida until Hartford purchased them. Hartford had the Cloisters reconstructed stone by stone – a process which took a year because there were no written instructions. Today the graceful columns and worn, delicately carved capitals form approximately the same serene square they did in France, though now roofless, with manicured grass growing between the paving stones. It is a romantic spot and serves as the setting for wedding pictures of countless Nassauvians. The Cloisters overlook the

Gothic mystery of the Cloisters.

eastern end of Nassau Harbour, with the eastern New Providence Island visible a half mile (0.8 km) across the water.

Hartford invested $10 million in improvements to Paradise Island, building not only Hurricane Hole, the Ocean Club and Versailles Gardens but an 18-hole golf course, riding stables, a restaurant, and installing a water-taxi service from Nassau embellished by a dockside garden. He also transformed Wenner-Gren's boathouse into an elegant French restaurant. It remains open to diners today, with candlelit terraces overlooking Paradise Lagoon, music and dancing.

When these extravagant plans did not pay off and severely strained even Hartford's resources, he finally sold everything to the Mary Carter Paint Company. Through political maneuvering the paint company obtained the gambling permit that would be the key to investors' success on Paradise Island.

Hartford had enjoyed a brief heyday in his paradise, surrounded by starlets, with friends (rather than paying guests) filling the rooms of the Ocean Club. Too soon his dream drew him into a morass of debts and crumbling plans.

Sand traps and solitude

East of the Cloisters, Paradise Island Drive leads to the 18-hole Paradise Island Golf Club built by Hartford, where the small clubhouse still retains the intimate poshness he so obviously valued. Along the southern boundary of the golf course runs a shady, romantic drive with views of the water. At the **Paradise Island Stables** on this road you can rent a horse to explore this wooded, relatively untrampled part of the island. The stables were another of Hartford's projects; his wife was a devoted equestrienne.

Victoria Beach (also called Honeymoon Cove) is a small cove at the island's southeastern corner. A road along the north side of the golf course reaches another secluded cove, the best snorkeling spot on the island. There a fringe of trees grows nearly to the water's edge; standing on the beach one might think the world contained nothing but this strip of sand, these trees and this sea. Like the far western end of the island with its private homes and yoga retreat, the eastern end retains something of the spirit and enchantment that first made people think of Hog Island as Paradise.

Mother and Child in Versailles Gardens.

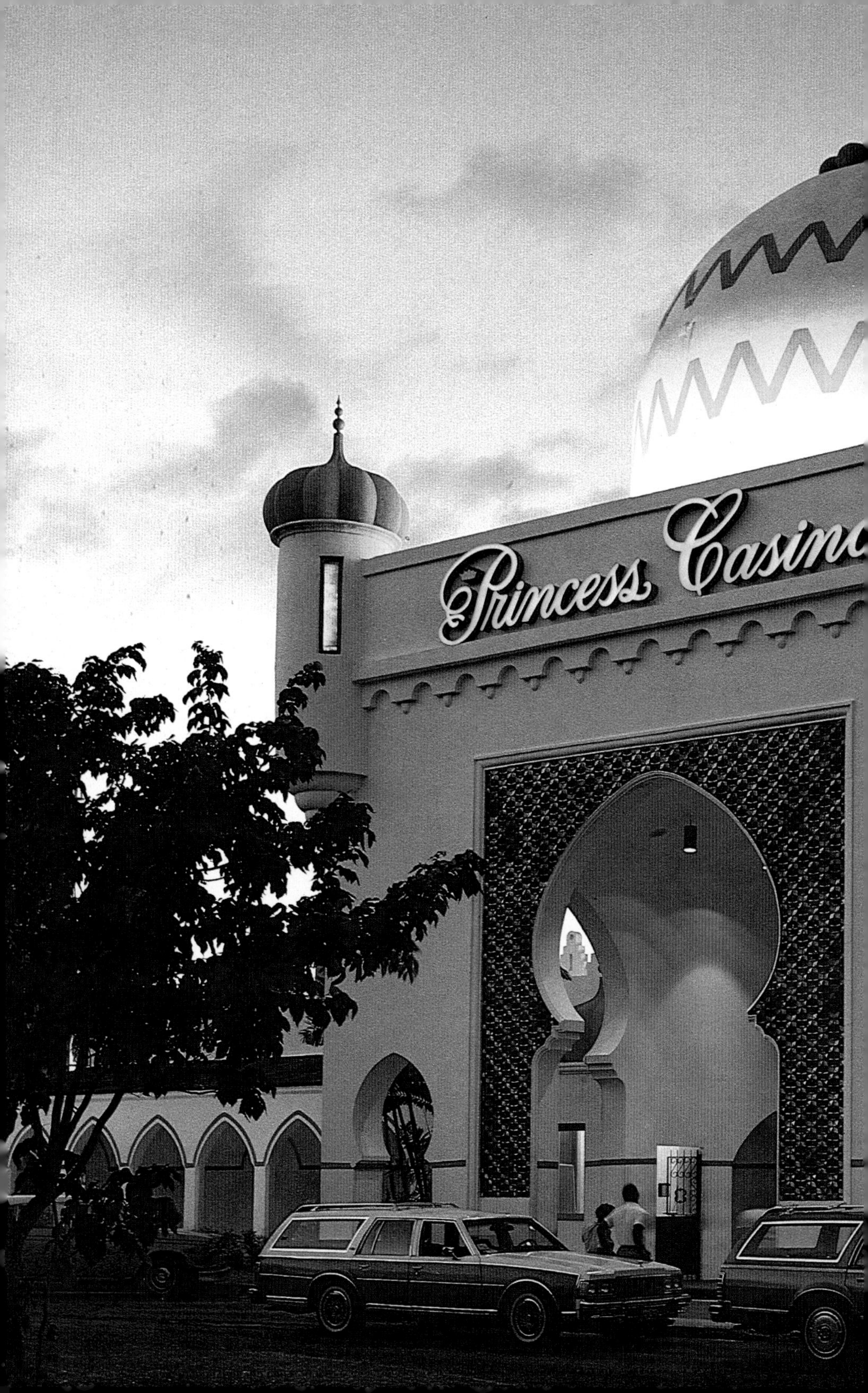
Princess Casino

GRAND BAHAMA ISLAND

Floating like a green iguana on its back at the bottom of the Little Bahama Bank, Grand Bahama is regarded by many as a maverick cousin to the rest of the Bahamas. Largely developed by American commercial interest in the 1960s, it's sometimes thought of as non-Bahamian. But continental drift has not made it a part of Florida – yet.

After New Providence and Paradise islands, Grand Bahama is the most popular tourist destination in the Bahamas, and with good reason. Miles of sandy beaches, layers of comfortable hotel rooms in soaringly ambitious hotels, gambling casinos and a world-class scuba diving facility make it a favorite long-week-end vacation spot. Among the modern shops and offices of Freeport, the suburban neighborhoods of Lucaya and the good-natured opulence of the large hotels, most Americans will feel right at home. Travel beyond the wide, landscaped thorough-fare of Freeport/Lucaya, and you will find that the island has even more in store...

A network of fascinating limestone caves at the Lucayan National Park, blue holes, piney forests, East End and its nearby cays, all these offer a taste of the "old" Bahamas, and a tranquil "Out Island" atmosphere. On Grand Bahama you will not get away from it *all,* but you will surely find some special treasures.

GRAND BAHAMA

With a maximum elevation of 50 feet (15 meters), Grand Bahama does not have the visual impact of many of the world's volcanic islands. Grand Bahama had a more peaceful genesis. Formed under the sea by oolitic faeces supplemented by coral detritis, it is part of a limestone platform thousands of feet thick.

Grand Bahama is the most northerly island of the Bahamas and is thus the first island most visitors from the north will see when they first visit the "Island Commonwealth." However, only recently has Grand Bahama become convenient to visit, and in early times it was a place to avoid. Before lighthouses and modern navigational aides were introduced, there was constant danger of shipwreck on the outer fringes of the Little Bahama Bank. The island of Grand Bahama lies along the southern boundary of this vast expanse of shallow water where the ocean floor is some 10 to 30 feet (three to nine meters) below the water surface.

Seaborne traffic around the Bank, and especially through the 65-mile (106-km) wide Florida Channel, was plagued by numerous wrecks. Indeed, for over a century salvaging wrecks was a way of life in the Bahamas and the government even recognized and regulated the occupation. And, if faulty navigation – aggravated by deliberately confusing beacons – was not the cause of a wreck, there was the constant danger of pirates. With the decline in piracy, the building of lighthouses, including the Great Isaac Light in 1859, and improved charting of the seabed, the possibility of making a livelihood from wrecking ceased.

The people of Grand Bahama returned to subsistence living, but, always astute in the ways of the world, they soon reaped a bonanza by acting as a supply depot for Confederate forces in the American Civil War. Later they tried their hands at sponging, assisted mightily in providing liquor to the United States in the 13 years of Prohibition and most recently have become a conduit for the supply of illicit drugs to North America. But let us return to the less worldly-wise original inhabitants of the island.

The original settlers of the Bahamas were the Siboney, a primitive stone-age culture which disappeared with the arrival of the Lucayan Indians. The Lucayans were a branch of the Island Arawak Indian group, who first colonized the Turks and Caicos Islands, then later the entire Bahamian archipelago. How many lived on Grand Bahama we do not know, but when Ponce de Leon visited Grand Bahama in 1513 he found only one old woman "*la vieja*" at or near what is today West End. The remainder of her people had probably died from diseases brought by the white man to which they had no immunity, or they had been transported to work in the mines of Hispaniola and Cuba, where certain death awaited them.

Ponce De Leon left two men to explore the northern island further for the fabled "Fountain of Youth." Meanwhile, Ponce de Leon traveled to the mainland peninsula to the west, which he called Florida (for *Pascua Florida*, the Easter Day of Flowers or Easter Sunday). He returned to Puerto Rico, and then to Spain where he received the title of *Don* and *Adelantao* of Florida

Preceding pages: Garden of the Groves; casino fit for a sultan; Lucaya's best advertisement. Left, caddy tests the Jack Tar Village green. Right, where to get off in Eight Mile Rock.

and Bimini which presumably included the island of Grand Bahama. With his demise the Spanish seemed to lose all interest in Grand Bahama.

Treasure Ships: Grand Bahama takes its name from the Spanish *gran bajamar* (the great shallows or, literally, the vast underwater). The Spaniards had reason to note the shallows, for the reefs and shoals on the island's outer edge were to be approached only at grave peril. Later the entire country derived its name from these shallows.

It is interesting to speculate that Grand Bahama may have been the only land base many pirates ever knew. They lived their harsh, cruel lives aboard ship, but from time to time they needed to refit their vessels. Remote, uninhabited islands like Grand Bahama would make passable havens, even though safe channels and anchorages were minimal. The pirates took a grisly toll on shipping, but the elements, too, sent many a ship to the bottom.

In 1628 a Dutch privateer made an audacious raid at Matanzas Bay in Cuba and carried away several treasure ships. For reasons unknown, one of the prize ships broke away and sank in shallow water off the south shore of Grand Bahama. It was found in 1965 and contained 10,000 silver coins, valued anywhere from $2 to $9 million.

In 1655 a large convoy set sail from Cartagena en route to Spain. It refitted and sailed from Havana on Jan. 1, 1656. Three days later *Nuestra Señora della Maravilla* sailed into shallow water near Memory Rock north of West End and tried to warn the other ships. In the confusion that followed, the *Maravilla* was struck by another ship and started sinking in 50 feet (15 meters) of water. The winter weather had turned foul, and salvage operations were delayed for six months. About 480,000 pesos of treasure were eventually discovered before the search was called off.

More salvage attempts were made, but it was estimated that only a quarter of the treasure was recovered. The *Maravilla* was rediscovered in 1972 and became the richest treasure found in the Bahamas in recent history. Work began anew on the site in 1984, continuing through 1988, with the richest finds retrieved in 1987 and 1988.

Governor Phenney, writing in 1721, confirms that Grand Bahama had no population but noted that the island had fine timber (indeed the island is even today largely covered by pine forest) and "white land" along the south coast which,

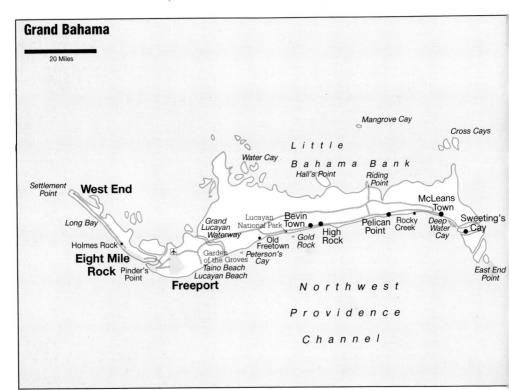

Grand Bahama

20 Miles

he predicted, would yield fair crops of corn. In 1772 a sale of 240 acres (96 hectares) to one Joseph Smith was recorded, and the island started to be permanently inhabited in the early 19th Century.

First Settlement: The first Bahamian habitation took over approximately where the Lucayan habitation left off: **West End**. By 1836 the island had a population of 370. Though the census of 1861 recorded a population of 858, the riches to be made in Nassau by blockade running the U.S. Civil War soon caused an exodus. These cash-poor times gave rise to the expression "a shilling in Grand Bahama is worth a pound of money." **Golden Grove** became the administrative center of the island, presumably because of its central location and the small channel entrance which could accommodate skiffs but not much else.

Almost a century later the population was a mere 1,700, but in 1919 the United States passed the Volstead Act (Prohibition), and things started to change. West End became an important center for transshipment of liquor. As many as 400 boats ran the cordon of U.S. Coast Guard cutters to deliver liquor to prearranged rendezvous in Florida. There was even a dirt runway for daredevil aerial bootleggers. The boom ended in 1933 with the repeal of Prohibition. The Commissioner who had been relocated to West End to "administer" the nest of bootleggers was moved to Eight Mile Rock near the mouth of Hawksbill Creek.

West End's main street is lined with bars, shops and houses. There is a service station, a small clinic and a straw market. This is a good place to go bonefishing — a pastime especially reserved by the government to tourists. Mountains of conch shells suggest the principal food staple of West Enders.

At the western end of the coastal road is the **Jack Tar Village**. It is one of the most self-sufficient hostelries in the Bahamas, with its own private jetport, marina, PGA ranked 27-hole golf course (with nine links holes) and commissary. The original buildings were constructed by Sir Billy Butlin (of English holiday camp fame) in 1948. In a master stroke of foresight, Butlin located his "holiday camp" on the nearest point of Grand Bahama to the United States. For a time it seemed that West End would enjoy the tourist surge that Nassau was attracting. But with construction delays, a devalu-

Roadside stall in West End.

ation of the British pound and finally jittery creditors, the hotel was closed down a year after it opened.

Rocks and Caves: The other settlements between West End and Freeport are positioned along the government road or **Queen's Highway,** to give it its proper name. Just after leaving West End you come to Bootle Bay, a small canal development which is partly developed. Not so the other "subdivisions" farther along this route which are rapidly being reclaimed by the bush. A good place to stop for lunch is Harry's American Bar, which occupies a beach front site and also offers rooms for rent. A mile farther east is the **Buccaneer's Club** which is the best restaurant on the island outside of Freeport. The owner/chef is Heinz Fischbaker, a transplanted German national.

There is good diving off the cays at **Deadman's Reef** near Holmes Rock, and from here there is almost continual development of a more modest sort all the way to the Freeport "bonded area" boundary. (The principal town on Grand Bahama Island, Freeport is the second largest city in the Bahamas. You can read about Freeport and its birth as a "company town" in the 1950s in the following chapter.) The small Catholic **Church of St. Agnes** is worthy of note just south of Seagrape, and farther down the same road, **Peace and Plenty** on the seafront provides excellent Bahamian cuisine. It is wise to telephone Mrs. Williams before visiting.

Eight Mile Rock is exactly that, eight miles of rocky foreshore stretching east and west of **Hawksbill Creek.** It is in actuality a dormitory suburb of Freeport, though it is now home to the Commissioner for the west end of the island. Across the Hawksbill Creek Causeway are Pinders Point, Lewis Yard and Hunters, the eastern half of the eight miles of rock immediately south of Freeport and outside the "bonded area." (But do not refer to the eastern settlements as being part of Eight Mile Rock since 8MR, as it is sometimes written, is the name reserved for the "towns" on the west side of Hawksbill Creek.) "Towns" in the Bahamas can consist of as little as two houses which often bear the names of the incumbents. Traveling along the oceanfront of 8MR you will see an interesting **"boiling hole"** next to the coastal road. Boiling holes in the Bahamas are entrances to subterranean cave systems, and this hole is no exception. They differ from "blue holes" since the water coming

Clutter of conch shells at Hawksbill Creek.

out of them is under pressure and appears to "boil." Visitors are invited to see the bottling and packing process. **Pinders Point** has a good Bahamian restaurant called **Freddie's** which serves dinner. The ambience is ho-hum but the food is usually excellent. Offshore is a boiling hole, the **Chimney**, which creates a vortex in both directions depending on the tide. Below is an extensive cave system, but viewing is best accomplished in the company of a qualified cave diver.

Williams Town and **Russell Town** occupy a beautiful stretch of beach just south of Freeport, at the southern end of Beachway Drive (a road much used by equestrians from the Pinewood Riding Stables). Here deaf and partly blind Joseph Williams resisted all attempts at removal by the Port Authority, and he even built a small Catholic church dedicated to Saint Jude on the beach road – a pointed indication of his intention to stay.

Nearby a cemetery contains the mortal remains of many of the villagers including William Russell of the "town" of the same name. Just outside the cemetery is a simple monument surmounted by a cross which reads:

"In memory of our twenty-one Haitian brothers and sisters who died at Sea 19th, July 1973. Ke pose yi." The unfortunate Haitians drowned just off Williams Town while seeking to sail to the United States to enter the country illegally.

The small beachfront communities **Smiths Point** and **Mather Town** are geographically in Freeport but outside the "bonded area." The White Wave Club is the place for a cool drink in Smiths Point. The Caribe Club in Mathers Town on the other side of the canal entrance has good native food and fronts right onto a gorgeous white sand beach. It is an excellent venue for brunch.

Diversions: A worthwhile excursion might be a visit to Water Cay, situated just east of the bulge in the north coast of Grand Bahama. Access is difficult. If you have a boat you can get there from Hawksbill Creek or via the Grand Lucayan Waterway. Another less sure way of gaining access is to drive through the Lucaya "country" subdivisions to the north shore dock. With luck, a returning resident or an alert boatman might pick you up. A trip to the cay is worthwhile since it is the most unspoiled settlement of Grand Bahama, with simple dwellings, luxuriant vegetation and no vehicles.

Low tide at Taino Beach.

A less arduous and very rewarding side trip is **Lucayan National Park**. It is only 13 miles (21 km) from Freeport's Garden of the Groves (discussed in the following chapter), but the journey through the pine forest may seem endless. The route will take you over the **Grand Lucayan Waterway**, a $30-million canal which bisects the island and stands as a monument to the confidence the early developers had for the future of Freeport Lucaya. When the straight road through the pine forest finally curves south (right) look out for a Film Studio on your left hand side. (No, the Bahamas' own Sidney Poitier is not on set — the studio was stillborn when the Freeport bubble burst in the late 1960s.)

At the next bend in the road — this time left — take the turn-off for **Old Free Town**. The villagers were removed when their land was purchased by the Port Authority and were relocated in New Free Town. All that is left are a few walls, a hibiscus bush or two and some fruit trees. Of primary interest in Old Free Town are the **blue holes**. Left of the turn-off road is a long innocent looking swamp which actually is the entrance to a cave system. Nearly a mile west of the cut-off road is a concealed pathway to **Mermaids Lair**, another surface opening to an underwater cave system. Farther inland (and joined to Mermaids Lair by water-filled caves) is the bell-shaped **Owl Hole**, a "cenote" of impressive proportions. The mouth of this hole is 35 feet (11 meters) above the water, and the walls dumbell inwards with small limestone stalactites hanging down.

As you continue along the main road towards the Lucayan National Park, stay alert for the sign. Pull off into the parking area and consult the visitor orientation signboard which illustrates the pathway system and gives some background information on the park. Yes, that's right, "the largest explored underwater cave system in the world" right under your feet! The Park has an extensive "figure eight" pathway system which takes visitors into two caves and up to a lookout point. (The second cave opening has yielded some Lucayan Indian artifacts and human bones now preserved in the Grand Bahama Museum close to Freeport.) South of the road the pathway leads to a bridge which crosses **Gold Rock Creek**. A trip by canoe down the two-mile (three-km) long creek has to be one of the most memorable inland sights of Grand Bahama, and some might say,

Blue hole, Lucayan National Park (left). Snorkeling sights (right).

of the Atlantic. Once across the bridge and through the mangroves, the sea and the small islet **Gold Rock** become visible. The dunes are among the highest on the island and the deserted beach is exquisite – a kind of proof that it may indeed be, as the locals claim, "Better in the Bahamas."

Another Bahamas National Trust property which is worth visiting is **Peterson's Cay National Park**. This is located a mile or so east of the entrance to the Grand Lucayan Waterway. You will need a boat, a mask and snorkel tube are also essential. The reef around this cay is spectacular, and an underwater trail is slated for 1987. Remember to bring suntan oil; something to drink would be a good idea too. Opposite the cay is **Barbary Beach** and the uninhabited Hermitage (originally a church built in 1901) occupied in the early days of Freeport by an ex-Trappist monk.

About the only point on the north coast that is easily accessible is **Dover Sound**, on the opposite side of the island from here. An enterprising Welshman, Dr. Peter Bizzell, has converted some canals near here for use in his fish-farming venture. Bizzell hopes to raise African tilapia fish in the freshwater of the canals. If all goes well his company should be on a sound commercial footing by the late Eighties.

Eastern Rocks: On leaving Lucayan National Park and the eastern boundary of the Port Area, for a moment you are in a U.S. military base. This is Gold Rock Missile Tracking Station, and though it is not overly active nowadays, the base shows evidence of its former importance when it was the first down-range station from Cape Canaveral. This general area is called **Gold Rock** (formerly known as **Golden Grove**) and incorporates a small village of relocated islanders: **New Free Town**.

The most impressive structure in New Free Town is the "Baptis (*sic*) Church, Ded. Sept. 13th, 1981, Rev. Cleveland Cooper Pastor," says the sign. A little farther down the road is the remaining facade of Zion Baptist Church. Groceries, in New Free Town, may be purchased from "Chicken Man."

Farther down the road is Bevin Town with the Three Sisters Restaurant and the Star Club. Most important here though is the service station — the only place where vehicle repairs are possible in eastern Grand Bahama.

The administrative center for the east end of the island is at **High Rock**. This is

Domino players at High Rock.

a charming little village situated on a low bluff above the sea some five miles (eight km) east of the Port Area. The sign says it all:

Welcome to High Rock where the scenery is beautiful and the people peaceful and friendly so enjoy your stay with us.

—The residents

Ezekiel Pinder's Oceanview Restaurant is the place to eat. If you wish, you can carry your meal across the shore road to a palm thatch hut and look at the sea while the waves crash on the rocks below you. Some of the older frame houses are worthy of note at High Rock. Also note that the settlement has a police station, a public library, a cemetery and a side-by-side public "john." From High Rock the road eastwards gets progressively worse. Cast your eyes upwards for a moment and you will see Fat Albert, the World War Two barrage balloon peeping through the clouds in the service of the Drug Enforcement Administration. The balloon is tethered at the Burmah Oil Transhipment Depot which, in more optimistic times, was intended by the government to be the nucleus of another industrial area on the island. **Pelican Point** is situated on what is probably the widest beach on the island. This is also the last place that gasoline is available.

Leaving Pelican Point, a new graded road serves the east end of the island. The beach track is much more interesting, but check that the tide is not high, and avoid it if there has been recent rainfall unless your vehicle has four-wheel drive.

Now that the new road has been constructed, it is easy to miss the turn-off to **Rocky Creek**. This would be a pity because the settlement consists of three or four small houses but more significantly includes a **"blue hole"** in an inlet off the sea. The blue hole is a natural sea aquarium for many species of marine life.

Just Cracking: Finally, or almost, the intrepid explorer arrives at **Mcleans Town**, the last mainland settlement on the island. This community has good shallow water anchorage and is famous for its **Conch Cracking Contest** held every year on Columbus Day.

"Cracking" a conch is a three-step technique. First the conch has to be hit with an axe or similar object at exactly the right spot to break the shell where the animal is attached. This leaves the characteristically oval-shaped hole seen on most conches not in their customary marine habitat. Then the conch is "jewked" (removed) from the shell by grasping the "claw" or foot (actually an operculum). Then the slimy foot-long (30 cm) animal is cleaned and dumped in a bucket. An expert conch cracker can dispose of about 20 in five minutes.

North of Mcleans Town a small airstrip has suddenly appeared. The people of Mcleans Town are not exactly jetsetters, so island cynics have their own ideas as to who and what makes "Mcleans Town International Airport" tick.

Farther exploration from here must be by boat. Just across Rumers Creek is the **Deep Water Cay** development which has some small guesthouses and a bush-pilot airstrip. The most easterly habitation of the island is at **Sweeting's Cay,** which is a neat and tidy place indeed. It was settled when sponging was the primary industry of the Little Bahama Bank. There are a few places for refreshment, including the Travellers Rest and the Seagarden Bar. Nearby is a small tourist development which offers cottages for rent. Like Water Cay, there are no vehicles on this tranquil "out island" cay.

Jewking a conch, left. Conch meat and shells, right.

141

FREEPORT

In just over a decade a forest of scrub pines was converted into the second city of the Bahamas. Freeport was first a clearing in a pine forest some five miles (eight km) from Hawksbill Creek; later, when it reached the "take off" phase it became more like a frontier construction camp, and, today, despite condos and country clubs, there is still a certain rawness to the place. Indeed it is no coincidence that its principal streets are named for adventurers, settlers and pioneers.

Freeport was the brainchild of Wallace Groves, a Virginia financier. Groves bought a lumber company in 1946, and, at his island retreat, Little Whale Cay, in the Berry Islands, he pondered the island of Grand Bahama. It seemed to have much going for it. It was large and unencumbered by private owners; it was near the United States, and it had large reserves of ground water in addition to the natural resource of lumber. If that wasn't enough, it was a British colony with a benign pro-business government and, as an additional bonus, it had sea, sand and sun in abundance.

To make his dream come true he needed a concession from the government, but Groves knew that would not be forthcoming unless he could offer something in return. Bargaining after all is a two way street. So to the government he went — represented by his lawyer Sir Stafford Sands, who was at that time the Minister of Tourism — with a bold plan.

Groves's proposal was the development of a free port on Grand Bahama. He asked for, and received, concessions on the importation of duty-free materials and guarantees that there would be no taxes of any kind. He also signed a lease purchase agreement for 50,000 acres (20,000 hectares) of land. In return he promised to dredge a deepwater harbor, encourage industry, pay for all government personnel employed within the Port Area (as the land became known) and reimburse the government for all other government services. The contract became the Hawksbill Creek Agreement and was signed into law on Aug. 5, 1955.

Early development was slow, but Groves was fortunate that shipping tycoon D.K. Ludwig had the unlikely notion that he would like to build large ships near the

Caribbean. Ludwig paid for the development of a commodious harbor in exchange for 2,000 acres (800 hectares) of land. The harbor was never used for shipbuilding, and D.K. Ludwig continued to purchase his ships in Japan, but Freeport had gained a harbor.

Industry was slower in moving to the island. The first major industry was a ship-bunkering terminal which fitted nicely with the deepwater harbor. Due to a quota imposed by the U.S. government on all residual fuels imported into the United States, it was worthwhile for shippers to bunker in Freeport. The strategic location of Freeport brought a bonanza, and in one month alone the terminal exported nearly 1 million barrels of duty-free oil. Other industries were small, catering mainly to the service sector, but in 1961 work began on a giant cement plant on the western side of the harbor. Foreign entrepreneurs and workers poured into the island.

Five years into the venture the Grand Bahama Port Authority, the company founded by Wallace Groves, found that things were good and could be even better. The original Hawksbill Creek Agreement had envisioned an industrial community on Grand Bahama, but Groves

Churchill Square
RESTAURANT AND BAR

realized that there was potential in tourism. So he went back to the government with another plan. The result was the signing in 1960 of the Supplemental Agreement.

This recognized that the Port Authority had performed as agreed under the principal agreement, and it now required the Port to build a luxury 200-room hotel and permitted it to purchase more land. To accommodate this change in direction, Groves formed the Grand Bahama Development Company with Louis Chesler, a dynamic Canadian businessman. Chesler put $12 million in cash into the deal, and Groves' Grand Bahama Port Authority contributed 102,000 acres (41,300 hectares) of land. The Development Company land became known as Lucaya.

The luxury hotel called the Lucayan Beach Hotel was completed on schedule and opened its doors to the public on New Year's Eve 1963. The hotel was strangely different from other hotels in the Bahamas of the time, for it incorporated a large gambling casino. The Certificate of Exemption required for the gambling license had been furtively obtained from the white minority government. When the government changed, a Commission on Gambling studied the manner in which the Cer-

tificate was obtained and pointed out that there was strong evidence to suggest that undesirables had been involved in the operation, that "skimming" seemed likely, and it further expressed concern "that the consultants who were members of the Council (government) should have allowed themselves to be put in a position where conflict of interest would surely have arisen." The slap on the wrist was merely for the record, for under black majority rule it was highly unlikely that former Council members would ever hold political office again.

In 1965 when lawyer Lynden O. Pindling (who would later become the first Bahamian Prime Minister under majority rule) threw the Speaker's Mace out of the upper-floor window of the House of Assembly, the Port Authority and other foreign companies and individuals noted the mood of the country with apprehension.

For a time it was business as usual. A $100-million oil refinery was built shortly thereafter in Freeport, but by 1970 things started to come unglued. The recession in the United States sent a shock wave through the local economy, and due to the government's Bahamianization policy, foreigners found that their re-entry permits

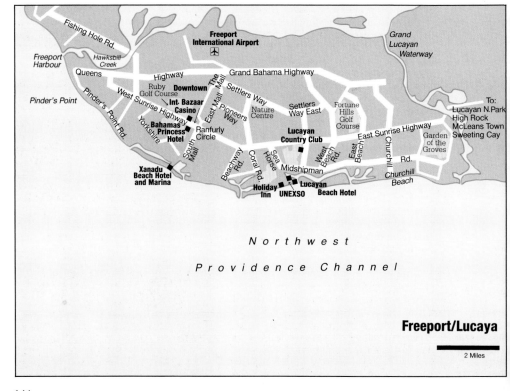

Northwest

Providence Channel

Freeport/Lucaya

2 Miles

were called in, and the new permits that were granted were subject to payment of a fee. Some were not reissued. For a time the licensees of the Port Authority were in revolt and threatened to challenge the government. After much pressure the Port Authority agreed to pay for arbitration proceedings. But the challenge did not last long. The new Prime Minister Lynden Pindling wanted the licensees to "bend or be broken." Many foreigners realized they were destined to play no part in the new Bahamas, and they left.

The Port Authority meanwhile looked overseas to diversify. It formed an appropriately named company, the Intercontinental Diversified Corporation, listed on the New York Stock Exchange, and added to its portfolio a Philippine gold mine company (Benguet), some tract land in Florida, the Canary Islands and California. Intercontinental Diversified also acquired the outstanding shares of the Grand Bahama Development Company.

The new overseas adventure was short-lived. The Philippine government forced the nationalization of Benguet. The foreign real-estate ventures were sold off with small financial gain. In 1970 Wallace Groves, in his 70th year, retired as Chairman of the Port Authority. When the Bahamas gained its independence from Britain on July 10, 1973, the Bahamians from other islands who had sought to make a new life in Freeport found that they needed to make considerable adjustments to their previous lifestyle.

Company Town: The unprecedented birth of Freeport as a foreign "company town" put several characteristics in place which carried over, even though with independence there was a fundamental change in the complexion of the city. The open planning of Freeport does not encourage "street society." With wide streets and liberal yards it is not easy to hail your neighbor; there are no corner shops, almost no neighborhood bars and, perhaps most regrettable of all, few people walk anywhere anyway. This is a mobile society, completely reliant on the automobile. Visitors from other islands have few places to socialize publicly, and, without family or friends in Freeport, feel the place to be alien, non-Bahamian somehow. Despite this they can't help noting that the streets are clean, and that water, electrical and telephone services seem to function without a hitch. Charitable commentators find Freeporters "private," "urbane" even. Other less charitable observers say they are "cold and indifferent." Because of the employment opportunities, Freeporters are seen as "materialistic" and "competitive," and they demonstrate more variety than other Bahamians in their choice of life-styles.

The island is unable to receive Bahamian television beamed from Nassau, and so the islanders tune into Florida stations or pick up a myriad of programs on backyard dish antennae. This in turn makes Grand Bahamians more aware of the world and its ways — they have even been accused of being less nationalistic than other Bahamians.

Princesses, Pioneers: If you arrive in Freeport by air you may hear the grinding of the hydraulic system as the landing gear locks into place. If you could then see directly downwards you would find yourself over the outer navigation beacon at the Deep Water Harbour. A few more minutes and (with luck) a smooth touchdown, and you will have your first contact with Grand Bahama Island.

By car you will almost certainly enter Freeport by circumnavigating Independence Circle which bears a sign saying that "It's Better in The Bahamas," a proud boast and one still to be proved. The Grand Bahama Promotion Board qualifies this

Wallace Groves, global magnate and founder of Freeport.

sign with one of their own which states more simply "It's nice to have you here."

Proceeding down the Mall ("Keep left except when Overtaking," the sign says, but nobody on the dual carriageway heeds its message) you will pass the Civic Centre site, soon to have a court house and several government offices. Next, three Canadian-owned banks occupy the west (right hand) side of the road, with the Main Post Office just visible behind the Royal Bank of Canada. (Canadian banks hold 80 percent of all deposits in the Bahamas.)

The next set of traffic signals marks the intersection with Pioneers Way, the center of the city. On the left, in a pseudo-colonial building painted lurid pink, the Grand Bahama Port Authority has its headquarters.

A mile farther south down the Mall, you arrive at **Ranfurly Circus**, a traffic circle named for a popular British colonial governor of the 1950s. Here is located the International Bazaar, the Princess Country Club and the Princess Tower Hotel and Casino.

This area is a must-see for visitors, if only for the sake of curiosity. The **International Bazaar** is an architectural melange which was better when it was new. Every shop now seems to be touting tee-shirts,

and the "merchandise-to-fit-the-architecture" rule is largely ignored. Nevertheless the Bazaar still retains some charm. In the words of Jay Mitchell, a local musician:

"down to the Bazaar
get what your hearts desire
because it Freeport, Freeport/Lucaya
down to the Bazaar
all the places you want to go,
we got Spain, France, Africa...
we even got Mexico!"

Cameras and photographic equipment are available at the Ginza in the Oriental section, and a great selection of emeralds and jewelry may be bought at Colombian Emeralds. There is even a free walk-through workshop for anyone interested in seeing the dirty-finger-nail side of jewelry making. The French Quarter bears a French facsimile street sign, *Place des Wallons*, and features Michel's, a French-style sidewalk cafe which surprisingly has a lot of atmosphere. An energetic steel drum band sometimes plays nearby. The Spanish section isn't very Spanish, though Casa Miro sells Spanish leather and porcelain. On the Churchill Pub side of the Bazaar a Bahamian Straw Market is a hive of commercial activity. The straw ladies are always busy sewing on pom

The International Bazaar.

poms, chasing their children and hawking their wares often all at the same time. Locally made straw products are good, but a lot of other merchandise, not made locally, has slipped. The Bazaar area is now the venue for a European-style motor race which promises to be an exciting yearly event.

The Moorish-style **Princess Casino** next to the Bazaar represents Sodom and Gomorrah for some. But if gambling is for you, the gaming hall has it all.

On the opposite side of Sunrise Highway is the 565-room **Princess Country Club**. Its rooms are arranged like the spokes of a wheel around a delightful plaza with hot tubs and a fanciful swimming pool, including a waterfall. Adjacent is the John B, an open-air dining room and bar, a charming place to dine or to sip a rum punch especially in the late evening.

Private Xanadu: West from Ranfurly Circus will take you through D.K. Ludwig's Bahamia (18-hole championship golf courses north and south), to the refinery and the deepwater harbor. On the channel entrance to the harbor is Pier One, which is built on stilts over the water like a New England fish warehouse and is a pleasant place to dine and watch the cruise ships dock. Continuing straight down the Mall the visitor sees the ocean for the first time and **Xanadu Beach Hotel** — formerly the private domain of Howard Hughes, who lived on the sealed-off 12th and 13th floors in total seclusion until his death in 1976. The Xanadu has a marina and there is another — the Running Mon — nearby.

Travelling east from Ranfurly Circus you will pass the Pub on the Mall (one of Freeport's three English-style pubs), a **Shrine** at Mary Star of the Sea Church, recently erected by Wallace Groves, the small Sunrise Shopping Centre (open after the downtown supermarkets are closed), and the Freeport High School. To the right some undistinguished housing completes the streetscape of this gateway road.

Lucayan Sand, Sun: Another mile and another circle, this time Lucaya Circle, and you reach the Groves/Chesler area of Lucaya. A right turn (south) will bring you to the **Lucayan Beach**. Here, situated on a beautiful white powder sand beach, are the principal beach hotels of the island.

The **Lucayan Beach Hotel and Casino**, the first Hotel on the island, was empty for many years but is now part of

Freeport's waterfall, at the Bahamas Princess Hotel.

the area's burgeoning new growth. The multi-story Corbusier-style Swiss owned **Atlantik Beach Hotel and Casino** occupies an adjacent beach front site, and next door is the 516-room **Holiday Inn**.

The new festival marketplace at Port Lucaya opened officially in June 1989. With 85 shops and ongoing entertainment, its popularity grows. Besides the traditional straw market and branches of other stores, there is a refreshing emphasis on local Bahamian ingenuity.

To the north, across from the hotels, is an extensive man-made canal system which has several small waterfront hotels and the largest yacht basin on the island: **Lucayan Marina and Hotel**. A stone's throw away are two more 18-hole golf courses: the original championship Lucayan Country Club and the Bahama Reef and Country Club.

The Lucayan Beach area is where most of the action is. In the daytime there are organised boat trips for fishing and snorkeling, and the **Underwater Explorers Society** (UNEXSO) offers splendid facilities for scuba divers. If just sitting in the sun is not enough, you can parasail or hire a Boston whaler, windsurfer or Hobe Cat. And at night there is the Pa-

nache Night Club in the Holiday Inn and the cabarets, bars and restaurants to the Lucayan Beach Hotel, and of course the half-acre arena devoted to "Lady Luck."

Flamingo Pink: If a quieter more contemplative mood is required, do not despair. Taxi and bus operators will take tourists around Freeport identifying "Mr. Grove house" (now owned by a wealthy German industrialist), the Sir "Union" Jack Hayward abode, some upper-middle-class housing and a glimpse of downtown. Some of these trips end up with free drinks and the opportunity to sign on the dotted line for time-sharing privileges or whatever. Others take the adventurous to the small settlements engulfed by Freeport or to the pleasantly tranquil Taino and Fortune beaches.

Perhaps a better way to see Freeport is to rent a car. The **Rand Nature Center** is centainly worth seeing. Quite near the center of Freeport, this nature reserve has interesting nature trails and a low key, knowledgeable Bahamian guide who explains the flora and fauna of the island. Another trip should take in the **Garden of the Groves** and the **Grand Bahama Museum**. The Garden of the Groves is a spectacular botanical garden completely designed from scratch but none the worse for that. It boasts exotic (labelled) trees, plants and shrubs from all over the world and cascading waterfalls, flamingos and a fern gully. The Grand Bahama Museum captures the history of the island and features reconstructed caves and audio-visual presentations. There is a marine exhibit (which could use some reorganization) and artifacts from the Lucayan Indian culture and the era of piracy. A working model of the south shore slip and the original Hawksbill Creek Agreement are preserved behind glass. In the small garden attached to the museum is a native house reconstructed from local pine lumber. The wood was actually cannibalized from the first airport terminal of Freeport. On the way out, note the driving wheels of a steam locomotive that once served the lumber industry of the island.

Freeport, in its short existence, has certainly known the boom-and-bust cycle that has typified much of the history of the Bahamas. Still, with all its natural attributes — not to mention its resilient population — it now seems poised to soar to the next economic peak, which just might even put the zooming Sixties in the shade.

Playing the one-armed bandits, left. Plumage at the Garden of the Groves, right.

THE FAMILY ISLANDS

You've survived the storm; your ship is battered, but you finally limp into a quiet, deserted cove and drop anchor. On the shore you see a hand-lettered sign: "Columbus landed here." The scene is imaginary, but not impossible, for the paths of early explorers indeed crisscrossed these islands — Columbus, eyes peeled for the gold and spices of Cathay; Ponce de Leon in search of the Fountain of Youth; pirates needing secluded landfalls to rendezvous, take on water, hide treasure.

Known traditionally as the "Out Islands," the Family Islands are remote, beautiful, mysterious. To many people they are the real Bahamas, the heart of this complex and diverse country. They are hardly "out" for travelers with a sense of adventure.

It would take years to discover all the secrets and pleasures of these islands — the friendly settlements of the Exumas; the piney woods of Andros; sunbaked Bimini; the trim seafaring villages of the Abacos — but the following chapters are designed to give you a head start.

We start the coverage of the Family Islands in the Bimini, the island closest to the United States, and travel in a leisurely fashion to the farthest, the strange and fascinating island Inagua. It is doubtful, however, that any but the most hearty yachtsman would wish to visit the Bahama islands in this order. Travelers with a week or two to spend should concentrate on one or two islands. Today, as throughout the Bahamas' history, island hopping, or a whirlwind multi-island tour, is not a practical enterprise.

Clear as wellwater in a china cup, borrowing dappled ribbons of color from the blue of the sky, the pristine sea around the Bahama islands is a thin skin covering treacherous reefs, bars and shoals. Covering over 90,000 sq miles (230,000 sq km), it makes every island a castle — surrounded by a moat with no drawbridge.

Linking the Chain: For most of the Bahamas' history, communication and commerce between the islands was difficult and sporadic. The Out Islands were truly "out," and in the mid-19th Century even Nassau did not enjoy regular steamship connections with New York. (An Act of Parliament in 1851 offered an annual bounty of £1,000 to anyone who would provide a "good, substantial and efficient" steamship service between New York and Nassau.)

Sailors knew how to read these waters — sandbars, grassy patches, deep channels are all described by the sea's color — and if they didn't, they joined the many shipwrecks in the Bahamas' "Davey Jones' locker." Boatbuilding was both an art and industry in the Out Islands, but the best building and sailing skills could not keep these islands from being chronically isolated. The words of the old spiritual, "In the sweet bye and bye, we will meet on that beautiful shore," must have had a temporal as well as a religious significance. To sail from Miami or Fort Lauderdale to Bimini took (and still does) a good 12 hours; from Nassau to Long Island, several days.

When a man named Arthur Burns "Pappy" Chalk began flying a three-seat bootlegging clientele. Judy Garland, Errol Flynn and Howard Hughes flew Chalk's seaplanes to the Bahamas — taking off in a foamy wake, droning low over the water, landing with a splash. And Chalk's is still flying today. A flight to one of Chalk's three current destinations — Bimini, Cat Cay and Paradise Island — can be a sightseeing tour in itself. Fishing boats, reefs, fish and starfish glide by beneath the wings. Even the shadows of big fish are visible on the ocean bottom.

With its perfect safety record (except for one hijacking to Cuba in the early 1970s) and reliable adherence to schedules, barring weather conditions that might make flying unsafe, Chalk's International Airlines is a top choice for Bahamian travel.

Stinson Voyager between Florida and the Bahamas in 1919, a new era in Bahamian travel began. Pappy's chief customers on the Voyager and a Curtiss HS-2L floatplane were bootleggers; the cargo was whiskey and rum to slake the thirst of Prohibition in America. At the time probably no one suspected that Chalk's Airlines would still be in operation decades later — the oldest continuously operating airline in the world.

By 1933, when Prohibition was repealed, Pappy Chalk was still in business with headquarters on Miami's Watson Island. Flying military surplus Grummans (Widgeons, Geese and Mallards) Chalk's International Airlines

For travel to most of the Family Islands, most Bahamians opt for the national carrier, Bahamasair. A sight more common than the elusive flamingo is one of Bahamasair's blue and yellow Hawker Sidleys. These British-made planes carry up to 48 passengers, and they're almost always filled with businessmen, grandmothers, children, tourists, suitcases and cardboard boxes. When the two propellors start to whir, get ready for a ride over

Preceding pages: Marsh Harbour evening; minimal breeze at Treasure Cay; and a front yard float collection on Man-O-War Cay. A Chalk's seaplane splashes down (above), and a mailboat unloads cargoes (right).

some of the world's most colorful seas on what's essentially an inter-island bus. The conventional wisdom warns that only the first flight of the day is on time. (Like most adages, this one has a basis in truth.) These workhorse planes fly from 7:30 a.m. until night, linking the islands with a little confusion and a lot of goodwill.

Tying loose: Old-timers, however, remember when travel to another island meant not "taking off" but "tying loose." In the early part of this century, Bahamian-built two-masted schooners plied the turquoise seas, serving as mother ships for fleets of sponge fishing dinghies. In the 1920s they made rum runs to the United States. Single-masted fishing smacks, 20 to 40 feet (six to 12 meters) long,

Blanche is carrying you home, or on an adventure, she can seem like a goddess.

One of these goddesses can be yours for 25 to 35 dollars for a one-way ticket, which you can purchase at the harbormaster's office at Potter's Cay, Nassau. The price is hardly cheaper than Bahamasair, and the boats' safety record is not as good, but that is the price you pay for adventure. You can look over the boats and crews at Potter's Cay dock, where they all begin and end their journeys, and where you will soon learn that these sometimes fickle ladies are not wedded to a fixed schedule. A bunk to sleep in and store your belongings on are the only amenities guaranteed to passengers, but on some boats you will have clean sheets, home-cooked

also sometimes carried travelers between the islands. Fish voyaged to market in watery darkness in live wells in the hulls, while above them seven to 10 passengers and crew cooked, ate and slept on the open deck.

The government mailboats provided the only regular service to most Out Islands — first by sail, later by diesel power. Today these battered boats with their peeling paint and roughneck crews are still the link that gets the mail sack, cars, chickens, pianos, diesel drums and foodstuffs to the far flung islands. *Bahama Daybreak, Bimini Mac, Current Pride, Big Yard Express* and others make weekly trips between Nassau and one or two of the Out Islands, and if the old *Willaurie* or *Lady*

Bahamian food, congenial companionship, and always the sea and the stars.

However you reach the Family Islands — by yacht, chartered plane, scheduled flight or by mailboat — the first thing to remember as you step ashore is that these are the islands most Bahamians will always call home. Ask a Bahamian, whether in Nassau, Freeport or New York, "Where are you from?" and in the response you will almost always hear a note of pride and nostalgia. "I come from Eleut'ra," "I was born in Mangrove Cay," "I'm from Marsh Harbour, Abaco." And these are indeed islands to speak of with pride. Perhaps the sign on the empty beach says not "Columbus landed here," but "Home at last."

THE BIMINI ISLANDS

The Bimini Islands are the only group in the Bahamas whose deep-water "weather" side faces west. In the long summer of 1935, Ernest Hemingway told friends that the discovery of Bimini was one of the great events in his life, and he got these island down on paper in the novel *Islands In The Stream*, no less true, he might argue, for its being fiction. At the closest point they are less than 50 miles (80 km) from Florida; and from North Bimini on a clear night you can see the glow of Miami's lights. Since the 1930s the rich and talented from Key West to Wall Street have made it their lawless vacation suburb – a place where Ernest Hemingway fought, drank, brawled, bullied, fished and wrote his way through several seasons – a long fraternity party paid for by the heirs of DuPont, Maytag, Kodak and Bessemer Steel.

The islands are flat as bonefish, and the string extends 28 miles (45 km), with large North Bimini and South Bimini on the top, running down to Turtle Rocks, Piquet Rocks, Holm Cay, Gun Cay, North and South Cat Cays, Sandy Cay and Ocean Cay. Seen from the air the upper arm of North Bimini looks like a giant gray-green crab claw floating low on the surface of the sea.

Alice Town: Wearing a girl's name is all that is feminine about this flea-bitten, raucous, charming, big-game town where a good boat, a good catch, or, lacking that, a souped-up Mitsubishi pickup truck with heavy chrome fog lights on the cab roof will get you farther than any sweet talking. If you dock at the Bimini Big Game Fishing Club, Weech's Bimini Dock, Brown's Hotel and Marina, or Bimini Blue Water Limited, or fly in by seaplane to **North Bimini,** the first street you will see in **Alice Town** will be the narrow, dusty King's Highway where the bars outnumber the shops, and traffic is two way only if both drivers are willing.

A stroll down **King's Highway** takes a lot of its character from the time of day: early morning the town seems empty, the sandy street golden, the shuttered buildings (mostly pastel except for the rust colored Red Lion Pub) contrite. A sunburned man in a T-shirt walks by carrying an ice chest.

Preceding pages, a Bimini beach. Below, flying in.

160

Someone has started the coffee in **Captain Bob's Conch Hall of Fame** and a few people are inside at the lunch counter. By the time the sun's full up in the sky the fishermen are out on their boats; the town can daydream or go back to sleep as the sun heats up the street and clapboard walls.

Later on, women come out to sell fruit and straw baskets in the shade of the tin-roofed marketplace. The children are in school, and the potcakes (Bahamian mutts) move from sunny doorsteps to lie in the shade. The day is heating up to be hot and dusty. When the Chalks seaplane roars in from Miami on schedule at 12:45, winging over the island and landing with a splash in **Bimini Harbour**, a handful of water between North and South Bimini, it's like Big Ben chiming in the afternoon. A few new tourists arrive; Biminites head for the terminal to pick up packages, to pick up a cab fare, to greet arriving friends or relatives. By this time, the best place to be is at the beach or in a bar.

(In the bar) *"it was cool and almost dark after the glare of the coral road and* (he) *had a gin and tonic water with a piece of lime peel in the glass and a few drops of Angostura in the drink. Mr. Bobby was behind the bar looking terrible. Four Negro*

Monument on King's Highway.

boys were playing billiards, occasionally lifting the table when necessary to bring off a difficult carom... Two of the crew of the yacht that was tied up at the slip were in the bar and as Thomas Hudson's eyes adjusted to the light it was dim and cool and pleasant." (From *Islands In The Stream* by Ernest Hemingway.)

The **End of the World Bar,** with its sand floor and back door open to the harbor would be a good place for the first drink, or a good place to wait for people to come in off the boats. *("How many of them are there?" "Seven with two girls. One nice-looking and one wonderful...")*

When the sun starts to set the fishing boats come in with their sunburned, beer-bellied fishermen, tan women; and once it's dark the mosquitoes come out, and then the town begins to hop.

Compleat Angler: The hotel where Hemingway used to stay is not content to remember; it likes to live up to its reputation. The bar in the **Compleat Angler,** with its polished wood walls, red leather-cushioned stools and captains' chairs is where most visitors to Alice Town whoop it up. Personalized auto license plates — BIGDADY, MARLENE, BILLY2, GO CUBS — decorate the wood paneling, and the rows

of bottles behind the bar beckon yachtsmen in blues and whites and other sundry folk. It's after dinner when the walls begin to shake, so if you're early you might check out the library dedicated to Hemingway memorabilia — snapshots of the writer posing beside monstrous fish, smiling in gracious camaraderie with friends, everyone sophisticated sportsmen and women of the 1930s. These are scattered on paneled walls that gleam with varnish like the most fastidious sea captain's cabin, amid cracked leather upholstery, a pair of back-gammon tables and a few tattered volumes. It's an outdoorsman's library, no question. Back in the entrance hall, a local band – calypso, rock, amplified – is setting up, and tough luck for anyone who thinks he's going to hole up in the library or climb those polished wood stairs and get some sleep.

Outdoors, in the palmy moonlight, a few Biminites roar up and down the narrow street in Mazdas, Datsuns and pickup trucks, radios blaring; it's party time.

The local action at the **Hy Star Disco** is heating up. If you're not up for that, you might pop into the **Red Lion Pub** for a bowl of conch chowder beneath framed newspaper articles on world-record size marlin, signed photos of Miami Dolphin football players and plaques promoting brands of beer. The tables and walls are the battered sort where you might find some boozy fisherman has carved his girlfriend's name.

Back out in the wild night, a few yachtsmen are relaxing on their boats at the dock.

"It was a fine night and after they had eaten dinner they sat out in the stern with coffee and cigars, and a couple of other people, both worthless sporting characters, came over from one of the other boats with a guitar...There was quite a lot of celebration going on at Bobby's place and you could see the lights from the open door over the water."

Don't forget as you revel in the haze of a warm, festive night that the people out on the docks are the reason for most of the action on Bimini. By sunrise most of them will be up, and sportfishing will be the island's undisputed king. If you want to get out on the water the next day, you had better find a bed at Brown's Hotel, the Anchorage, or the Bimini Big Game Fishing Club.

Bimini Big Game: The center for fishermen is the **Bimini Big Game Fishing Club,**

Below, Captain Bob in his restaurant. Right, Hemingway relics at the Compleat Angler.

HEMINGWAY IN BIMINI

Before Ernest Hemingway discovered Bimini in 1935, the island was not unknown — as some of the writer's fans, and perhaps Hemingway himself, liked to think. Sportsmen in the know, mainly ones with a good deal of money, fished the Gulf Stream and stopped off for rest and relaxation on this little island throughout the 1930s. According to Hemingway's biographer Carlos Baker, the inimitable writer-adventurer heard of Bimini in 1933 or '34 when he was spending time in Key West, Florida, but he needed a boat to get there. So in 1934 he bought the *Pilar*. She was a 38-foot diesel-powered cruiser that could do 16 knots on a flat sea; her cabin slept six, with room for one more in the cockpit. She was painted black.

On the first trip to Bimini, on April 7, 1935, Hemingway set out on the *Pilar* with John Dos Passos and four others. They trolled on the way, and when Hemingway hooked a large shark he brought it alongside the boat and blasted its head with a barrage of bullets. As he fired, the gaff broke, Hemingway slipped, and he shot himself in both legs. In Baker's words: "Instead of Bimini, Ernest went to bed."

Hemingway arrived in Bimini a week later and spent much of that spring and summer there. He reeled in a 785-pound (355-kg) mako shark and boasted to his editor, Maxwell Perkins, that his expertise had changed the "whole system" of sportfishing on Bimini. He also indulged in his passion for boxing, offering $250 to any Negro who could stay in a ring with him for three three-mintute rounds. Despite several challenges, he held on to his $250. He was not above fistfights with the rich sportsmen whose sleek yachts crowded Bimini Harbour. The tale of his knockout victory over wealthy publisher Joseph Knapp was memorialized by a black calypso band whose improvised lyrics lauded "the big fat slob" from Key West.

A Bimini Celebrity: Even if he had not been a famous writer, he would have been a celebrity in Bimini for his fishing prowess. When, in 1936, he sailed in with a 514-pound (233-kg) tuna he hooked off Gun Cay, it is said the whole population came out to admire the fish. This excitement aside, he was still Hemingway the writer, and in June 1937 he was also at work in Bimini, revising the manuscript of *To Have And Have Not*. His lifestyle in Bimini did everything to enhance a career that put a generation in what biographer A.E. Hotchner called "Hemingway Awe."

In the novel *Islands In The Stream,* which remained unfinished at his death, Hemingway captured in fiction the seedy charm of Alice Town, North Bimini, and the mysterious power of battling a big fish in the Gulf Stream. The novel's central character, Thomas Hudson, is several degrees calmer and more peaceable than "Papa" Hemingway was himself in those Bimini years, but the novel still served to prolong the spell he cast over the island. Though he did not "create" big fishing in Bimini, it never would have been the same without him.

ERNEST HEMINGWAY WITH TWO SAIL FISHES

where the good-sized swimming pool, expensive, subdued restaurant and liveable rooms are all secondary to the action on the docks (67 slips) and the walk-in freezer for the day's catches. At dawn the bleary-eyed fisherman can take inspiration from a mural on a wall near the pool which commemorates some Bimini greats, including Bonefish Willie, a seasoned, genial boat captain who is also a gospel minister. Sequestered from King's Highway by a discreet wall, the club is almost sufficient unto itself. You could go from dock to hotel to restaurant without seeing another bit of Bimini, though there would be little point in that.

May 7 to June 15 is the prime season for bluefin (giant) tuna, the long-lived fish that spend their winters up the Gulf Stream off New England. The ultimate opponent for sportfishermen, they swim fast and grow up to 1,800 pounds (900 kg). June and July are the best for blue marlin, winter and spring for white marlin, summer and fall for tarpon, so there is almost always a big fish to chase here.

For true bluefin and billfish aficionados, no visit to the Bimini Islands would be complete without a visit to the southern Biminis. It was off **Gun Cay**, nine miles (14 km) south of Bimini Harbour, that Ernest Hemingway caught with rod and reel the giant bluefin tuna that he claimed galvanized Bimini fishing into what it is today (or was in the Thirties). In 1931 in the middle of the Depression, Louis Wasey founded a club on **Cat Cay** where he and a few friends could get away from golf on the nine-hole course, formal banquets in the Tudor-style mansion, cocktails at the Kitten Cay Bar. To a few friends he sold land for getaway homes. Still a private club today, though owned by a group of businessmen, Cat Cay is a place where DuPont heirs and the like get down to the serious business of catching bluefin tuna. Here the fishing goes on in style with His and Hers Tournaments, boat captains and coaches, yacht parties and celebrations in luxurious vacation homes.

Sidetrips: Compared to Cat Cay, **South Bimini** (North Bimini's next door neighbor) is more of a backwater, with a bit of farming and a few vacation homes. But the island holds fast to the claim that the explorer Ponce de Leon searched for the fabled "Fountain of Youth" there. People have at times claimed rejuvenating powers for a pool called **Healing Hole.**

End of the hunt.

At the far southern end of the Bimini chain, man has added to nature's work by building Ocean Cay. Aragonite, a very pure lime sand, is dredged here from the ocean floor, to be used in the making of cement, fertilizers, glass and other products. Tall cranes and other equipment make it a landmark for yachtsmen.

Back in Port: Back on north Bimini after a stint at sea (or a night in the bars), Alice Town is easily explored in an afternoon on foot. At the far south end of the King's Highway you will find a roughly painted sign indicating that if you pass beyond the fence you should fear for your life. So that is as far south as you can go. (You can see South Bimini and some homes along its shore from here.) Nearby to the west, overgrown with a spongy, grass-like moss, is a small graveyard with some of the older headstones sunk deep, so only their caps show.

The pink stucco Government Complex, a few steps down King's Highway, burned in the late seventies and is in the process of repair.

Walking down King's Highway you will pass a lagoon shaded by coconut palms and fenced by chain link, a number of small shops and bars, and an impressive outdoor patio extravaganza with lots of tables, trees, and hanging lanterns that looks like it could be lots of fun for a goombay-calypso-luau evening. You will pass a concrete arch that proclaims Bimini the Gateway to the Bahamas.

At the **Anchorage**, the Cape Cod clapboard hotel at the highest point on the island, is a pleasant restaurant with windows overlooking the water. Once it was the large home of Mike and Helen Lerner. Lerner, who was a friend of Hemingway, was a philanthropist whose projects included the Lerner Marine Laboratory in Alice Town, a branch of the American Museum of Natural History. From its opening in 1947 until its closing in 1974, scientists at the lab studied the behavior of sharks, dolphins and fish and made significant contributions in the fields of microbiology, icthyology and marine ecology.

With its commanding location and sea views east and west, it was undoubtedly the Lerners' home that inspired Thomas Hudson's house in *Islands in the Stream.*

"The house was built on the highest part of the narrow tongue of land between the

Bonefish Willie, esteemed Bimini boat captain, left. Collecting coconuts, right.

harbor and the open sea. It had lasted through three hurricanes and it was built solid as a ship...and on the ocean side you could walk out the door and down the bluff across the white sand and into the Gulf Stream."

The Anchorage, on its knoll, is still ship shape, with guest rooms added in a modern wing. No one with a day to spend on Bimini should miss the beach on the deepwater side. It has coarse white sand, starting below the Anchorage and extending in either direction. The waves here are large enough for body surfing and can make visibility for snorkeling rough unless you swim beyond them.

"It was a safe and fine place to bathe in the day but it was no place to swim at night. At night the sharks came in close to the beach, hunting in the edge of the Stream and from the upper porch of the house on quiet nights you could hear the splashing of the fish they hunted and if you went down to the beach you could see the phosphorescent wakes they made in the water."

You should not miss taking a walk on the pathway above the beach. Here you cannot help but notice the trim, white and green clapboard **Wesley Methodist Church,** founded 1858. Its French doors open on-

to a clean, simple nave with polished pews. There's a small belltower on the roof with dusty, old-fashioned looking loudspeakers aimed out. A walk south on the path above the beach or on the King's Highway will take you to **Bailey Town.** This is where most of the population of North Bimini lives, and on a walk there at dusk you will see children on shiny new American bicycles playing outside old wooden homes, well-kept churches and at least a dozen ambitious new frame houses or duplexes freshly painted beige, yellow or tawny brown. At some new houses, cars fill the short driveways, curtains cover the windows, beneath an unfinished second floor. In the dusk, people pass on foot, on bicycle or motorbike, on their ways home; in the air you smell a waft of marijuana and aftershave.

There is money on Bimini, and it's hardly a secret where it comes from. A fast boat can carry a cargo of marijuana or cocaine to Florida in a matter of hours. So the island fills with new cars, new motorbikes, new construction and hip new clothes. In March 1986 motorcycles with horsepower above 125 cc were banned from Bimini, so, as the island fills with cars, people wonder what they will do next with their money.

Back in Alice Town you will be able to smell your way to Estella Rolle's fresh bread, which she bakes and sells in a blue wooden hutch about five feet (1.5 meters) square and lays out for sale on the doorsill. She makes bread with raisins, regular white bread, and delicious coconut rolls.

Down the King's Highway, someone is dancing on the sand floor of the End of the World Bar. The sun is setting, and the fishermen are back. Some barefooted sportsmen pass, carrying open bottles of beer. In the purple dusk, someone is revving the motor of a flashy new car. In one of the shops where they sell T-shirts some of the local girls are keeping the place open while they plan their evening, and light spills out on the street. You take a few steps starboard to the docks and you're where you want to be. Out on the boat, if it weren't for the dock lights, you could see the stars.

Ah, Bimini!

(All quotes in italics from Ernest Hemingway, excerpted from *Islands In The Stream.* Copyright © 1970 Mary Hemingway. Reprinted with the permission of Charles Scribner's Sons.)

Cruising the King's Highway, left. School uniforms, right.

THE BERRY ISLANDS

The Berry Islands lure a special breed to their shores. Low-lying, rocky, with little water or arable soil, these are islands for people who already have everything.

Except for Bullock's Harbour on Great Harbour Cay, most of these 30 islands, if inhabited, are enjoyed by foreigners who have the means to create "worlds" on their own private cays. Other cays remain private paradises for wildlife. Terns, pelicans, and noddies make them favorite nesting grounds. Beneath the waters, sailfish, blue marlin, and giant bluefin tuna roam, tempting sports fishermen to this lovely, desolate chain of cays. They are known mostly to yachtsmen who favor them as a stopover on trips between Florida and Nassau.

Barely 500 souls make the Berry Islands their permanent home. Most of these islanders live in **Bullock's Harbour** on **Great Harbour Cay**. Politically, they are tied to the North Andros constituency, with which they share a representative in parliament. In reality, they seem to float free with the tides and trade winds on the Great Bahama Bank. The largest of the Berry Islands, at six miles (10 km) long and 2.5 miles (four km) wide, Great Harbour Cay saw its first residents in 1836 when Governor Colebrook founded a settlement there for homeless ex-slaves. For a 19th Century agrarian community, this tiny island offered a harsh life. Poor soil and little water left room for hardly more than a bare existence, supplemented only by the abundance of the sea.

In recent years, economic difficulties have kept facilities of yachtsmen and other visitors to a minimum. However, The Great Harbour Cay Marina has been refurbished, so the lull in activity may be coming to an end.

Passing Ships: Cruise lines also have seen the attraction of the Berry Islands as a pristine landfall on the way to Nassau. When the great white ship appears on the horizon, **Great Sturrup Cay** comes to life as a setting for "castaway for a day." A picnic, a swim and "native" entertainment (generally non-Bahamain fun like limbo dancing) complete a frolic on the **Abandoned on Great Sturrup Cay.**

cay's unspoiled beach.

Great Sturrup Cay also marks the northernmost tip of this hook-shaped chain. Here a lighthouse beams its white light to passing ships. Less romantic, but more effective, is the red light on the tower of the United States Tracking Station which is visible to boats at sea for 18 miles (30 km).

At the southernmost end of the chain, tiny **Chub Cay** sits on the very edge of the Great Bahama Bank, overlooking the deep sea trench, the Tongue of the Ocean. Here you will find the only resort in the Berry Islands currently set up for tourists – the semi-private Chub Cay Club. Founded by a wealthy Florida horsebreeder, Chub Cay and its club became a favorite gathering place for sportsmen and women with the time, money and guts to pursue the big fish. Some people call Chub Cay the bill-fish capital of the Bahamas, but it is interesting to note that the founder and first owner of the club was an avid bone fisherman whose research into the habits of bonefish led him to this spot. You can charter a big-game fishing boat here, or hire a boat and guide for bonefishing. With an airstrip, marina

A lone castaway.

and dive facilities, poolside hotel rooms, restaurant, tennis courts and driving range, the Chub Cay Club can proudly claim to have everything anyone could reasonably want on a postage stamp-sized island.

Private Paradises: Between Great Harbour Cay and Chub Cay, a number of cays are privately owned, and landing on any of these is by invitation only. **Bird Cay**, with its plantings of tall coconut trees, casuarinas and fruit trees, shelters several luxurious homes. **Whale Cay** is being developed as a private resort. **Frozen Cay** and **Alder Cay** are a paradise for birds – and bird lovers – when at sunrise and sunset the air around them fills with terns. Pelicans and brown noddies also nest on these cays, which are accessible from anchored yachts by dinghy. They are also private property, so remember to leave them as natural sanctuaries, free from litter.

On **Little Whale Cay**, Wallace Groves (multi-millionaire and founder of Freeport) has an elegantly landscaped estate with an airstrip, and, among other amenities, an aviary for exotic birds including flamingos, pheasants and peacocks.

THE ABACOS

A lovely group of islands, situated approximately 106 miles (170 km) north of the capital of the Bahamas, Nassau, and about 200 miles (320 km) north east of Miami, Florida, the Abacos are the most versatile of the Bahamian island groups. Thoroughly saturated with the quaint and harmonious atmosphere which is a trademark of the Family Islands, the Abacos also offer the visitor some of the conveniences of "city" life in Marsh Harbour, the third largest town in the Bahamas. In the Abacos you can take a yacht out to sea by day and dine onshore in a fine restaurant at night. You can let your hair down and enjoy the islands thoroughly, but if you want to recapture a chic appearance for the trip home, there is a hair-styling boutique at your service. From Walker's Cay in the north all the way down to Hole-in-the-Wall in the south, the Abacos simply offer a unique experience.

Once a prime shipbuilding center, also with a fine agricultural tradition, Abaconians have always been self sustaining. They have long had the reputation of being some of the most ambitious people in the country. Abaconians like Bunyan Key and the late Albert Lowe built such sleek craft that they became something of a legend in their time. Both learned boatbuilding from older relatives in the early 1900s. The Abaconian three-masted schooner, when completed, was a vessel of tremendous beauty and typified the craftmanship of the Abaco boatbuilder.

The people of the Abacos have always been an enterprising lot, and whatever they set out to do, it was done with great finesse and pride. So proud are Abaconians of their own abilities and their islands that at one point in the early 1970s, many supported a move to secede from the rest of the Bahamas.

When the Bahamian government officially announced plans for the Bahamas to become an independent nation a great number of Abaconians were quite upset. Expressing their profound loyalty to the Queen of England, they started a movement to avert the historic milestone – independence – that became a reality in 1973. A group called the Greater Abaco Council initially led the movement, and members traveled to London in Decem-

ber of 1972 to the Bahamas Constitutional Conference to petition against independence. When that venture failed the council soon disbanded, to be replaced by the Abaco Independence Movement (A.I.M.) which then tried for independence from the Bahamas. Of course, A.I.M. also failed. The controversy split the people of the Abacos virtually in half, with one group advocating going it alone as a small nation, and the other preferring to remain a part of the Bahamas.

But the conflict did not dampen the enterprising spirit of the Abaconians. They continued to strive and develop the islands, and today, with boatbuilding and farming taking a back seat to tourism, the Abacos have perhaps the highest employment rate in the Family Islands.

A number of attractive marinas have made the Abacos a popular resort area. All year and especially during peak season, the **Treasure Cay Marina**, the **Conch Inn Resort and Marina** and **Green Turtle Yacht Club and Marina** are inhabited by a dazzling array of boats. Many of their owners return repeatedly and often several times a year.

Early Settlers: Many of the people of the Abacos are descendants of the British Loyalists who left the United States following the Revolutionary War. They came in the 1780s; however they were not the only early settlers. Putting down roots around the same time were a group of Harbour Islanders. Some say it was the pretty Loyalist girls that attracted these Harbour Island men, plus the prospect of a developing area with plentiful resources. Prior to the Loyalists' arrival in the Abacos, these islands were a cruising ground for pirates, and before that, home to Indians, who gave the island its early earmark of Yucayonequi.

It was the Loyalists, however, who should be credited with starting the agricultural tradition in the Abacos. Thanks to them, farming gained a strong foothold, and from that time to today, agriculture has been able to supplement other means of survival for the Abaconians.

When the Harbour Islanders (whose forebears had been among the first settlers of the Bahamas 150 years before) arrived in the Abacos they married into the Loyalist families. Soon life in the Abacos was an amalgam of old island ways and "modern" Loyalist ambitions, with the old ways growing stronger all the time. The set-

Preceding pages, pastel on Green Turtle Cay. Left, the girl next door gets married in Hope Town.

tlements on the mainland were not successful, and soon most everyone was living on the offshore cays, engaged mostly in boatbuilding and fishing — the two old island standbys.

If you travel to the Abacos by air you will land at either Treasure Cay on the north end of Great Abaco or Marsh Harbour in the island's center. In either town you will be near the site of one of the earliest Loyalist settlements. The first arrivals stepped ashore not far from Treasure Cay.

Carleton Site: Records indicate that about 600 Loyalists of both black and white ethnic backrounds left New York City around 1783 and came to a stop on the outskirts of Treasure Cay, with the intention of using the land to produce enough commercial value to sustain a self-sufficient township. They named their settlement Carleton, as a tribute to Sir Guy Carleton who at the time was a noted representative of the King and the top Royal official in all of North America. According to a statement from the group, the settlement was supposed to evolve into a great community for those whose allegiance to England had made them outcasts after the American revolution.

The Loyalists must have felt some of the same kind of an uncertainty that Christopher Columbus knew 300 years before when he first came to Bahamian territory: he didn't know what to expect. The difference between Christopher Columbus and his crews on the *Niña, Pinta* and *Santa Maria*, and the Loyalists is that on the one hand you have a group of explorers, just looking around to find new discoveries to report when they returned to Spain. On the other hand you have a rather desperate group of people, some more dejected than others, hoping to begin a new life which would wipe out the bitter memories of the American Revolution.

Many conflicts developed among the Loyalists, and their plans met many obstacles, including a devastating hurricane that totally destroyed the first settlement. Nothing of Carleton remains today, but if you drive a mile or so north of **Treasure Cay** you will be able to see what is believed to be the settlement's site.

Treasure Cay (which is not a cay, but on the mainland of Great Abaco) is perhaps the most modern, complete resort facility in the Family Islands. Started in 1959, by a native Abaconian when the site's prin-

Man-O-War Cay, ship shape as a New England fishing village.

cipal attraction was a lovely three-mile (five-km) beach, the resort now features a hotel, an 18-hole golf course, shops, and well-landscaped roads along which a number of Americans have built vacation homes. Jets fly directly from the U.S. to Treasure Cay; yachts from Florida and ports farther afield tie up in the marina. One of the resort's slogans was "60 minutes from Florida...a million miles from cares."

From a historic point of view, the Loyalists who settled in the Abacos were hardly a million miles from cares. Fortunately not all suffered the same fate as the Carleton group. Some of the first Loyalist settlers split up from the original group at Carleton, and traveled south to found the settlement of Marsh Harbour.

Land of Water: More than one third of the island of Great Abaco is marshland along the western coast, making it difficult to judge where the water ends and the land begins. Therefore most of the settlements of Great Abaco dot the solid ground of the east coast with **Marsh Harbour**, the island's commercial center, smack in the middle. Available to all residents and visitors in downtown Marsh Harbour are modern food stores, equipped with every-

thing a chef could desire. There are department and hardware stores, two banks, restaurants, a beauty salon, an exclusive dining room, gas stations, a plush motel and time-sharing facilities. The shops of Marsh Harbour draw customers from distances of 50 miles (80 km). Two adjoining communities, **Murphey Town** and **Dundas Town**, complete the spectrum of life in Marsh Harbour and give it a population of nearly 3,000 – making it the third largest town in the Bahamas. Despite this distinction, it is still a relatively quiet place, sprawled out along the large harbor.

The road linking the towns of Great Abaco was built in 1959 by the Owens-Illinois Company so they could transport logs from Abaco's forests to their mill in **Snake Cay**. This operation, plus an earlier lumber operation in **Wilson City**, caused the principal development of the area south of Marsh Harbour. From two licensed cars in 1959 to over 2,000 in 1970, Abaco sped into the automobile age, and Marsh Harbour and for a time the area south, rather than the offshore cays, became the hub of activity.

South of Marsh Harbour, **Spring City** and Snake Cay were built by Owens-Illinois

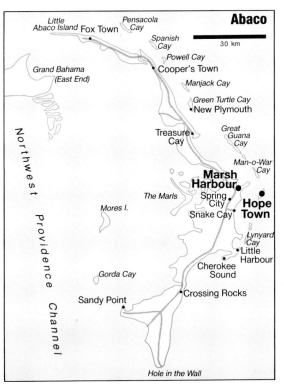

to house workers for their lumber and sugar cane enterprises. These were not the first "company towns" in the Abacos, for in 1906 an American company developed Wilson City, which attracted workers from all over the Abacos and the Bahamas, and produced 15 to 28 million feet of lumber annually until 1916. Later on, the work was carried on by the Bahamas Cuban Company and the Abaco Lumber Company and finally Owens-Illinois. Today, in these old lumbering areas, abandoned by the Owens-Illinois in 1970, the few residents devote themselves mostly to farming, and of course fishing. **Cherokee Sound** and **Sandy Point** are basically fishing settlements. There are no settlements south of Sandy Point, but the lighthouse at Hole-in-the-Wall is one of the most important navigational lights in the Bahamas.

Until the construction of the road on Great Abaco, the Abaco cays were the island's hubs of activity. None was more important than **Hope Town**, on **Elbow Cay**, which was the life of the Abacos and seat of the islands' Commissioner until 1960.

Hope Town: Located a short ferry ride across the water from Marsh Harbour, Hope Town is a picturesque village of

freshly painted wooden homes with picket fences. The red and white striped Hope Town harbor lighthouse is probably the most photographed in the Bahamas, and the small town of about 350 residents, mostly descendants of the original Loyalist settlers of the Abacos is one of the most fascinating. A quiet pride in the past permeates this town, where a few families – the Russells, Lowes, Bethels, Sawyers and Malones – have dominated for two centuries. They have preserved a taste of the early life in the **Wyannie Malone Historical Museum** which occupies an old Hope Town house. Named for the widow Wyannie Malone, whose four children formed the basis for much of Hope Town's later population, it contains a fascinating melange of old furniture and artifacts collected from residents.

Cars are not allowed on the streets of Hope Town; this contributes to the impression that on making the short trip from Marsh Harbour you have made a voyage into the past. In the old days residents farmed, fished and won occasional windfalls from the practice of "wrecking." The reefs around the Abacos proved dangerous to passing ships, and as soon as one ran aground on a reef the Abaconians were out

Triplets at Treasure Cay.

on the water to rescue the luckless mariners and seize the cargo. By law the cargo was sold in Nassau, with a certain percentage of the receipts paid in tax to the government, a large portion to the wreckers, and the remaining bit to the hapless ship owner. The natives of Hope Town depended so much on this source of livelihood that they went so far as to sabotage the construction of the Hope Town lighthouse in the 1830s. Today the lighthouse is important for tourism, particularly since it is one of the few in the Bahamas that has not been automated. You should be sure to climb the stairs to the top for the view.

A number of foreigners have found Hope Town a delightful place to build second homes, and today over half the houses on Elbow Cay are owned by non-Bahamians. Three inns provide rooms for visitors.

Man-O-War: Elbow Cay's next door neighbor, **Man-O-War Cay** is famous for ship-building, which had its peak in the 19th century. Through the years, the natives have proven their ability to design and produce first-class vessels, whether large ocean boats or dinghies for harbor work.

With a slightly more disciplined at-mosphere than Hope Town, Man-O-War is a ship shape settlement at all times. Proud of their heritage, and determined to preserve it, Man-O-War residents have allowed no hotels to be built on their island, and until recently they allowed no blacks to remain on the island overnight. No liquor has ever been sold there. The people are known for their efficiency and ingenuity, and many yachtsmen from the United States have their craft regularly hauled up for painting and repairs on Man-O-War Cay, where they know they will get quality work.

One enterprising Man-O-War citizen changed the face of life in the Abacos by instituting **Albury's Ferry Service,** which is the main mode of transportation between the Abaco cays today. Travel in the Abacos has always been by boat, and some Family Islanders say the Abaconians could not help but develop a special talent for producing sea worthy and quality boats. Yet, though Abaconians had been ferrying themselves and their families to visit relatives to and from the cays and islands for many years, an actual ferry service for tourists and natives who did not have their own boats did not take root until the late 1950s. As ironic as it may seem, the open-

Candy stripes of Elbow Cay's landmark lighthouse.

BOATBUILDING

The pine forests, the watery distances between the cays and the ambitions of the first settlers made the Abacos the first boatbuilding center in the Bahamas, and the most famous. Marsh Harbour, Cherokee Sound, New Plymouth, Hope Town and Man-O-War Cay are all names that sound long and clear throughout Bahamian nautical history. Dinghies, smacks, sloops and even large cargo schooners built in these settlements have cut wakes through the Atlantic for over 150 years.

In the 1980s boatbuilders on Man-O-War Cay turn out sleek fiberglass boats, but old-fashioned boatbuilding, with local lumber and hand tools, persists on a smaller scale.

There are several steps in building the famous Abaco dinghy the traditional way. First the builder selects and cuts the wood for the boat's frame. He usually uses corkwood trees, which are plentiful near Hope Town, but the hardwoods madeira (mahogany), dogwood and horseflesh also grow in the Abacos and were traditionally used. He works without plans, making use of the crooks of trees for the frame, the natural curve of the wood providing the structure with extra strength. He imports pine boards for the planking, though in former years Abaco pines provided this material. He tamps cotton into the seams, paints them and applies caulking; for sailing models he constructs a rudder, mast and boom. The finished boat is one of the prides of the Bahamas — eminently seaworthy, simple and beautiful.

The dinghy is a modest creature compared to the creations of the early part of this century — two- and three-masted schooners which were both glorious achievements and something of an anachronism in their time. Born in 1886, Jenkins Roberts was perhaps the most famous of these master builders. He built the twin-masted *Albertine Adoue,* which served as the Abacos' mailboat until the 1920s, and in 1922 he launched the 130-foot (40-meter) *Abaco, Bahamas,* the largest ship ever built in the Abacos.

Many other Abaconians — Edwin Carey, Dickie Roberts, William Albury, Albert Lowe and others — made their marks as shipbuilders over the years when travel and commerce in the Bahamas usually meant voyages by sea.

ing of two airports, in Marsh Harbour and Treasure Cay, actually opened the market for ferrying as a business.

Prior to the opening of the airports, sea planes landed twice a week at Green Turtle and Man-O-War cays. When larger planes, carrying more passengers and transporting tons more provisions, started landing at Treasure Cay and Marsh Harbour, seaplane service became obsolete. Yet there was still a need for mainland people to get to the cays, especially when tourists began landing in Marsh Harbour and Treasure Cay, interested in exploring the cays. So, after the opening of the airports, Marcel Albury, from a distinguished line of Abaconian boatmen, purchased a vessel in the 40-to-50-foot (12-to-15-meter) range and wrote an important page in the island's history. He started the Albury Ferry Service, initiating a venture which was soon to be duplicated by several other natives who were perhaps more at home in boats than under the roofs of their homes.

Today many visitors enjoy taking a ferry boat to one of the cays for an afternoon or longer.

Twice a week Albury's Ferry travels to **Great Guana Cay**, where about 100 people make their homes, mostly fishing and farming for a living. There is a hotel, the Guana Beach Resort, and many deserted beaches.

Green Turtle: New Plymouth, on **Green Turtle Cay**, once rivalled Hope Town as the hub of the Abacos. Like the other cays, it was known for boatbuilding; the residents also had a reputation for growing pineapples. Today the pineapple industry is no longer, and New Plymouth on Green Turtle Cay is primarily a quaint little fishing village, attractive for visitors. The New England-style saltbox houses — sometimes brightly painted — seem to belong to another century.

New Plymouth's quaint and friendly atmosphere has attracted foreigners to build homes, as they have in Hope Town. Also like Hope Town, New Plymouth boasts an interesting small museum.

In 1980 New Plymouth was the site of a Fine Arts Exhibition, for which many of the town's citizens donned attire reminiscent of 18th Century Loyalists. The exhibition was held at the **Albert Lowe Museum**, which is owned by Alton Lowe, an artist and one of the sons of the soil of whom Abaconians are most proud. Highlighting the exhibition were some of

Rough Waters, a famed racer built on Man-O-War Cay, left. The Albert Lowe Museum in New Plymouth, below.

Alton Lowe's paintings of Abaconian subjects, and artifacts from the Loyalist settlers and their descendants. The museum, housed in a 150-year-old building, grew in stature because of the exposure. In 1984, it formed a partnership with Treasure Cay resorts and a group of archaeologists to locate and excavate the first Loyalist settlement, Carleton. Visitors to the museum will find interesting models of Abaconian ships, built by New Plymouth native Albert Lowe, displays of Loyalist artifacts and early photographs.

New Year's Day is a special time on Green Turtle Cay, when everyone celebrates the capture of Bunce — a character who according to local folklore, lived in Abaco's pine forests. There's a parade and a day of festivity for residents and visitors alike.

Yachtsmen make Green Turtle Cay and its lively restaurants and bars a favorite stop. For land-based travelers there are several charming hotels. Those who like a lot of action should plan well ahead to be on Green Turtle Cay for the regatta sponsored annually by the Green Turtle Yacht Club. Ferries make the trip from a dock near Treasure Cay to Green Turtle Cay.

Towards Little Abaco: The north end of Great Abaco, north of Treasure Cay, and the adjoining island of Little Abaco are little traveled, but the cays offshore are a favorite cruising ground for yachtsmen. North of Green Turtle Cay, the nearest mainland settlement is **Cooperstown** on Great Abaco. Five miles (eight km) north, across a causeway bridge, is the island of Little Abaco and the villages of Cedar Harbour, Wood Cay, Mount Hope, Fox Town and Crown Haven. Neither Cooperstown or the settlements of Little Abaco have deepwater harbors, so the inhabitants long lived in relative isolation from the rest of the Abaco chain. Since the road was built connecting them with Treasure Cay, some of them work at the Treasure Cay resort; others have found prosperity in the booming business of crawfishing. Unlike those on the Abaco cays, the settlers here were primarily blacks, brought into the islands with the Loyalists in the 18th Century.

North of Green Turtle Cay only two cays are inhabited — Grand Cay and Walker's Cay — and the sailing between them is breathtaking. **Powell Cay** is private property, but uninhabited, and according to the 1989 Yachtsman's Guide to the Bahamas there is a fine anchorage off its high bluffs, the beach is beautiful, but the mosquitoes are unusually voracious. The mud flats and mangrove roots along the edges of the habor on **Great Sale Cay** are home to barracuda, sand sharks, bonefish, snappers and other fish. Some yachtsmen make the harbor and small settlement at **Grand Cay** a base for fishing. A number of the people who live in Grand Cay commute to work - by boat - to the resort at Walker's Cay. Here, on the northernmost point in the Bahamas, the **Walker's Cay Club** caters mainly to fishermen from the north who fly in to the private airstrip or sail in on yachts. Perched on a bluff, the club offers fabulous views of the sea.

From Walker's Cay it's a short step to the Mantanilla Reef, then off the Little Bahama Bank and into the Gulf Stream. It's a step Abaconians have taken in the past — for jobs in the U.S. and opportunities beyond their islands, yet today more are returning and remaining. The Abaconians take great pride in their heritage and as a people have done more for themselves than any other island in the Bahamas. Whereas New Providence and Grand Bahama had tremendous outside influence in their development, the people of the Abacos have made their strides largely on their own.

Abaconian memories at the Albert Lowe Museum, left. Maintaining the traditional colors, right.

ELEUTHERA, HARBOUR ISLAND AND SPANISH WELLS

In 1649 a group of religious dissidents from Bermuda set to sea. Information is sketchy as to whether Eleuthera was their intended destination, but when their vessel wrecked just off the northern end of the island they went ashore. Taking shelter in a limestone cave, they faced fear, hardship and privation, and they settled officially on the island of Eleuthera.

These first settlers, like the Puritans who colonized New England, were British subjects who fled religious persecution at home to establish their own colony. They called it Eleuthera — the Greek word for freedom. Known as the Eleutherian Adventurers, they were to later split ranks and move to nearby islands. They became the first settlers in Eleuthera, Harbour Island and Spanish Wells.

The population of these islands grew when colonists in Bermuda exiled troublesome slaves and all the island's free Africans to Eleuthera. These were the first blacks to live in the Bahamas, and they arrived as free men and women. In the 18th and 19th centuries, British Loyalists from the new United States of America joined these first settlers. Some brought slaves with them.

Today the descendants of the Eleutherian Adventurers, the freed slaves and the Loyalists can be found throughout the island of Eleuthera and the adjacent cays — but nowhere is the melting pot of cultures, old and new, as delightful as on **Harbour Island.**

With its fine natural harbor, Harbour Island is thought by some historians to have been the intended destination of the Eleutherian Adventurers. Located just off the northeast coast of the island of Eleuthera, it is well protected from rough weather by the treacherous reefs that destroyed the Eleutherian Adventurers' ship. More of the Adventurers eventually settled on Harbour Island than on Eleuthera.

The hardy nucleus of Eleutherian Adventurers was bolstered by the arrival of British Loyalists from the American colonies. Bringing with them expertise in shipbuilding and agriculture, the Loyalists helped launch there the most prosperous economy in the late 18th Century Bahamas.

From the 18th Century until World War Two, ships built on Harbour Island plied the seas of the world. By the 19th Century the island's main settlement, **Dunmore Town,** was the Bahamas' second city, exceeded only by Nassau in population and wealth. Islanders built everything from dinghies to swift three-masted schooners. In 1922 they built the largest ship ever constructed in the Bahamas, the four-masted *Marie J. Thompson.*

A striking measure of Dunmore Town's prosperity and subsequent decline are the population records which list 2,500 residents in the 1870s and little more than 700 in 1943. Today Harbour Island is a sleepy community of about 1,000 people, far removed from the hustling and bustling era when trading was a by-word. It is an island for passing the afternoon on a shady porch or on the lovely pink sand beach, for chatting with a neighbor over the garden fence, for watching the many flowers bloom. Fishing and farming occupy the time of some of the population, while others are employed domestically or by the government. There are also a small number of ferry operators who transport people to and from North Eleuthera.

Friendly Willie Gibson, a long-time Harbour Island native, perhaps most aptly described Harbour Island today: "Harbour Island is a place of native peace, a place of joy, a place of harmony with lots of friendly people." Gibson himself is the prototype of the life nowadays. A fruit vendor, he hits the street for short periods each day with his trolley, but mainly he sells from his home, where he can most often be found, just relaxing the time away.

Then there is Earl P. Johnson, the local Justice of the Peace. He strolls around the island visiting residents and processing legal documents when the Commissioner of the Island is out of town, or otherwise just giving advice and reliving the aristocratic Harbour Island past. "This was the first capital. The seat of the Governor was here and this town (Dunmore Town) was named after Lord Dunmore. When I was a young man, there were certain levels, and you had to live up to them to earn a certain respect. There is great history in this place. When our men went to Nassau and took it over from the Spaniards who had gained possession, that was the finest achievement at the time of a group of Bahamians. That incident will forever live in our history," Johnson said.

Today the only evidence of the "fighting spirit" of the men of Harbour Island are some of the old-style wooden-frame houses which served as headquarters for the military. They stand as sturdily as the determination of those soldiers who sailed into Nassau two centuries ago under Colonel Andrew Deveaux, and drove the Spanish conquerors away, liberating the city and taking control for the British.

Today in Dunmore Town you will find a remarkable mix of characters and colors — pastel clapboard cottages, several small hotels and restaurants and the three-mile (five-km) beach famous for its pinkish sand. This is a town for days on the beach, twilight strolls along the harbor, or perhaps a noonday bicycle ride to explore the place at greater speed.

As one of the oldest settlements in the Bahamas, Dunmore Town has many quaintly beautiful buildings. Those along the harbor are especially noteworthy, some of them carefully restored. A house two centuries old has been converted into a well-loved bar. For vacationers, life in Dunmore Town is one of evenings in such bars, lunches by the pool, dinner on a terrace or by candlelight, rooms with ceiling fans. For everyone it is a place where bougainvillea and hibiscus bloom along white picket fences, and the pace is friendly and leisurely. The **Romora Bay Club,** with its ancient tropical garden, is a favorite among visitors, as are the **Pink Sands** resort and **Valentine's Yacht Club.** Divers come especially to enjoy the nearby reefs.

Devil's Backbone: The sharp reefs off the coast of North Eleuthera snagged the Eleutherian Adventurers' ship, and have been the nemesis of dozens more. So it is easy to see why one reef earned the name Devil's Backbone. Divers, however, will find them a paradise. Parrotfish, giant groupers and angelfish glide through the hulk of a 250-foot (75-meter) freighter. Divers can also explore the train wreck, the remains of a barge which, as it was carrying a train locomotive to Cuba in 1865, ran aground on a reef. There is also an 1890s passenger steamship that sank on the reef during a tropical storm.

Even for experienced yachtsmen, a sail along the north coast of Eleuthera, between Harbour Island and Spanish Wells, is a treacherous one. Sailors making the trip for the first few times will probably need the help of a local pilot. But this should not deter anyone who visits Harbour Island from making the trip to Span-

Spanish Wells, between the sea and sky.

ish Wells. (Visitors who arrive by plane in North Eleuthera have an easier time of it. It's a short taxi ride to the ferry and then a 10-minute ferry ride to Spanish Wells.) In Spanish Wells you will hear traces of a British accent and diction centuries old, spoken by the descendants of the original Eleutherian Adventurers who have made the place their home since the 17th Century. Spanish Wells is unique to the Bahamas in that in over 300 years the makeup of its population has hardly changed. The people still make a living mostly from small farms and the sea.

Rich Sea: The people of Spanish Wells are unique in another significant way. They form the richest society in the Commonwealth of the Bahamas.

In Spanish Wells a youngster at age 22 could very well be a millionaire. The fishing business is extremely lucrative, and young men learn fishing habits from an early age. Lobsters are the prime catch and biggest money maker, and boats from Spanish Wells scour the Bahamas in search of them. Some divers call these lobsters "bugs," but a better name would be "gold bugs." So lucrative is the business, and so much has it influenced the entire community, that educators have a

difficult time convincing the young children to stay in school.

Many of them, by the time they are 14 or 15, have opted to skip classrooms in favor of fishing trips which could net them as much as $20,000 each.

The situation is a source of great frustration for noted educator Philip Pinder, the Headmaster at the Spanish Wells All Age School. So attractive financially is the fishing business (lobsters and large groupers the primary sale items) that even Pinder does not have a solution for the educational dilemma.

"If you talk to the captains of the boats and you hear the figures they talk about, you would wonder why we are sitting down teaching at school instead of all being out there on the water. The money filters right on down the line. The children who stay in school have to deal with the sarcasm from their former classmates who throw jeers from their new car or the back of a motorcycle. 'You're still in school, but I've just been paid $20,000.'"

However, the situation does cause Pinder to reflect with pride on the skills of the men of Spanish Wells on the water. "I guess you can correctly say that we are proud that here in Spanish Wells are

A seafarer's steady gaze.

Eleuthera

Spanish Wells
Harbour Island
Lower Bogue
Dunmore Town
20 km
Current
Upper Bogue
Glass Window
Gregory Town
Current I.
Alice Town
James Cistern
James Point
Governor's Harbour
North Palmetto Point
South Palmetto Point
Savannah Sound
Windermere I.
Tarpum Bay
Powell Point
Rock Sound
Cape Eleuthera
Green Castle
Deep Creek
Wemyss Bight
John Millars
Bannerman Town
East End Point

perhaps the best fishermen in the entire country. I would prefer the youngsters to complete school, but it is traditional for them to leave early, and they seem to be doing alright with their lives. There is little anybody can do about effecting a change," Pinder said.

A paradox indeed, when you consider that Pinder, a native of Spanish Wells, has been engrossed in learning and teaching practically all his life. A veteran teacher of 30 years, he got his primary and secondary education right in Spanish Wells. At 19, he was among a group of students who were sent to the United Kingdom for two years of study. He attended Sheffield Teachers Training College, returning to go full time into teaching. He has pursued further studies at the University of the West Indies Mona Campus and later completed a degree in education at the University of Miami. So, indeed, Pinder is well educated. But some of the kids he had in the 10th grade last year are now tripling his earnings as a school principal.

But life on Spanish Wells has not always been so easy. The settlement, which got its name from the Spanish galleons which frequented the area to take on water supply, bred a people nurtured in the ways of the sea because their very lives depended on it. The first settlers, the Eleutherian Adventurers — religious dissidents who came to the Bahamas in search of political and religious freedom — endured great hardship to survive on this cay which is less than two miles (three km) long and a quarter-mile wide. Later, during the American war for independence, British Loyalists from the American colonies joined the original inhabitants. But those Loyalists who were slave owners were turned away on principle, it is said, because of the original settlers' abhorrence of slavery.

Tropic Cape Cod: Like their counterparts in New England, the Puritan settlers in Spanish Wells built ship-shape Cape Cod-style cottages — only many of these are painted blue, yellow or pink. Blond, blue eyed, hard-working, most natives of Spanish Wells are Methodist or Anglican (belonging to an offshoot called the People's Church). Out of a population of 700, a large proportion share the surnames Pinder, Albury, Higgs or Sweeting, and tangled family trees. In this quiet, insulated utopia, hardly a newspaper is delivered (people get the news from television), hardly anyone locks their doors or even takes the keys out of the car ignition.

Easy going philosophy on Harbour Island.

For visitors there are bicycles for rent (no cars) and accommodations in two casual hotels — **Spanish Wells Beach Resort** and **Spanish Wells Harbour Club** where you enjoy yourself mostly by sunning, swimming, eating, drinking, and getting to know the friendly locals. Needless to say, the fishing is excellent off Spanish Wells. A number of men there are available for hire as fishing guides to the waters off nearby Royal and Russell islands.

On **Russell Island,** the island's nearest neighbor, a small group of Haitians live and grow produce which they sell to the people of Spanish Wells. It's interesting to speculate that perhaps they endure many of the hardships known to the area's earliest settlers, who toughed it out on the tip of North Eleuthera, just a couple of miles away.

Preacher's Cave: When the Eleutherian Adventurers lost their ship and supplies to the winds and waves, they found shelter ashore in a cave. For months they lived on food foraged from the land and sea, until their leader, Captain Sayle, set off in a small scallop with eight men to obtain help from the Puritan settlers in the colony of Jamestown, Virginia. When he returned with supplies they were able to survive for

Unspoken camaraderie in Governor's Harbour.

two years longer, until, desperate, they appealed again for aid from the colonists in Massachusetts. (These were the "Pilgrims," who landed at Plymouth Rock in 1620.) The New Englanders generously sent supplies, and the Eleutherians thanked them by returning the ship loaded with hardwood. They asked that proceeds from the sale of the wood should be used to benefit Harvard College. Thoughout these early years, **Preacher's Cave** was used first as a makeshift shelter, then as a place of worship (from which it derives its name). You can travel there today by a rocky, unpaved road which leads north from the settlement of **North Eleuthera,** a journey of about 10 miles (16 km). In the cave you will see a large rock which the settlers roughly shaped to approximate a pulpit. Light filters gently down from holes in the cave roof. This quiet spot might be said to be the location of the first government of the Bahamas. Operating under a document called the Articles and Orders, which called for a Governor, a Council and a Senate, the Adventurers breathed the first air of democracy in this part of the world.

Eleuthera developed slowly but steadily through the centuries, and on the northern part of the island the settlers hung

on to life by tenaciously farming the rocky soil. Eleuthera tomatoes and pineapples are synonymous with quality in the Bahamas.

Traveling south from Preacher's Cave you will pass through two small farming settlements, Upper Bogue and Lower Bogue. From here it is not far to one of the most stunning land formations of the Bahamas, the **Glass Window.** Here Eleuthera nearly becomes two islands. The bluffs of North Eleuthera and the rest of the island break apart in a steep drop, connected only by the thinnest of threads at sea level. A bridge links the northern and southern bluffs. Below, on the eastern side of the bridge waves crash against the rocks, while on the western side the sea may be smooth as glass.

A few miles south of the Glass Window you will reach **Gregory Town,** a quaint fishing settlement on the coast. It was also a pineapple growing center in the 19th Century and the site of a pineapple canning factory in this century, but is known more enduringly for production of a pineapple rum known locally as "Gregory Town Special." Several more miles will take you to **Hatchet Bay**, which naturalists find interesting for its bat cave. Here, thousands of leaf-nosed bats roost in the

midnight black cave, waiting to fly out at night to search for food. In the 1930s and 1940s Hatchet Bay was one of the major workplaces in the country with a large poultry and dairy industry. When the company closed down the economy practically died. Today it is on the upswing due to a government farming and produce exchange. As you continue south you will find that the rest of Eleuthera is also on the road to recapturing its glorious past.

Old Mortality: A fading Victorian beauty, **Governor's Harbour** was once one of the Bahamas' most prosperous towns. Founded by some of the original Eleutherian Adventurers, with the arrival of the Loyalists it became a hive of activity. Ships loaded with Eleuthera pineapples and other fruit set sail for Baltimore and New York, to return with the fruits of America's burgeoning 19th Century industries Food and building supplies, cloth, tools and household items entered the Bahamas by way of Governor's Harbour. According to Bahamian historian Paul Albury, ladies traveled from Nassau to Governor's Harbour to buy the latest fashions.

Job posting in Governor's Harbour.

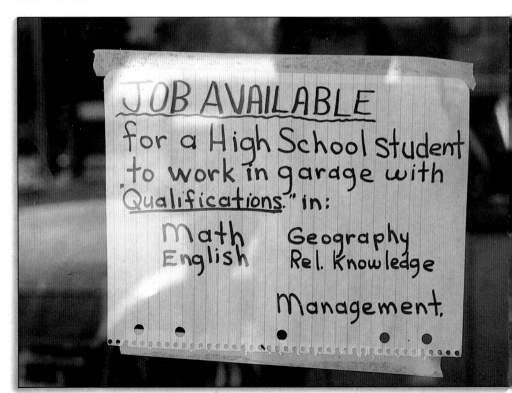

Today you may also spot some of the latest fashions across the harbor on **Cupid's Cay** where Club Méditerranée runs one of its holiday outposts. Outside the club grounds, large casuarina trees, poincianas and bougainvilleas shade the quiet streets of one of Eleuthera's oldest settlements. You can cross a little bridge from Governor's Harbour to reach Cupid's Cay, where the colonial homes are charming, if a bit tattered by the years of use.

Tattered would hardly be the word for the digs a few miles south on **Windermere Island.** Preppie is the by-word at the understated, comfortable Windermere Club where well-heeled vacationers enjoy swimming, sunning, tennis, afternoon tea and dressing for dinner. "Preppie" is perhaps also an understatement for some of the clientele, who would be better described as "royal." Prince Charles and Princess Diana have vacationed here, as have a number of titled or distinguished guests like the Duke and Duchess of Abercorne, Countess Mountbatten and the British Astors. Edwin Moses, the Olympic gold medalist track star, has also enjoyed some rest and relaxation here. In addition to hotel facilities, there are several private homes on the island. You can reach the island by bridge from the small settlement of **Savannah Sound**.

Several miles south of Savannah Sound you will reach **Tarpum Bay,** an old settlement which had its heyday when Eleuthera was a booming exporter of pineapples. The then Assistant Resident Justice, Joseph Culmer, of Tarpum Bay, even composed an essay on the pineapple industry in 1904. "Select good men as cutters and draggers-out of the field, avoid the injurious practice of breaking off the pineapple from the stem by pressure of the knee, cut the stem at the base of the fruit; pass the pineapple over to the attendant who will lay them carefully at the fence or margin of the field..." he instructed. Regrettably, this care was often taken for naught, as pineapples were normally packed by the thousands in the holds of large schooners, and the ones on the bottom did not always arrive at port in the best condition.

Throughout the 19th Century, Eleuthera led the Bahamas in pineapple exports and know-how, and is credited with introducing the crop to Cat Island and Long Island. It was largely pineapples that gave life to towns like Tarpum Bay, where today the dock no longer bustles with activity. In the words of an Eleutheran pine-

Tarpum Bay, prepared for Christmas.

apple grower: "It was from the Bahamas that the Americans took pineapples to Hawaii and it was from Hawaii that the Bahamas received most of its competition which ultimately led to the decline of the industry." Today, the ramshackle ginger-bread houses and shady casuarina trees make Tarpum Bay a pleasant place to stroll the quiet streets.

Farther south, **Rock Sound** was another pineapple center, where as recently as 1964 Bahamas Best Products was canning B. B. Brand sliced pineapples and pineapple juice. Today Eleuthera pineapples are still delicious, but they are grown mostly for consumption within the Bahamas. Rock Sound today is an enjoyable place to visit, with a modern shopping center that the local people and yachtsmen find pleasingly complete. There are several restaurants in town and two popular resorts nearby: the **Cotton Bay Club** – with an 18-hole championship golf course – and **Winding Bay Beach Resort**.

Just over one mile (1.6 km) east of Rock Sound, down a narrow road, you will find **Rock Sound Ocean Hole.** Like other inland "ocean holes" or "blue holes" in the Bahamas, this pool is reputed to be so deep it has no bottom. Actually, it is connected by

underground caves and passages to the sea. Seagoing fish like grouper and yellowtail travel the watery ways to swim around in this "lake."

From Rock Sound, you have the option of travelling either to **Cape Eleuthera** or **Eleuthera Point,** which are like the opposite tips on the tail of a fish. In between, along the bottom of the fin, are several small quiet villages: Deep Creek, Delancy Town, Weymss Bight, Bannerman Town and Millar's. There are no resorts along this "tail" of the island, but bonefishermen will find blissful fishing in the many creeks that are favorite homes for those wily fish. In the villages here and in the other villages farther north on the island – Upper Bogue and Lower Bogue, Gregory Town, Alice Town, James Cistern – life ambles on much as it has for years throughout the Family Islands. A middle-aged man, with the experience of many years, deftly skins a goat which hangs from a tree beside the road. Fresh "local mutton" will soon be on the dinner tables in his settlement. A child stands outside his modest thatched roofed home overlooking the sea. He has never seen television, but he eats fresh fish and conch and is robust and healthy. An elderly woman pats two loaves of dough into an iron pan and, using a stick of wood, guides the pan into an outdoor stone oven which she claims will bake the tastiest bread anywhere in the hemisphere.

In the larger settlements, like Rock Sound, Tarpum Bay and Hatchet Bay, friends greet each other in a shop. In old Governor's Harbour, dusk is falling, and the lights in the houses begin to come on. At Club Med a volleyball game continues in the fading light. At the Windermere Club, perhaps a princess is donning her jewels. Off Spanish Wells an experienced seaman has just guided a sloop safely between the reefs towards port in Harbour Island. In Dunmore Town a girl plucks a hibiscus flower. At the Glass Window bridge a teenage lad peers out at the expanse of ocean, and the sight of the deep water surging around the rocks on one side, while the water on the other side is calm and peaceful.

Such is the unique beauty of Eleuthera – an island of calm and storm, old and new, where the Bahamas lived a glorious past, and where wonders continue in the smile of a child or the gold of a sunset.

Girls in Tarpum Bay, left. Last light in Spanish Wells, right.

CAT ISLAND

Imagine walking down a country road on a sun-washed morning, the sky above you blue, the air soft and fresh, the day ready to unfold. You eat lunch in the shade of tall casuarina trees beside a deserted beach, explore a ruined plantation house where the walls are green with vines, search for buried treasure, spear fish for your supper, watch the sun set over a sheltered bay. Imagine the perfect summer day.

Then think of watching clouds scuttle across the moon as you listen to a ghostly tale and the roar of wind in the trees. Imagine the thick darkness of a night beyond the edges of the scientific, citified world.

Shrouded in mystery, bathed in sunlight, Cat Island is among the least known islands in the Bahamas and the least travelled. Most Bahamians can tell you little about this long-forgotten island, except that it is about 50 miles (80 km) long and shaped like a pirate's boot or a lady's stocking. The summit of one of the hills, every Bahamian knows, is the highest point in the Bahamas. And then they will tell you enticingly, mysteriously, "There's lots of stories about Cat Island."

The island was named for a pirate, Arthur Catt, who used to rendezvous there at Port Howe with his friends Henry Morgan and Edward Teach (also known as Blackbeard). So some of the stories concern buried gold and jewels. "Some years ago a yacht came into Port Howe," one such story begins. As told by Frances Armbrister, who has been collecting folklore of the island for the past 50 years, the yacht captain got into conversation with a very old woman on shore, who told him that her father had been overseer for the Richman Hill-Newfield plantation, and that he had told her where treasure was buried. She described the location, they organized a treasure hunt, and they found an old chest full of silver coins. The captain took the chest away and left the woman to mourn: "They gave me only one piece." Some Cat Islanders say that if you get close to buried treasure, ghosts will "move the treasure."

Preceding pages, waves crash against rocks at Exuma. Below, bird's eye view of Fernandez Bay.

Many other stories concern ghosts and the supernatural powers of hexes and curses. Though most Cat Islanders are zealous church goers, around the island you may see trees with bottles hung in the branches. Graveyard dirt, hair, fingernails and other articles inside the bottles are meant to protect the owner's property from robbers. Known throughout the Bahamas as a big Obeah island, Cat Island is inhabited by some powerful Obeah men and women — practitioners of this traditional Bahamian form of witchcraft or magic. If somebody "puts a witch" (hex) on you, watch out! The island abounds with tales of illnesses, deaths and retribution meted out by the powers of Obeah: hands coming from nowhere to strangle someone in the night, sperrids (spirits) and zombies rising out of graves.

Another story islanders like to tell is that Cat Island is where Columbus first set foot on the New World. It is indeed true that old deeds and maps name Cat Island "San Salvador," which was Columbus's first landfall, and call the present San Salvador "Watling's Island." (Watling, like Catt, was a pirate.) The large lake at the ankle of the

Cat Island to Nassau flights.

boot and the huge bay on the island's west side fit Columbus's enigmatic journal descriptions of "San Salvador" just about as well as the geography of the current San Salvador. The huge bay, which was perhaps the one Columbus meant when he wrote of a harbour that could hold "all the ships in Christendom," would make a fine place to begin an exploration of the foot of this boot shaped island. Depending on your desire for leisure, this could take the better part of a day or more (not including a walk to the Hermitage, which will be discussed later).

Called **the Bight**, this immense bay laps on the shores of two villages, New Bight and Old Bight. In **New Bight** you will notice some small shops for groceries and supplies, the Catholic Church and the Commissioner's house. **Old Bight**, more quaint, lies inland from a beautiful, lazy curve of beach. Not to miss along the north end of the Bight are the ruins of **Pigeon Bay Cottage**, a plantation house dating from the early 19th Century when, for a few short years cotton was king on the island, the way it was in the American south. Now white goats wander amid the tumbledown walls, and the two-story house on the graceful rise above the road clings

to but a glimmer of its proud past.

When Britain's abolition of slavery and the cotton-eating chenille bug combined to put an end to the plantation way of life, most plantation owners abandoned the island. A man named W.E. Armbrister remained, however, and put his field hands to work growing fruit, vegetables and sisal. Midway down the road along the Bight, you will pass cross Armbrister's Creek. Close by, in a settlement called **The Village**, W.E. Armbrister had a small factory to extract the fibers from the sisal plant, which was then shipped to foreign ports to be made into rope. A narrow gauge railroad, the remains of which can be seen here, carried sisal from the fields on the other side of the island.

If you follow the road as it veers inland, you will have a fine view of the ocean again at **Devil's Point**, a ragged pretty village on the sole of the boot and the southernmost point on the island. As in many Cat Island settlements, the thick-walled stone houses are painted white, yellow or pink, with roofs made of palmetto thatch.

Also interesting along this coastline of windblown shrubbery, crumbling cliffs and sea views are the ruins of the Richman Hill-Newfield plantation, Port Howe and the Deveaux house. Traveling east from the Cutlass Bay Club you will pass the villages of Bain Town and Zonicles. Past Zonicles the gray stone ruins of **Richman Hill-Newfield** plantation are just visible from the road. The walls you see once formed the overseer's house. The road to the plantation is totally overgrown, but under better conditions you can see garden walls, slave quarters and a main house. The plantation's lands encompassed 2,000 acres, stretching from the lake that lies just inland to the ocean.

A couple of miles farther you will reach **Port Howe**, known for the delicious pineapples grown round about it each summer. In the past it was known for wreckers, who used to lure ships onto the offshore reef by shining false and confusing lights. When the ships foundered and broke up, they reaped the bounty of the cargo. These wreckers were among the earliest settlers of the island. In 1768 Governor Thomas Shirley, describing the population of the island, declared that there were "in all supposed to be 30 people who have gone thither [to Cat Island and Exuma] to make a trial of the soil and for the convention of wrecking."

A more illustrious early citizen was the

Faded splendor of the Deveaux mansion.

famed Colonel Andrew Deveaux. He received grants of land on Cat Island as a reward for capturing Nassau from the Spanish in 1783 and lived near Port Howe as lord-of-the-manor in a fine house he built in the late 18th Century. The *Bahamas Gazette* in April 1799 reported in an "Extract of a Letter from a Cotton Planter" that "the best specimen of practical rural economy that has met my observation is afforded by the elder Mr. Deveaux's plantation in St. Salvador [Cat Island].....His is a plantation of Georgia cotton without bugs; and his crop is gathered, in the barn, clean and white. Indeed the dreadful outcry against Georgia cotton on account of bugs must be silenced by the actual state of nearly all the St. Salvador plantations." Deveaux and his family lived in fairly grand style in a two-story plantation house with a detached kitchen and a smaller one-story addition next door. In the 1930s the house still had its balconies, a staircase and random-width plank floors, and two Catholic priests lived there. Today shrubs grow through the open floor, and in the kitchen a tree has strung its twisted roots around the fireplace. In the parlor, only a ghostly trace remains of the once elegant staircase, a

faint stain that rises up the wall, step by step. Afternoons, the faded pink walls catch the last of the sunlight before slipping into the shadow of the school that has been built next door.

The coast near Port Howe affords splendid views. Cliffs drop sharply to the sea; the low, thick undergrowth shines waxy green in the bright light. A couple of American business magnates have built second homes here. Though no road goes there, you should know that about three miles from Port Howe is the easternmost point of the island, the heel of the boot. It points towards Spain and is called **Columbus Point**.

Holy Solitude: Back on the calm, western side of the island, above the village of New Bight, you will find another spot with a gorgeous view. In the early part of this century a man named John Hawes, who later took the name Father Jerome, built churches throughout the Bahamas — notably two on Long Island and St. Augustine's Monastery in Nassau. He was an Anglican who converted late in life to Catholicism, and, near the end of his days he retreated to Cat Island to live essentially as a hermit. A tall man, he slept in a short, narrow bed to mortify his body; he wore san-

The Hermitage, a monastery in miniature.

dals and a long robe in all weather. It seems he was humble in everything but the choice of a site for his hermitage, which he built on the highest point in the Bahamas. At 210 feet (64 meters), with a view of ocean both east and west, **Mount Alvernia** feels like the top of the world. To get there it is well worth the short drive on a dirt road which begins next to the Commissioner's house in New Bight, and then the steep climb past the stations of the cross Father Jerome carved by hand. From a distance, the chapel, bell tower and adjoining buildings seem about three times their actual size; up close they are an Italian monastery of surprisingly small size, that would be perfectly proportioned for a child. Two or three grown people could sit in the chapel; the living quarters consist of three main rooms, none much larger than a closet, with small windows from which you can glimpse the sea. From a covered outdoor passage, between the stone arches, you can see the dusky green of the north island and the bright blue of The Bight.

Back down at the bottom of the heavenly hill, if you drive about three miles (five km) north of New Bight you will arrive at **Fernandez Bay Village**, a small, gracious resort with several guest cottages built of local stone among the casuarina trees. In each cottage, large glass doors open onto the sandy curve of beach along Fernandez Bay. Walk this sheltered stretch of beach between the rocky spits that form the bay, and you may decide, like a few people who have homes here, that there is no place you would rather be. At dusk the sinking sun fills the whole bay with gold and silver-blue, as if it were a giant turtle shell filled with all the gleaming fish in this warm, shallow sea.

A fine place for dinner is the dining room of Fernandez Bay Village, where you will sit in a panelled room beneath mahogany beams and most likely dine on fish caught that day.

Journey North: A trip up the leg of the boot is a fine outing for another day. There are no hotels on this long, skinny shin of the island, so, unless you have friends there, you must plan to return south in the evening. The road north along the water passes one quaint settlement after another: **Tea Bay**, with wooden dinghies pulled up on the beach beneath the coconut palms; **the Bluff**, with its outdoor stone ovens whitewashed like miniature houses; **Bennet's Harbour**, one of the island's larger and oldest settlements.

At the north end of the island, **Arthur's Town** lacks the charm of the other villages, but it boasts a perfectly paved 7,800-foot (2,400-meter) airstrip, several provisions stores, and a telephone station. It was the childhood home of Sidney Poitier, who relates some fond memories of his parents and Cat Island relatives in his book *This Life*. Like many Cat Islanders then and now, his parents were farmers. Using the traditional cut-and-burn method to clear the ground of undergrowth, farmers create small plots — usually no larger than one or two acres (less than one hectare) where they grow mostly tomatoes and pineapples, but also pigeon peas, bananas and melons. Plots are often a considerable distance from home, and the trip is often made on foot, though horses were sometimes used in the past. Today, more and more people buy pickup trucks. Fishing supplements the very small profit gained from farming, and some people have been known to keep a Cat Island turtle (*Pseudemys felis*) in the bottom of a well as insurance against hard times. Islanders call these turtles "peters," and consider their meat delicious. These freshwater turtles have experienced hard times of their own throughout the Bahamas, and the muddy, shallow ponds of Cat Island have become the last refuge of this particular species.

At times it seems Cat Island is a distant, sheltered, hidden pool, not for turtles, but for an old Bahamian way of life. But time has not stood completely still here. Beside cinder-block shops and houses a few satellite dishes have sprung up. The three small resorts on the island provide regular work for some people on the island, as do government jobs. Yet some things remain much the same. In the villages farmers set out mornings for their fields — leaving behind their thatch roofed houses, their whitewashed outdoor ovens, their children studying in a one-room school. On the long afternoons, the coconut palms, casuarina trees, palmettos, pineapple plants and the rocky limestone soil seem to lie beyond time, warming in the tropical sun. As the rest of the world moves on, grinding through the day's momentous and trivial events, life on Cat Island shuffle steps through its age-old dance, readying for evening, for night.

It's a sweet slumber on this island, caught between midnight and dawn.

Tomb of Father Jerome, the Cat Island hermit.

200

SAN SALVADOR

On the decks of the three Spanish vessels men were tense, straining all of their senses to locate the first vestiges of land. The day had been exciting; they had seen land birds overhead and green branches floating by.

It was ten o'clock when all hands were awakened. Could they see that small light ahead? Then a shout came from the masthead, "a light, a light!", and to Christopher Columbus' elation another person had seen the flickering light, which even he had been afraid to tell himself was not just another mirage.

At two o'clock the white cliffs of High Cay were clearly visible. The day of European discovery of the New World had begun. With a prudent mariner's skill Columbus ordered his fleet to hoove-to until daylight when the rising sun would reveal dangerous coral reefs tying High Cay to its sisters, Low Cay and Nancy Cay, on the southeastern corner of a much larger island. These small cays, visible from San Salvador's shore and easily reachable by small boat, are now the graveyard of numerous ships whose captains were not as skilled as Columbus.

Continuing westward, Columbus skirted **French Bay,** missing the poorly visible break in the reef leading into an anchorage which is safe during winter northwest storms. Visitors today find French Bay well worth a visit. Shelling and tidal pools attract beach walkers; outstanding elkhorn coral reefs beckon snorkelers and scuba divers; and the ruins of Watling's Castle provide food for thought for the enthusiastic history buff.

Traveling south along the west coast of the island on the Queen's Highway leads you to the Government Dock on French Bay. Here beachcombers can walk to both right and left in complete privacy, and even the most timid snorkelers can view exciting back reef areas. For more vigorous swimmers and divers a trip to the western tip of **Sandy Point** where the fringing reef across French Bay attaches itself to the headland, is a must in calm weather. Reached from a small road off the Queen's Highway which parallels the bay, this pristine reef consists of massive stands of elkhorn corals and numerous reef fishes.

Outlined against the sky, on the hill

Monument to Columbus, left. Bay of discovery, right.

overlooking French Bay are the ruins of **Watling's Castle.** Although the island tourist trade has promoted the legend that John Watling, a pirate, built this "castle" in the 1600s, history and archaeological facts reveal they are the remains of a Loyalist plantation. Following the American Revolution many southern planters who remained loyal to the British Crown migrated to the Bahamas and reestablished slave-run cotton plantations. This migration played a major role in populating San Salvador, since emancipation in the 1830s resulted in the remaining landowners leaving the island in the hands of their ex-slaves.

Watling's Castle, more properly called the Sandy Point Estate, consisted of numerous stone buildings, including several for industrial or storage purposes as well as a main house and a cookhouse for the master. One can climb the hill to the west of the Queen's Highway and walk among the ruins of these buildings. To the east of the highway are located the slave quarters, which were small, one-room stone dwellings, with no distinguishing features. It is difficult to visualize what the entire plantation looked like because of the dense vegetation covering some of the

buildings, but a visit is well worthwhile for anyone even remotely interested in the past history of the Bahamas.

Landing at Long Bay: As Columbus rounded Sandy Point he prudently avoided the outer reef, yet anxiously sought a break in the corals which would allow his fleet access to the sandy shoreline. Finally a break was revealed, permitting the three vessels to enter what is today called **Long Bay.** Columbus brought his boats as close to the beach as he dared, thus providing cannon support for a landing party if the inhabitants of the visible village proved unfriendly. A bronze monument is now located under the sea at Long Bay to mark the spot where Columbus anchored on Oct. 12, 1492.

Upon reaching shore Columbus knelt and gave thanks, declaring the land to be property of the King and Queen of Spain, and naming the island San Salvador. Today a large white cross, erected in 1956 by Columbian historian Ruth Wolper, marks this spot. Nearby is the Mexican monument which commemorates the transferral of the Olympic flame to the New World, on its journey from Greece to Mexico City in 1968.

The Indians who met Columbus came

Columbus scholar Ruth Wolper entertains her favorite subject.

from a village near the shore, the remains of which have recently been excavated by archaeologists from the College Center of the Finger Lakes' Bahamian Field Station. Artifacts unearthed include bronze buckles, glass beads, and pieces of European crockery, all items Columbus described his men trading with the Indians. These original inhabitants of the island, which they called Guanahani, were Arawakian speakers related to other Indians of the Caribbean and South America. Specifically they were Lucayan, a peaceful people who lived by fishing and the raising of manioc or cassava.

Explorations: As Columbus stood on the deck of the *Santa Maria* he described the rocks along the shore to the north as "suitable for the construction of government buildings." These rocks are still visible today, though we know now that their friable composition precludes their use in construction. However, because these rocks seem to move in and out of the water during wave and tidal action, they have been termed **Riding Rocks,** and gave their name to the principal hotel on San Salvador, the **Riding Rock Inn.** This hotel is located just north of Cockburn Town, the main community and government center for the island's 1,000 residents.

To explore the island Columbus used his long boats, rowing northward along the coast. On rounding a point on the northwest corner of San Salvador he described a group of Indians coming from their homes. Archaeologists have located an Indian settlement here and named it **Palmetto Grove.** Artifacts from this site and others on the island are now housed in the **New World Museum,** owned by Ruth Wolper, and located near this point and the present settlement of North Victoria Hill.

A northeastward course brought Columbus into Graham's Harbor which he said "would hold all the ships of Christendom." To the east he beheld **North Point,** a long spit of land jutting northward. The end of the point Columbus felt would make an excellent fortification since it could be easily separated from the mainland by digging a moat. Nature itself later provided the moat, separating **Cut Cay** from North Point sometime in these last 500 years. And in fact, a fortress may have occupied this site at one time, since a cannon was brought up from the sea near Cut Cay and cannon balls have been unearthed along its shore. A walk along North Point reveals the vast contrast in the

"Watling's Castle," actually a ruined plantation house.

ocean, with the calm waters of Graham's Harbor on one side and the fierce, crashing waves of the open ocean on the other.

On the hill overlooking the western end of Graham's Harbor is located the grave of the first priest to bring Catholicism to San Salvador, Fr. Chrysostom Schreiner. Fr. Schreiner is probably best known for his extensive Columbian research which resulted in the name of the island being changed from Watling's Island back to Columbus' original, San Salvador.

Fossils and Missiles: A large complex of buildings are now located along the beach of Graham's Harbor. These house the **College Center of the Finger Lakes' Bahamian Field Station**, a research and educational institution involved in studies of the island's biological and geological features and its historic and prehistoric past. This consortium of United States colleges and universities provides housing, laboratories, and related support facilities for scientists and students throughout the world to study and learn in this unspoiled and unique environment.

The facilities of the CCFL Bahamian Field Station were originally built by the United States Navy in the late 1950s and early 1960s as a submarine tracking station.

Also built during this same time period were the U.S. Pan American Base and airport on the northwest side of the island, and the U.S. Coast Guard Station on the northeastern corner of San Salvador. These military bases were constructed on what was then British Crown land under the lend-lease agreement between the United States and England in World War Two. When the missile tracking operation of the Pan American Base and the Loran A system of the Coast Guard Station became obsolete, these facilities were turned over to the Bahamas Government, as was the Navy Base on Graham's Harbor. Today the CCFL Bahamian Field Station leases its campus from the Bahamas Government.

The effect of this influx of U.S. military and civilian personnel on San Salvador in the 1950s was phenomenal. Prior to this influence the island was accessible only by boat, and transportation on the island was by dirt trails and small boats plying the inland lakes between settlements. Today the airport provides the major link to the outside world, with twice weekly commercial flights from Nassau and numerous air charters and private planes from the U.S. The weekly mailboat brings produce, freight and surface mail from Nassau.

Delicate skin of the water.

The departure of the U.S. personnel in the late 1960s also altered the local lifestyle. Many young men and women had to leave San Salvador to find employment elsewhere. Those who remained found positions within the rising tourist industry. A small hotel, the Riding Rock Inn, had been built south of the airport in the late Fifties to accommodate relatives and friends of the military personnel. This was purchased by a land development company out of Florida, which used it as a base while developing large tracts of land at the southern end of the island.

The Second Landing: Thousands of Americans, Canadians, and Europeans were transported to San Salvador by Columbus Landings Company, accommodated in the expanded Riding Rock Inn, and sold lots in the four subdivisions of the future Columbus Landings communities. The landscape of the southern portion of the island was greatly altered, with streets, avenues, and a golf course bulldozed into existence. When the roads were built and the land sold, Columbus Landings Company departed leaving behind 12 condominiums, 20 private homes, and an overgrown golf course.

The Riding Rock Inn continues to operate under new ownership, catering now to divers and underwater photographers who flock to the pristine reefs of San Salvador, considered by many to be the best in the Caribbean. The steep submarine canyons off Southwest Point and French Bay are a special attraction.

When not in the water visitors enjoy walking through the narrow, charming streets of nearby **Cockburn Town** (pronounced Kō burntown), or taking a bus tour to numerous points of interest around the island. Cockburn Town, home to about 250 souls, may be easily explored on foot.

Lookouts and Salt Lakes: Directly east of the Riding Rock Inn a road leads inland to a **lookout tower** from which most of San Salvador is visible. A sight of beauty and wonder are the numerous inland lakes which were once the main transportation network of the island, but today are peaceful and seldom visited. Across the lakes to the northeast you can make out the large community of United Estates and the lighthouse, which are now reached by the paved Queen's Highway which encircles the island.

The **Dixon Hill Lighthouse** was built in 1856 and is one of the few lighthouses still in existence which is entirely hand-operated.

Fisherman's son.

The light from a small kerosene lamp is beamed up to 19 miles (35 km) at 400,000 candle power by a set of prisms which floats on a bed of mercury. The double flash sent out every 25 seconds is controlled by a set of weights and clockworks which must be wound regularly by one of the two lighthouse keepers. A tour of the lighthouse machinery and a view from the top are a must for anyone visiting San Salvador.

If you walk eastward from the lighthouse, across a narrow causeway and over several sand dunes, you reach **East Beach.** This mile-long stretch of golden beach just awaits a beachcomber, since flotsam in the form of glass fishing floats and bottles with notes inside often come ashore here. For the venturesome, a walk to the south will lead to a rocky outcrop, **Crab Cay,** on which sits the oldest monument commemorating Columbus' landing on San Salvador in 1492. Overlooking the numerous reefs and rocks along this coastline, one wonders why anyone believed this to be the site of Columbus' first landfall. Yet, in 1892, *The Chicago Herald* built this monument to celebrate the 400th anniversary of this event.

Returning to the Queen's Highway one can continue south, though the road lies inland most of the way. **Storr's Lake**, a large muddy colored lake on the left is a good example of the many hypersaline, utrophic lakes which make up the interior of the island. Farther south the road parallels **Pigeon Creek,** a large lagoon whose opening is at the southeast corner of the island, opposite High Cay. Since this lagoon is flushed regularly by tides it is slowly filling with sands, but it still serves as a calm anchorage for small fishing boats. The mangroves along its shores form a unique ecological niche and serve as a nursery area for numerous species of large fish, including shark.

The trip down the east side of San Salvador leads through several settlements whose names reflect the history of the island, since they are called after old plantation names: Polly Hill, Fortune Hill, Holiday Tract, and Old Place. Other communities reflect a later history and the island's British past, like North and South Victoria Hill. But whatever the time period, past or present, San Salvador holds something for everyone, be it ancient Indian and early Spanish archaeology, historic ruins, unlimited opportunities for watersports, or time and space to relax on an unspoiled beach.

Agave braceana; its thorns can be used as needles.

ANDROS

Andros, the largest of the Bahamian islands, has always been described as a mystery. Lying in the middle of the Atlantic Ocean with its host of sister islands, cays and rocks, Andros is well endowed with everything a visitor could dream of.

About 104 miles (225 km) long and 40 miles (64 km) wide, Andros is situated to the west of the Bahamian capital of Nassau, New Providence, and has the third largest population in the Bahamas. Divided politically into three sections — North, Central and South — Andros features some of the most interesting sporting life in the Bahamas in the form of deep sea fishing and diving.

Christopher Columbus called Andros "La Isla del Espirito Santo," the island of the Holy Spirit. No wonder this cloud of mystery surrounds it. The huge island's modern name is believed to be derived from the British commander, Sir Edmund Andros.

The history of the island is as vague as it is tantalizing. There are numerous tales and Indian myths, the most famous being the chiccharnies of Red Bay, North Andros. Possibly, the tale of these little red-eyed tree dwelling birds originated with Seminole Indians who migrated from South Florida to Red Bay in the 17th Century.

According to legend, the chiccharnies, birds with beards, are responsible for much mischief and build their nests by tying the tops of pine trees together. They are also said to hang from the trees by their tails.

Least known of all the Bahamian islands, from Morgan's Bluff in the north to Mars Bay in the south, Andros has a great many tricky shoals on the western side rendering it almost unapproachable by boat. The eastern coastline has the world's longest coral reef outside the continent of Australia.

Andros has four airports for easy travel to any part of the island, which is divided at several points by long, narrow creeks. There are airports at San Andros (serving the north), Andros Town and Mangrove Cay (for the center) and Congo Town for flights to the south. In addition, there are three official ports of entry: Fresh Creek (central), Mastic Point (north) and Congo Town (south) servicing boats, aircraft and seaplanes.

Spectacular Dives: Offering a variety of sports, Andros has always been top on the list with scuba divers for its 140-mile (225-km) long **Great Barrier Reef**. The second longest coral reef in the world (only Australia's Great Barrier Reef is longer) attracts hundreds of visitors throughout the year. Lying on the eastern shore, the reef divides the 12-foot (3.5 meter) waters of the Great Bahama Bank from the depths of a great ocean trench, the **Tongue of the Ocean.** Plunging two miles (three km) into watery darkness, the Tongue of the Ocean is an anomaly in the shallow Bahamian seas. Geologists speculate that it was once a prehistoric riverbed, something like the Grand Canyon of Arizona.

The coral gardens, drop-offs and wall dives here are among the most spectacular in the world. The **Small Hope Bay Lodge** at Fresh Creek has become one of the diving centers on the island; there are also instructors and dive masters at **Nicholl's Town.**

To cap off a breathtaking diving experience, there are numerous blue holes where freshwater springs well to the surface in the middle of the ocean floor. A 1981 exploration of the blue holes of

Mysterious moonlight at Small Hope Bay, left. Enchantingly romantic bridesmaid at Nicholl's Town, below.

Andros by a team of expert British and American divers was described as one of the most original, exciting and important underwater adventures in recent memory. **Conch Sound**, with more than 3,000 feet (900 meters) of passage, was explored during the expeditions and has been revisited for exploration of distant passages. Experts described the blue holes as the longest, deepest and most beautiful submarine caves on our planet.

Water also wells up to form some spectacular inland blue holes of great depth where the mirrorlike waters reflect the tall trees and sky. Evil spirits called *lucas* which, according to folk legend, resemble octopi, are said to live in these blue holes, lying in wait in the dark pools to pull unsuspecting divers and small boats down to the depths.

Nets and Spears: In addition to diving, Andros has also established a name for itself as "Bonefish Capital of the World," with miles of flots. The center for this activity is the **Lowe Sound** settlement in North Andros.

In former times the people of Andros used nets to haul in fish, but spearfishing among the reefs has become the most fashionable form of fishing, with reelfish-

ing from yachts rapidly on the rise. Offshore reefs attract a large variety of fish, including mackerel, snapper, amberjack, grouper and yellowtail. Inhabiting the Tongue of the Ocean are sailfish, wahoo, dolphins, tarpon, marlin and jack.

Although the traditional regatta at Andros has not been held for many years, its demise hasn't halted the boating fun that many visitors enjoy. Skiffs, sailboats, sunfish and larger and faster speedboats such as Boston Whalers and Abacos, explore the island's many inlets, bays and creeks. Several small boat marinas are available to fishermen and small boaters.

Adding further excitement for a few sports lovers is the six-month September to March hunting season, when hunters can take advantage of the island's large wildbird preserves. **Green Cay**, located 20 miles (32 km) east of Deep Creek in the Kemp's Bay Area, holds the second largest breeding colony of white-crowned pigeons in the world. The pigeons, one of the hunter's prime targets, fly to Andros in search of food and water. They breed and rest in July and August, finishing in September.

Since early times when settlers needed

An inland blue hole.

pigeons for food, the yearly white-crowned pigeon hunt has been a Bahamian tradition. In the 19th Century these birds flocked to the area in such abundance that C.J. Maynard, an ornithologist, counted over 10,000 nests on a single one-acre (half-hectare) cay. He wrote:

"The rocks were mostly covered with a scanty growth of low bushes and with a more luxuriant growth of cacti, and upon both plants and bushes the birds had placed their nests, and some were on elevated portions of rock, while a few were placed on the naked ground. So completely covered was the southern and northern portion of this key that the nests were nowhere over two feet apart, and often nearer than that."

Since Maynard's time the population has been much depleted, and laws have been instituted (including a 90 day residency requirement for foreign hunters) to protect them. (You may obtain a copy of the Wild Birds Protection Act from the Government Publications Office, Bank Lane, Nassau.)

Bird watchers in Andros have also spotted rare types of tern and the rare whistling tree duck.

Finally, there are tennis courts, lighted for night play, bicycle and scooter rent-als, and several individuals who provide car rentals to visitors who wish to ride from settlement to settlement.

Subs, Bays and Bluffs: North and central Andros hold the most interest and variety of any part of the island. At the northernmost tip, in addition to the Lowe Sound settlement, there is nearby **Morgan's Bluff**, believed to be named after the pirate Sir Henry Morgan who, it is claimed, hid a valuable but as yet undiscovered treasure there.

To the west, across vast mud flats, unreachable except by boat or unpaved road, is **Red Bay**, a village whose inhabitants are of mixed Seminole and Negro descent. They are believed to have arrived here in the mid-19th Century as runaway slaves from the United States. **Nicholl's Town**, with its tall casuarina and evergreen trees, is the largest population and commercial center on this end of the island, with about 500 residents. You will be able to buy groceries and other supplies here; there is also a clinic and a telephone station.

About 30 miles (50 km) south, by way of a fairly well paved road, is **Fresh Creek**, the main population center of central Andros. But don't miss stopping by the village

North Andros forest.

of **Staniard Creek**, which you'll find about half way to Fresh Creek. It's a lovely settlement, by a white beach framed with coconut palms.

At Fresh Creek, you will find the settlement of **Coakley Town** on the creek's north bank and **Andros Town** on the south. Andros Town, as discussed, is the site of the **Small Hope Bay Lodge,** the center for dive excursions to the Tongue of the Ocean reefs. Some people regard it as their favorite place to stay in the Bahamas.

Just south of Fresh Creek is **AUTEC** (Atlantic Underwater Testing and Evaluation Center), a $160 million joint exploration venture between the United States and Great Britain. It is the busiest and best underwater testing facility in the world and is being utilized increasingly by the Royal Navy to test their most advanced antisubmarine weapons. Yachtsmen should beware that this area and harbor is off limits for casual sightseeing.

For dining, the Small Hope Bay Lodge and the Chickcharnie Hotel serve good food, and just about every settlement has a one room local bar or nightclub with dancing and music.

Land of Water: Midway down the island is an intricate tapestry of creeks and inlets.

This is a sparsely populated, little traveled region. There may be more water here than land; three long inlets (North Bight, Middle Bight and South Bight) snake between dozens of cays – Water Cay, High Ridge Cay, Linda Cay, Pine Cay, Wood Cay and others – which lie among the creeks and inlets like pieces in the world's most difficult puzzle. **Mangrove Cay** is the largest of these cays, and its main settlement runs along the coast. The airstrip in **Moxey Town** on Mangrove Cay is served by Bahamasair. There are no rental cars here, but you can arrange with one of the the residents to take you around by car.

In south Andros, along the 28-mile (45-km) road from Drigg's Hill to Mars Bay, you will find tiny settlements and gorgeous beaches. **Congo Town,** the main settlement, has an airstrip served by Bahamasair and the comfortable Las Palmas Guesthouse on the beach.

Big Yard: Andros has been described in the past as the Big Yard because of its vast landscape, and the Sleeping Giant because of its low level of development. But it has now begun to awaken from its slumber.

Direct dial digital telephone systems

Morning light at Small Hope Bay.

were established in north Andros in 1979, in South Andros in 1983, and in central Andros in March 1984, placing residents and visitors in instant communication with people in any country in the world.

In October, 1985, Her Majesty, Queen Elizabeth II paid a royal visit to Fresh Creek, Andros, her first visit to any of the Family Islands, instantly putting Andros on the map. During her visit, the Queen toured AUTEC and opened a park in the settlement. In announcing the visit, the Bahamas' Prime Minister, Sir Lynden Pindling (who is also Member of Parliament for Kemp's Bay, South Andros), promised that big things were in store for the island in terms of development. In addition, Darrell Rolle, Member of Parliament for Mangrove Cay, announced major infrastructural plans to assist the development of the island. The development plans will complement fishing and farming, as well as tourism, which is currently showing signs of revitalization. There is also a local effort underway to build a new library; plans were announced at the 1989 Labour Day celebrations, attended by the Prime Minister.

By promoting tourism through the Hotel Corporation, the government is attempting to spur economic growth that will arrest the steady migration of Andros' population to Nassau and Grand Bahama in search of employment. Andros is making headway. The Las Palmas Hotel in Congo Town, South Andros is a comfortable destination for tourists. Another industry that has been developing on Andros over the past 12 years is batik and the manufacture of exquisite casual clothing in Fresh Creek. The company, called **Androsia**, began in a single room and now employs over 70 people who use the ancient Indonesian method for handpainting and dying natural fiber fabrics. If you visit the work place you'll see the process, including bright sheets of fabric hung on clotheslines to flap dry in the breeze. Androsia now has two retail outlets in Nassau, in the Cable Beach Hotel and the Grand Hotel; the womens' shop Mademoiselle in Nassau also sells Androsia products. The stunning blue, purple, green, yellow and pink prints are known all over the Bahamas. Though not a traditional product, they've come to represent a cheerful ingenuity that is indeed traditionally Bahamian, even, yes, Androsian.

Midday at the Androsia factory.

THE EXUMAS

Stretching in almost a straight line for some 90 miles (160 km), the Exuma Cays, which lie in a southeasterly direction from Nassau, are perhaps the most tantalizing of the Bahamas' island groups. They are known for their beauty, the amazing colors of the sea around them and their interesting people. An overview provides a kaleidoscope of different shades of blue and green waters lapping lazily onto the shores of some cays.

The Exumas today are inhabited by approximately 3,700 people, spread out on some of the cays but with the majority congregated on Great and Little Exuma. The largest single land mass of the Exumas is Great Exuma, which is connected to Little Exuma by a bridge across the narrow Ferry Channel.

There is one major airfield in the Exumas, in George Town, the principal settlement. However, flying over the cays you can spot a number of smaller airstrips. Of course you can also arrive by boat. If you travel by mailboat you will probably join several Exumians on the trip.

Many Exumians are as colorful, albeit more peaceful than the pirates who once made Great Exuma's large natural harbor a favorite rendezvous. A sign in one of the bars says "Rest Awhile, Live Longer," which might seem to sum up the philosophy of these islanders, but perhaps only on the surface. You could easily become engrossed in conversation with a number of Exumas' denizens: a midwife Minell Dames, whose brews of herbs have eased the delivery of scores of the island's babies, and who at age 90 was still going strong; a venerable farmer, Jeremiah Rolle, who at 83 was as bouncy as a young man and tending five acres of farm all by himself; World War One veteran Horace Rolle of Rolle Town; Church of God of Prophecy stalwarts Sisters Doris Curtis and Clara Rolle of Rolleville; an old sponger, Henry McPhee; of Rolleville's interesting younger generation, businessmen Kermit Rolle and Vernon Curtis.

Many Rolles: Visitors to these cays will soon notice that fully half of the residents go by the name Rolle, and that there are

Left, Exuma gentleman. Below, Lord Rolle, Exuma's first patriarch.

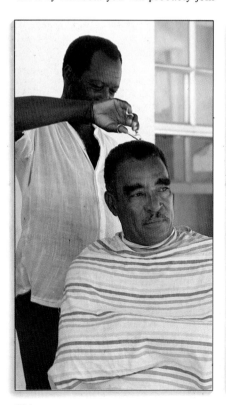

settlements called Rolle Town and Rolleville. There is a very significant connection. During the latter part of the 18th Century the British Crown granted an Englishman name Denys Rolle a total of 7,000 acres (2,800 hectares) on Great Exuma. Denys Rolle brought slaves and cotton seeds to the island and set to work building up five plantations. Rolle Town and Rolleville were the first; Mt. Thompson, Steventon and Ramsey followed. His son Lord John Rolle followed in his footsteps, and by the time of emancipation in 1834, he had some 325 slaves on Great Exuma. Legend has it that when cotton proved to be a dismal financial failure and the prospect of emancipation loomed, Lord Rolle generously deeded all his lands to his slaves. The slaves, following a custom of the day, adopted their master's surname.

According to Bahamian historian Dr. Gail Saunders, no such deed has ever been found, and Rolle's will, written three years after emancipation, asks his executors to sell all his lands in the Bahamas. In any case, the Rolle slaves effectively maintained their claim to the land. Both the land

Shades of colonialism in the Government Administration Building in George Town.

and the name have been passed down to their descendants since.

But this very special situation of the Rolles has not gone to their heads. Today, they coexist peacefully with the rest of their fellow Exumians, continuing the island's tradition of a tranquil atmosphere. Indeed, the former slaves were left by Rolle to eke out a living on the island as best they could, and because the land was deeded or claimed by them as a group, it has been almost impossible for many individuals to obtain clear title. The ownership status of some of the land remains in dispute today.

George Town: On landing at George Town airport the most noticeable landmark is a rustic bar-restaurant a few yards off the airstrip with a large block letter sign saying KERMIT'S. This establishment is owned by Kermit Rolle, one of the island's leading entrepreneurs. A self-made man who is a farmer, airport-lounge operator, taxi driver and general connoisseur of island life, he is one of the many refreshing qualities of Exuma.

It is a short taxi ride to **George Town,** Exuma's main settlement, where there are no traffic lights and where, under a gigantic tree at the center of town, a half dozen ladies are likely to be found displaying their

handmade straw goods and plaiting in the shade. A few yards away is the town's largest building, the pink and white **Government Administration Building,** which was modelled on Government House in Nassau. Eschewing sidewalks and curbs, buildings hug the main road as closely as possible, and many attest to the residents' fondness for decorating their walls with pink, yellow or turquoise paint.

The main road follows the curve of stunning **Elizabeth Harbour,** a large natural harbor protected by long, narrow **Stocking Island.** Known for its beautiful beaches and the Mysterious Cave, accessible only to divers, Stocking Island lies about a mile (1.6 km) offshore. Their fabulous harbor has prompted some Exumians to speculate that perhaps Columbus's first landfall in the New World was in the Exumas — not San Salvador, as currently believed — because he ebulliently described in his journal a harbor that could hold "All the ships in Christendom." Winter months today often find dozens of sleek yachts at anchor there.

A few steps north of the Government Administration Building, **St. Andrew's Anglican Church** graces a low rise. The lovely, fresh white 150-year-old building is an active place of worship today.

Peace and Plenty: The oldest hotel in the Exumas was a sponge market before the buildings were converted to a hotel in the late 1950s, and it still has a friendly lack of pretension — though it could claim to be the center of activity in George Town. It has welcomed its share of celebrities — from Jack Nicklaus to King Constantine of Greece — and its bar and dances are always enjoyed by a small crowd of visitors and Exumians. Well over a century ago, the bar's two rooms with their timbered ceilings and large fireplace served as a kitchen for the local slave market, but today nautical memorabilia clutters the old walls. From a wide sundeck, stone steps lead down to an azure sea. So the **Hotel Peace and Plenty** richly deserves its name, except during a week in April each year when the Out Island Regatta takes over George Town. In this now classic race, Bahamian work boats from all over the islands compete for the championship of the Bahamas. Since H.R.H. Prince Philip attended in 1959, the race has been more popular each year. For the three days of the regatta, plus a few days before and

St. Andrew's Anglican Church.

after, visitors mob the island, liquor flows freely, and there's plenty of everything in George Town except peace.

Farms North: Jeremiah Rolle was the first farmer in the Exumas to use a tractor on his farm and is considered the man who ushered in modern farming in the Exumas. One of his proudest accomplishments was having his produce displayed at the 1966 World's Fair. Some of his sweet potatoes weighed 10 or 11 pounds, he recalls. Queen Elizabeth II was visiting around that time and saw some of his crop at an exhibition. "She talked to me for about 15 minutes and after asking me a lot of questions, she asked for a few samples, and she had them sent to the fair," he remembers, and every so often in his home in Mt. Thompson, he sits back and reflects on his encounter with Her Majesty.

From Mt. Thompson to Rolleville, the land north of George Town has been scatteringly devoted to farming since the days of the Rolle plantations. To explore this picturesque area you can rent a car in George Town, or take the bus which runs from Rolleville at the north of Great Exuma to Williams Town at the south of Lit-

tle Exuma.

About eight miles (13 km) north of George Town you will come to an area known as **Jimmy Hill** which is not notable for a hill but for miles of empty beach, lovely for swimming. Past the village of Ramsey the beach continues until you reach **Mt. Thompson** where Jeremiah Rolle lives, and where local farmers bring their produce to the packing house to be crated for the trip by mailboat to Nassau. The hill there affords a sparkling view of the sea and the **Three Sisters Rocks** which rise unexpectedly from the water about 100 feet (30 meters) from shore. A mile north (1.6 km) of Mt. Thompson, a large bay called **Ocean Bight** laps at a treeless white-sand beach.

Hilltop Life: It is well worth it to press on a few more miles, passing through **Steventon,** a quiet village named for one of the Rolle plantations. You will soon arrive at **Rolleville.** Built on a hill above a harbor, the village of Rolleville has a curious old-world feel to it. The area has a proud history too, for according to Dr. Saunders, the Rolleville and Steventon slaves showed great independence and resolve in the face of cruel treatment. In her book *Bahamian Loyalists and Their Slaves*, she recounts that with the failure

Stocking Island's pier.

of cotton as a profitable cash crop, the Rolle slaves gradually gained time and freedom to pursue their own interests. They cultivated plots of land, fished and raised animals. When they were told with three days notice of a plan to move them to a plantation on another island, they objected. When that produced no results 54 of them, led by a slave named Pompey, fled to the woods where they hid for five weeks before stealing Lord Rolle's boat to sail for Nassau. Captured in Nassau, they were eventually returned to the plantations where they refused to work more than mornings, occupying themselves with their own projects afternoons. Their collective resistance continued until emancipation, forcing the Royal Governor several times to send troops from Nassau.

Today in Rolleville the **Hilltop Tavern,** owned by Kermit Rolle, is the center of nightlife for visitors and locals alike, and the churches play a significant part in the town's social life as well. Rolleville's Sister Doris and Sister Clara are fond of telling the story of how as young women they went out into the brush to dig and cut rock, then transported it by hand to the site of their church. It took many walks loaded down with rocks to accumulate enough to build Rolleville's **Church of God of Prophecy**, but they persevered.

North of Rolleville the hamlet of **Barraterre** holds fish farming as its most recent claim to fame. In conjunction with Scientists at the Caribbean Marine Research Center on nearby Lee Stocking Island, residents have been raising tilapia.

Home for Iguanas: Exumians claim to count 365 cays in their island chain, one for every day of the year. The string begins with **Lee Stocking Island** and extends up to Sail Rocks. To the west there is a sharp underwater dropoff to the deep Exuma Sound, but between the cays the water's depth can measure as little as 10 feet (three meters). On some of these cays Americans have built vacation homes, and on Norman's Cay a Colombian named Carlos Enrique Lehder ensconced himself as ruler of a powerful drug smuggling ring. He was deported from the Bahamas in 1982. A more likable creature, the rare Bahamian iguana also makes his home on these cays. The Exuma Cays Land and Sea Park, which encompasses about 200 sq miles (500 sq km.), is devoted to this species' preservation.

At Lee Stocking Island, the interest in

Rolleville's beach.

growing a certain species of fish is just as strong as the efforts to preserve the iguana. John H. Perry, Jr., an American scientist-oceanographer found a way to mass produce the tilapia, a freshwater fish brought from Africa. The unique aspect of the fish project is that they are being sustained in saltwater cages. Tilapia culture, as the project is called by the locals, is doing quite well, with a recorded growth percentage of 20 percent and upwards.

Plantations South: An excursion south of George Town will take you through the territory of still another Rolle plantation — **Rolle Town.** Today the settlement of Rolle Town contains a number of brightly painted buildings over 100 years old, and some old tombstones just off the main road. Many of the inhabitants of Rolle Town grow onions, mangoes, bananas and other crops.

A little bridge links Great Exuma with **Little Exuma.** Cross it and you will find yourself in **The Ferry,** a small settlement on a hill with lovely views of the sea. A short drive farther south you will find **Pretty Molly Bay,** where, according to local legend, on moonlit nights a pretty mermaid may be seen sitting on a rock in the bay, combing her hair.

In the 19th Century, salt held the promise of wealth and livelihood for Exumians, and a few miles south of Rolle Town a 200-foot (60-meter) white obelisk marks the site of a "mining " operation. Residents of **Williams Town** built the marker to signal potential customers on passing ships. Beyond the salt beacon you will find Williams Town, today an old village known for the small, fertile farms round about it.

Approximately one mile (1.6 km) past Williams Town, the Exumas' only standing plantation manor house can be found at the end of a driveway marked by two evergreen trees. **The Hermitage,** or **Cotton House** as it is sometimes called, is nearly 200 years old, and is home to a local "squire." Its construction is largely original. Hardly a mansion out of *Gone With the Wind,* it shows that life on these plantations for neither masters nor slaves was particularly easy. One room slaves' cottages can still be seen nearby.

Though life has often been difficult for the people of Exuma, some combination of these cays' hardship, beauty and tranquillity has given many of them a resolve that has stood them in good stead for many years.

Rolleville's most prominent citizen, Kermit Rolle, at his hilltop bar.

LONG ISLAND

As you step down the narrow stairway of the twin engine Hawker Sidley airplane you might mutter to yourself, "Here we are in sheep country." Long Island *was* sheep country for some time, and the land still has that look: vaguely inhospitable yet with just enough vegetation to make one imagine some hearty breed could survive here. Before New Zealand and Australia made lamb their prime export, sheep meant profitable business for Long Islanders, who sent their animals live by boat to Nassau where they were butchered and the meat sold. Those days are gone, but sheep and goats still roam free about the island, and it is not unusual to see a house with several animals roped to a stake in the yard.

Some Long Islanders today make a meager living by farming, often using explosives or bulldozers to break through the ground's hardened limestone surface. Filling these "quarry pits" or "pot-holes" with rock, sand, vegetation trash and soil, they create plots that will support bananas, corn or pigeon peas. But none of this is immediately obvious on landing at **Deadman's Cay**. At the airport a couple dozen people are normally on hand to meet the plane, brought by a handful of cars, seemingly from nowhere. In the worn, one-room airline terminal a breeze filters through the open doors, across the pale tile floor, past the bare counter and the man behind it, who is custodian of the telephone – one of the few phones on the island.

This is the island the Arawaks called Yuma, and that Columbus named Fernandina. Though it is now called Long Island, and has a few modern flourishes like the bar with satellite TV just visible down the empty airport road, when the small gathering at the airport disperses it will be very quiet. If you need a taxi, someone will likely approach you. The taxis and freelance drivers here provide friendly service, at a bit above U.S. city prices, and will take you the two-hour bumpy haul to the Stella Maris Inn on the north end of the island, or wherever you might want to go.

The town of Deadman's Cay is home to about one third of Long Island's population of 3,300, and it is the only settlement

Freedom at Cape Santa Maria.

on the island that can claim to sprawl — a condition exaggerated by the fact that Deadman's Cay adjoins several smaller settlements: Lower Deadmans Cay to the north, and to the south Buckleys, Cartwright, McKenzie and Mangrove Bush. They blend into a haphazard skattering of cinderblock houses and shops, stucco or limestone walled churches, schools and government buildings.

Foreign Enclave: Most visitors, unless they have friends on the island, stay at the **Stella Maris Inn** on the north end of the island. (Note: It is possible to fly directly to Stella Maris, thus avoiding the costly and arduous drive from Deadman's Cay.) The Stella Maris complex includes a world renowned diving center, a marina, clubhouse, tennis courts, guest cottages and moderately priced vacation homes which attract a loyal following, particularly among active, middle-aged U.S. and European leisure-seekers.

He had a Dream
Out of Barren Land
He Created This Haven
And Named it Stella Maris

So says the plaque on a small memorial

Detained in Simms.

HER MAJESTYS PRISON

stone dedicated to Johann I Aufochs (1906-1977), a native of berg. The small memorial for whose romantic appellation for h means "Star of the Sea" occupies a small lawn at approximately the center of the Stella Maris Inn grounds. The German connection remains because, though the inn and development corporation changed hands in 1979-80, the new owner-managers are German too – energetic people who pride themselves on running a casual, athletic, organized resort. They employ between 80 and 200 Long Islanders, depending on the season; as Stella Maris' fortune rises and falls, so do those of many people on the island.

From a small lookout tower on a rise near the inn's main building you can get a fine view of the lay of the island — the mostly rocky coast and inlets, the low, dense bushes which on this end of the island grow too thick even for a machete. You can see below the gray ruins of **Adderley's Plantation,** the 19th Century plantation house, roofless, with crumbling walls and vacant windows. Here, as on many other Out Islands, Loyalists to the British crown who fled the newly formed United States attempted to run cotton plantations in the grand style. Today it would take a good deal of determination and a sharp machete to reach this old plantation house.

You can pleasurably swim at several beaches near the inn, but a drive about 12 miles (19 km) north will take you to the island's bold headland **Cape Santa Maria** and its miles of stunning white sand beach. To get there you will pass through **Burnt Ground,** a small settlement which some say contains the oldest building on the island — a two-story stone structure laced with vines, brightened by faded blood-red paint.

Some scuba divers claim the waters off Long Island are the clearest in the world. Just south of the Stella Maris Inn you will find the Stella Maris Marina and dive-boat operation which offers, as its most unusual feature, dives to **Shark Reef.** There, intrepid divers can watch in safety as a divemaster extends a speared fish; sharks smell the blood, glide in for the feeding, and when the bait it devoured, prowl away.

Bumpy Way South: To see Long Island south of Stella Maris, guests may rent cars at the Stella Maris Inn. (Warning: A 1985 editorial in the *Tribune* [Nassau] claimed, believably enough, that an old woman seriously injured herself falling in a pothole on Long Island's Queen's Highway, the principal road. These holes range from diameter of a basketball to the size of a car. Stretches of the road are not paved.) Driving south from Stella Maris you will pass through the small settlement of Millerton. About five miles (eight km) farther south you will reach **Simms,** with its shady casuarina trees and limestone walls. One of the oldest settlements on the island, it dates from the 18th Century. Just before reaching Simms you will see a sign indicating the side road to the government packing house. Once a week, on mailboat days, the tin-roofed packing house bustles. Farmers from all over the island bring papayas, bananas, tomatoes, pineapples and corn to be packed for the sea trip to Nassau. The farmers' sales are to the government, which buys the produce at a fixed rate.

Most Long Islanders live on the west side of the island, where the sea is shallower, quieter and where the northeast tradewinds have formed protective dunes and rocky hills. Unpaved roads and footpaths lead to fishing grounds among the coral reefs on the east coast. Passing a string of villages, some of which consist of just a few houses, you will reach Salt Pond in about 15 miles (24 km). But linger first at **St. Joseph's Church,** which stands pristine and white amid gravestones on a hill overlooking the sea.

Regatta Town: Salt Pond, the next main settlement south, is best known as the site of the annual Long Island Regatta. Held each spring on Whit Monday, the race is a major commercial and patriotic event on the island. The race itself, in which only Bahamian made boats may compete, is both a showcase for Bahamian nautical skills and a serious competition for prize money.

Unmistakable on the southwest corner of Salt Pond's single crossroad, the trim, suburban-looking Harding's Supply Center is the town's most prominent feature when the regatta is not underway. Standing on the well-stocked store's front porch, the proprietor may point out the mailboat docked a few hundred yards away and tell of the years in the 1950s when he worked on the Long Island-to-Nassau mailboat. Until the mailboats converted from sail to motor power, the trip to Nassau took eight days.

Continuing south from Salt Pond you will pass through the small settlements Pinders, Bowers, Grays, Andersons, Old Grays, Lower Deadman's Cay, Deadman's Cay, Buckleys, Cartwrights, McKenzie and **Sunday dinner.**

Mangrove Bush. This last village is the home of Laurin Knowles, one of the most respected and celebrated boatbuilders in the Bahamas.

Two Churches: Before the airport opened at Deadman's Cay, most people reached Long Island by boat, landing at the sheltered bay at **Clarence Town**. The town still serves as the island's capital, though its business activity and population has been surpassed by Deadman's Cay about 12 miles (19 km) north. Clarence Town's signal landmarks are two white churches on opposite hills, built in what some call Moorish and others call Mission style, one accented with red trim and the other with blue. These are the creations of John Hawes, otherwise known as Father Jerome. In the early part of this century the Anglican minister-architect, who later converted to Catholicism, built churches throughout the Bahamas. He died as a hermit on Cat Island. **St. Paul's Anglican Church** perches on a hill at the western end of town, with a wide view toward the south and a glimpse of the bay. Slightly taller and more imposing, **St. Peter's Catholic Church** gleams on the near eastern hill. Father Jerome built his Cat Island hermitage on the highest point in the Bahamas, and here too he shows his affinity for a site with a sweeping view.

Clarence Town - quiet, more spread out than its population of 200 warrants – feels like it's the end of the earth. But there is more beyond. An hour's walk on a footpath near Clarence Town will take you to a large blue hole–one of the Bahamas' seemingly bottomless pools. The Stella Maris Inn divers sometimes conduct expeditions here. Just south of Clarence Town, the Public and Chancery Ponds contain old salt pans where Long Islanders have evaporated sea water to obtain salt since the 18th Century. About 10 miles (6 km) farther south in Hard Bargain, the Diamond Crystal Salt Company had a more extensive operation, but today the concentration pans, each several acres in area, are used as a shrimp farm. Foreign visitors are few on Long Island and become oddities south of Clarence Town, mainly because one would be hard pressed to make the round trip from Stella Maris by car in a day. These settlements endure with few amenities, largely beyond reach of the outside world. But there are plantation ruins here, and lovely beaches at **South End**.

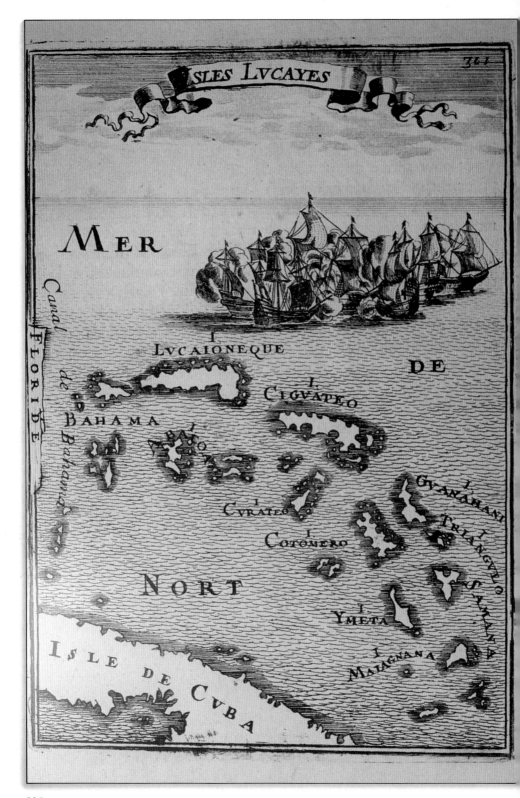

ISLES LVCAYES

MER

DE

Canal de Floride

Canal de Bahama

LVCAIONEQUE

I. CIGVATEO

BAHAMA

CVRATEO

COTONERO

GVANAHANI

TRIANGVLO

SAMANA

YMETA

MAIAGNANA

NORT

ISLE DE CVBA

226

THE SOUTHERN ISLANDS

On a good day, the hazy bulk of Cuba to the southwest is just visible from the observation platform of the Matthew Town lighthouse in Inagua. Turning a few degrees to the left, you see only the unbroken horizon over the ocean, yet only some 75 miles (120 km) away lies Tortuga Island off the north coast of Haiti.

Through these waters have passed the treasure-laden ships of Imperial Spain, as well as countless freighters and merchants plying their trade between the Caribbean and North America.

The route is hazardous; low-lying cays and shallow reefs await the unwary, and those poor souls hopelessly driven on by the forces of storm and hurricane. A few miles north of Great Inagua, the rusting hulk of a freighter sits perched atop the treacherous Hogsty Reef, while the remains of many more vessels scatter the reefs and ocean depths to the north and west.

Southernmost of the Bahamian Islands is **Great Inagua.** Sandwiched between Cuba and the Turks and Caicos Island, its salt flats and low hills spread across the peak of an isolated undersea mountain rising almost 10,000 feet (3,000 meters) from the ocean floor.

The terrain of Inagua is harsh. With little freshwater, low rainfall, and constant trade winds, only the most hardy vegetation can survive. Yet it is these very factors that have brought comparative prosperity to the island. Nature has been concentrating salt in Inagua's shallow lakes for thousands of years. Today, the Morton Salt Company speeds up the process by controlling water flow, and produces some 1 million tons of sea salt annually.

It was salt that first brought settlers to this, the largest of the southern Bahamian Islands, and the third largest island in the entire archipelago. Bahamian historian Dr. Paul Albury writes that the name of the island was most likely derived from two Spanish words *lleno* (full), and *agua* (water). An English corruption of these words, Henagea, apparently persisted for some time, and was the name of the island when settlers first came there to harvest salt. In 1803, it was recorded that there was only one inhabitant on Inagua, and by

1848, a mere 172. However, the salt harvest and the sale of the commodity to passing ships was so successful that by the year 1871, the population had risen to 1,120 a number close to the present population.

These good times were not to last, for the mining of salt in the U.S.A., and protective tariffs imposed by that country reduced the market, and the Inagua salt industry went into decline.

G.C. Klingel, who was shipwrecked upon Great Inagua in the 1930s, and who later described his experiences in his book, *Inagua,* wrote: "The place was a ruin. Vacant and broken windows stared at us from tumbled and deserted houses. Roofs careened at crazy angles, and through great gaping holes in their surfaces we could see golden splashes of sunlight that filtered into the darkened interiors. Flattened fragments of long-deserted garden walls lay in piles where they had fallen, dislodged by the elements and the flowers of these gardens had long since run riot and were strewn in hopeless profusion in a tangle of weeds and broadly padded Prickly Pear."

In the 1930s, the Erickson brothers revived the salt industry into a successful operation that was later taken over by the Morton Salt Company. Today, **Matthew Town** reflects its former prosperity and its residents enjoy a lifestyle unequalled in the southern Bahamas.

Some 12,000 acres are now set aside for salt production. Sea water is pumped into the island by powerful diesel engines, and carried to the interior through natural creeks lined with mangroves. Man-made dykes separate this sea water from the increasingly saline brine in the evaporating lakes.

Inagua's low rainfall and persistent trade winds are ideal for salt production, a natural process that is guided and assisted by man at every step. From the air, the ponds are a quilt of many colors. Different species of algae, minute floating forms of plant life, thrive in the changing concentrations of brine. Indeed their presence is welcomed, for by coloring the water, they increase the absorption of heat, and thus speed up evaporation and salt production.

At the end of the line, the brine flows into crystalizing ponds to a depth of some 18 inches (0.5 meters). When the salt has crystalized, the remaining liquor containing other mineral salts is pumped out into an adjacent area, a moonscape punctuated by the skeletal remains of dead trees. The salt left behind is harvested with heavy machinery, and carried away by trucks to an enormous pile where it awaits shipping.

The salt ponds may not only produce salt. Experiments are being carried out to grow various forms of marine life in the salty water. Brine shrimps, stonecrabs, and prawns are all potential harvests. The old salt-ponds to the north on Long Island have already been converted to this purpose.

Natural Aviary: Long before the lakes of Inagua were utilized by man for salt production, water birds gathered here to enjoy nature's bounty. Man, in his turn, has enjoyed the birds. In 1771, English naturalist Mark Catesby wrote about the flamingo: "....the flesh is delicate and nearest resembles that of a patridge in taste. The tongue, above any other part, was in the highest esteem with the luxurious Romans for its exquisite flavour... A man, by concealing himself from their sight, may kill great numbers of them, for they will not rise at the report of a gun, nor is the sight of those killed close by them sufficient to terrorise the rest, and warn them of the danger, but they stand gazing, as if it were astonished, til most or all of them are killed."

By the 1950s, Inagua's **Lake Rosa** was the last stronghold of the flamingo in the Bahamas. Fortunately for the species, an organization called "the Society for the Protection of the Flamingo in the Bahamas" was formed to protect the birds in a declared protected area. Later this organization became the Bahamas National Trust, and the flamingo reserve has become the **Inagua National Park,** a 287 sq-mile (741 sq-km) area comprising almost 50 percent of Great Inagua.

The flamingo, recently declared the national bird of the Bahamas, and appearing on the national coat of arms, has since made a spectacular comeback, and today as many as 30,000 of these birds may congregate at Inagua each spring to engage in their complex courtship rituals, and to raise their young. The Bahamas National Trust wardens have established a camp at the western edge of the Park, and some 23 miles (37 km) from Matthew Town, upon a low sand dune optimistically known as **Long Cay.** Here you can relax far from the cares of the world. While the constant breeze keeps away the bugs, flamingos, spoonbills, and other waterbirds parade past the observer in their search for food,

Flamingos in Inagua National Park.

probing the heavily organic mud for their supper. (Arrangements for a stay at the camp, and tours of adjacent areas may be made through the Bahamas National Trust at P.O. Box N4105, Nassau.)

At the eastern end of the lake are remote creeks, ponds, and luxuriant mangroves where myriad waterbirds build their nests. Here are cormorants, pelicans, spoonbills, herons, and the rare reddish egret, the local form easily distinguished from its North American cousins by its pure white plumage.

Rocks and Wind: Not all of Inagua is swamp or lake; the southern and eastern portions of the island are mostly raised a few feet above sea level, and covered with either low coppice or thorny scrub. There are more cactus here than in the rest of the Bahamas, from the tall elongated dildo cactus to the wooly-nipple cactus, a six inch (15-cm) ball of ferocious spines.

The rocky landscape, thin soil, and low rainfall make Inagua a harsh place for plants. Trees of possibly great age rise no more than a few feet above the rocky terrain. Such a growth form is even more exaggerated along the southern coast where the unrelenting trade winds, and the almost continuous salt spray from the jagged

rocks below have flattened the vegetation against the rocky soil. Mature trees, molded to the contour of the land, rise little more than a foot above the rock and blanket the ground with their trailing stems and branches.

From these rocky windblown slopes there is a fine view of one of the most graceful of seabirds, the white-tailed tropic bird. After spending months out in the Atlantic Ocean, this species comes ashore along the rocky cliffs of the eastern Bahamas to mate, and to lay its single mahogany colored egg. Wheeling and swooping, the birds utilize the air currents coming off the ocean as they search for a suitable nesting hole. Evidence from ringed birds suggests that they always return to the same nesting hole each year. The young bird, a fluffy white ball with a sharp beak, is fed by its parents upon a regurgitated mixture of partially digested fish, a concoction which it is only too happy to splash over those who disturb it.

Farther inland, and better protected from the influence of the sea, the taller broadleaf coppice is home to the Bahamas parrot, a species which today only survives on the northern island of Abaco, and here on the southern island of Inagua some 350

A shorebird's signature.

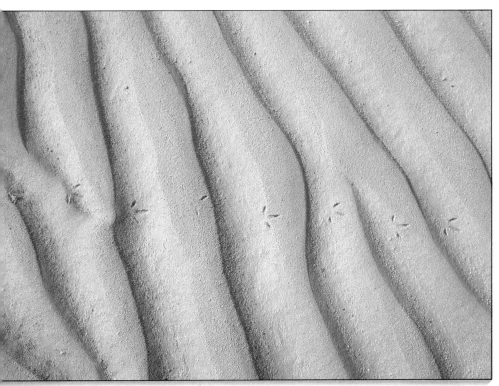

miles (560 km) away. The Bahamas parrot is closely related to parrots of Cuba and the Cayman Islands, and in its Abaco habitat, is the most northerly species of parrot anywhere in the world.

Just to the north of Inagua, and surrounded by water thousands of feet deep, is **Little Inagua,** an uninhabited wilderness of some 49 sq miles (127 sq km). Local stories have it that Henri Christophe, one-time ruler of Haiti, buried his treasure either on Little or Great Inagua.

Fishermen sometimes visit the island, and turtles come here to nest. Inland, in an inhospitable pothole terrain is found the only natural stand of royal palms in the Bahamas. The seeds may have been brought from the island of Hispaniola in the digestive tracts of birds.

Another World: Some 60 miles (96 km) north of Inagua across the Caicos passage is the island of **Mayaguana.** Although a medium-sized Bahamian island of about 285 sq miles (735 sq km), its population has always been small. Today less than 600 people live in the "capital" of **Abraham's Bay,** and the two smaller settlements of Betsy Bay and Pirate's Well.

Fishing, farming, and the few government positions are the only jobs on the island. Such being the case, many of the younger residents have left for Nassau to seek other careers. However, plans are afoot to increase tourism on Mayaguana and thus provide more jobs.

Interestingly, Mayaguana is one of the few Bahamian islands to retain its Indian name. Out in the coastal settlement of **Betsy Bay**, many of the homes have a rural innocence from another era.

Continuing to the north and west along the island chain you come to a small cluster of uninhabited cays. These are **Samana Cay,** sometimes known as **Attwood's Cay,** and the east and west **Plana Cays.** Two of these small islands are of particular interest for their plant and animal species.

Samana Cay has been inhabited seasonally by farmers from nearby Acklins, and by collectors of Cascarilla bark. This small tree, also known in the islands as sweet wood or Eleuthera bark, has a rich spicy aroma. Its bark is an important ingredient in the production of the popular liqueur Campari. Today Samana Cay ranks third in importance in the production of Cascarilla Bark behind Acklins and Crooked islands where many of these trees have been planted around homes for the later harvesting of the bark.

The roseate spoonbill dips its food from Inagua's saline lakes.

230

A somewhat barren and nondescript little island, **East Palana Cay** has an area of less than 1,000 acres (400 hectares). It was here in the mid Sixties that Dr. Garrett Clough, a rodent biologist rediscovered the unique Bahamas hutia, an animal long thought to have been extinct.

Hutias are plant eating rodents, and are about the size of a small rabbit. They have living relatives in Cuba, Hispaniola and Jamaica, but were only known in the Bahamas by their skeletons. In 1747, Catesby wrote about the hutia: "The Bahamas Coney . . . is a little less than the common wild rabbit, and of a brown colour without a mixture of grey hairs. Its ears, feet and tail resemble those of a rat, in the other parts it is somewhat like a rabbit, they feed wholly on wild fruits and vegetables, when surprised by hunters they retreat to holes in the rock. Their flesh is esteemed very good, it has more the taste of a pig than that of a rabbit."

In early colonial times, the edibility of local wildlife was of critical importance, for supplies from elsewhere were sporadic and unreliable. Even today, with American-style supermarkets on several of the islands, the first question many Bahamians will ask about animals is "Can it eat?" — local dialect for "is it edible?"

The population of between 5,000 and 10,000 hutias on East Palana Cay is still thriving. Smaller populations are also growing on two cays within the Exuma Cays Land and Sea Park. A small number of hutias were placed here a few years ago by scientists aboard the research vessel *Regina Maris.*

Sheltered Lagoon: The islands of **Crooked** and **Acklins** encircle a shallow lagoon known as the **Bight of Acklins.** Geologically this is actually the smallest of the true Bahamian Banks. Banks are shallow sandy platforms often bordered by narrow islands, and isolated from other shallow water regions by water of great depth.

Crooked Island was not settled by Loyalists until after 1783, but by the beginning of the 19th Century there were more than 40 plantations worked by more than 1,000 slaves who planted cotton. The plantations were short lived for the soil was thin and could not support crops for more than a few years. Soon the homes of the plantation owners began to fall into disrepair. Roofs collapsed, and stones from the walls were used for other purposes. Today, fewer than 700 people live on Crooked Island.

guanas
nhabit cays
n the Bight
f Acklins.

Most of them make a living from the land and the sea. At best, the plantation houses are now tumbled and scattered ruins. Two however are worthy of note. **Hope Great House** and **Marine Farm** have been left to the Bahamas National Trust by the late Herbert McKinney of Nassau, so that they may be preserved.

Located at the extreme northwestern tip of Crooked Island, Marine Farm overlooks the Crooked Island Passage, the deepwater channel dividing the southern and central Bahamas. It was close by here, at Bird Rock, that it is believed Columbus anchored during his passage through the islands on his first voyage of discovery.

In 1492, he spent several days in the area searching for "Samaot," a place where it was rumored that gold was to be found. Although he located an Indian village near to his anchorage, he apparently never found the Indian settlement on Acklins which undoubtedly was the place he sought.

Recent evidence shows that there was a major Indian community occupying 3.8 miles (6 km) of coastal Acklins between Jamaica Cay and Delectable Bay. This was quite possibly the largest Indian community in the entire Bahamas at that time. To this day there is no evidence to suggest that

gold existed on or had been brought to the island. Columbus called Acklins, "La Isabella"; later it came to be called Acklins Key (early 19th Century), and in more recent times Acklins Island.

Before the advent of steamships, the monthly packet from Jamaica to England would pass through the **Crooked Island Passage** en route to Britain. Here it would drop off and pick up not only the mail, but passengers and freight, for later transshipment to Nassau, and to other Bahamian islands.

The first General Post Office of the Bahamas was located at **Pitts Town,** close to both Marine Farm plantation and to Bird Rock.

Just to the south of Acklins are a small group of cays that still retain their original Spanish name. The **Mira Por Vos Cays** have never been inhabited, but are one of the most important seabird nesting sites in the entire Bahamas. On the cays is probably the most northerly colony of brown booby, a tropical gannet with a four-and-half foot wing span.

Getting There: If you wish to visit the southern Bahamas you will find it helpful to make arrangements well in advance either through a travel agent, or somebody with family or friends in the area. Inagua, Mayaguana, and Crooked Island, Acklins is only accessible by private plane or boat, charter plane or mailboat. The mailboats, privately owned craft under contract to the Bahamas Government, carry passengers and freight throughout the islands. Arrangements for travel on such boats must be made directly with the captain in Nassau.

On Inagua the Main House, operated by the Morton Salt Company has basic rooms and good island cooking. Ford's guesthouse is also occasionally open to guests. Arrangements on Crooked and Acklins should be made through the Bahamas Ministry of Tourism in Nassau, or privately upon reaching the island. Other than charters from the United States, all travel to the southern islands is from Nassau.

For those who require structured vacations, the southern Bahamas is out, but for those seeking a new experience, a new view of the interaction of man and nature, the southern islands offer much.

Lignum vitae (left), the national tree of the Bahamas, is common throughout the Southern Islands. Salt crystals of Inagua's lakes, right.

THE UNDERWATER BAHAMAS

Most of us will never walk on the moon or take a flight through space. But almost anyone can experience the indescribable feeling of floating "weightless" beneath the sea amid a panorama of remarkable beauty. Scuba (self-contained underwater breathing apparatus) diving is booming. Even greater numbers enjoy snorkeling, which requires only a mask, breathing tube (snorkle) and fins. With at least 100,000 sq miles (259,000 sq km) of crystal clear seas, the Bahamas is a diver's paradise.

Although sport diving in the Bahamas has only flourished in the past 30 years, the wonders under these seas were known back in the mid 1800s. John B. Green, "the celebrated submarine diver" as he called himself, took a break from his usual treasure diving in the Great Lakes to dive in these waters for treasure. He discovered the lost wreck he had been hired to find but wasn't able to bring up the silver because it had become so encrusted with coral. Green did find treasures of another kind that modern-day sport divers still discover when they dive in this incredibly beautiful area.

"On this bank of coral is presented to the diver one of the most beautiful and sublime scenes the eye ever beheld. The water varies from 10 to 100 feet in depth, and is so clear that the diver can see from 200 to 300 feet, when submerged with little obstruction to the sight," he wrote. He described the sharks, fish and corals which grow in profusion in these waters. He was clearly in awe as he swam among these creatures. Most 20th Century divers feel the same.

Floating slowly over one of the isles' many shipwrecks, a diver enters another world of natural beauty, wonder and amazement, a world divers are privileged to enter – if only for brief moments. Large Nassau groupers approach divers looking for handouts. Disappointed at not being fed, they back off a little but still tag along like friendly puppies or curious cats trying to be affectionate without getting in the way. Brilliant-hued parrot fish feed head down, crunching hard with their beak-like teeth. They are sand-makers; they graze on the stony surface of the coral, spitting out bits of hard exterior skeleton and devouring the algae growing there. This is a quiet world, and the parrot fish's crunching

Preceding pages: flamingo flight pattern; weathered limbs on Walker's Cay; and coral branches. Left, a boat becomes a sunken habitat for fish and an attraction for divers; and right, an instructor prepares a student to take the plunge.

sounds loud to divers who watch the scene from a few feet away.

A lifetime of diving would not be enough to explore the underwater world of the Bahamas. These isles offer ideal conditions for new divers, with many certified instructors and calm seas. There are also an amazing number of sites and experiences to fascinate even the most experienced diver; shallow reef diving, wall dives, shark diving, blue holes, canyons and more. Fish is so plentiful that they often appear as walls of color.

These islands feature one of the world's finest

fleets of live-aboard dive boats. These boats offer more dives per day and better access to remote reefs than do land-based dive operations.

Ships Claimed by the Sea: Wrecks liberally sprinkled throughout the islands give mute testimony to the extensive coral reef system that surrounds them. The history of the Bahamas is written in the wrecks and there is an "other world" quality to floating through a ship the sea has claimed and transformed into an artificial reef full of sea life.

There is something magnetic about a wreck, even an oft-visited one. Some wrecks date from the days when the islands were a refuge for pirates for almost two centuries. Rumors of hidden treasure abound in the southern Bahamas.

Filmmakers have flocked to Nassau to shoot James Bond movies including *Thunderball, Dr. No* and *Never Say Never*. Parts of *Splash!, Wet Gold* and *Cocoon* were filmed here as well.

Coral Cathedrals: Living coral reefs are enchanting and magical places, and the Bahamas abound in these special gifts of nature. To dive on a coral reef is to dream. Keep both eyes open to insure that you don't miss a single thing. Drift, soar, glide through sprawling cities. Domes of brain coral closely resemble their namesake. Staghorn corals forest the reef with their stony trunks and branches.

Greek mythology attributed corals to the seeds of seaweeds petrified by Medusa, whose hideous face turned all who saw her to stone. Early naturalists assumed corals were some sort of marine shrub. It was not until 1726 that

process. Over millions of years these tiny creatures have built major landscapes. Some coral heads are so huge divers can swim inside the cavernous structure. Once inside, you have entered one of nature's cathedrals. Tall dark and awesome, it is easy to feel dwarfed by its size and uplifted by the cascades of light. Elusive black coral that has become as rare as jewels elsewhere is prolific on some of these reefs. Vivid sponges grow in patches of bright orange, deep rust and florescent yellow. Tiny feather dusters and Christmas trees sprout from brain corals. Really the gills of burrowing worms, the slightest motion causes them to retreat into their homes.

Each coral reef is an entire community. Many reef dwellers are territorial, and divers can usually count on seeing the same curious

French naturalist Jean André Peyssonnel actually showed that a reef was made up not of plants but groups of tiny animals. Though they don't roam for food, corals are efficient predators and manage to reproduce, communicate, clean themselves and build reefs all within their rocky homes.

It takes all kinds of coral to make a reef: star coral in mounds, elkhorn and staghorn coral with spreading branches. Though it looks like a luxurious, overdeveloped garden, a coral reef is more akin to a marine housing development.

Coral reefs are created by polyp colonies building exoskeletons of calcium carbonate. The calcium waste has been deposited by countless generations to build a solid block of reef covered by a thin veil of living polyps continuing the

angelfish on each visit to a particular reef. Look carefully under a ledge and there will be a moray eel. Under another ledge is a spiny lobster. The reef is a fascinating mosaic of colors, forms, shapes and constant motion. It is also one of the most complex and delicately balanced communities anywhere.

Night Dives: The Bahamas are an ideal spot for an introduction to the fantastic and surrealistic world of the reef at night. During the day, with natural light, you dive in a kind of blue-tinged twilight. Colors disappear one by

A glide through coral gardens (above). The grouper's phlegmatic personality makes it "all in a day's work" for this fish to pose with three excited divers (right).

one as increasing depth steals light of varying wavelengths. Red goes first. At 30 feet (nine meters) a cut finger oozes green blood. Most coral polyps are nocturnal, withdrawing deep within their skeletons by day. But at night with a camera's flash or a dive light the pure intense light lets you see the true color of everything.

The reef is alive at night. It is also much noisier at night than in the daytime. Fish grunt, groan, click, vibrate. Lobsters and sea urchins march boldly across the bottom. Corals open their polyps for feeding. Some fish do sleep, allowing you to get very close to study and even pet them. They hang motionless under coral ledges, sleeping in spite of their open, lidless eyes. Some hide in packets of their own mucus that may prevent their scent from alerting

operators feature both windward and dive sites so if winds are up divers ca perience fine diving. Summer is a sp season with air temperatures ranging fr to 88°F (24°C to 31°C) moderated by cooling ocean breezes. The water can warm up to the high 80s (30° to 31°C) and the seas are usually calm and glassy. Visibility may pick up to as much as 200 feet (60 meters).

Photogenic Wrecks: Despite its population and development New Providence Island has some surprisingly fine diving and is one of the best kept diving secrets in the Bahamas. On the north side of the island, very close to Nassau, there are shallow reefs and several outstanding wrecks: the *Mahoney,* the *Alcora* and the *LCT.* On the south side is Clifton Wall, a dramatic wall near a dozen shallow and deep sites

predators. Turn off the divelight and you are in a void, insulated from the rest of the world. You see nothing and hear nothing except your own breathing.

Run your hands through the water and you will see the bioluminescence, the phosphorescent streaks and sparks that light up the sea. Reef sharks might be on the prowl for they roam at night. Time to turn the light back on.

The climate for diving varies according to the seasons of winter and summer—both are great but summer is even better. In the winter air temperature may range from 68°F to 78°F (20°C to 25°C) from November through April. The water temperature during this season may range from 70°F to 76°F (21°C to 24°C), and a wetsuit is definitely recommended. Many dive

clustered within a mile of each other.

The *Never Say Never Again* wreck formed a perfect backdrop for the James Bond film. The 110-foot (34-meter) freighter, which was seized as a dope runner by the Bahamas government, was sunk here by the film crew. It is one of the most photogenic wrecks in the Bahamas if not the Caribbean. The movie *Wet Gold* and several television commercials were also filmed here.

Just a few dozen yards away are the remains of the airplane prop created for *Thunderball.* The frame is carpeted with gorgonians with large basket stars clinging to them. Gorgonians are probably the most exotic of the corals. Plant-like seafans and seawhips form vast underwater coral "gardens." Their elaborately

ched colonies sway and bend with the
motion of the sea. Basket stars are a type of
starfish which resemble baskets with their
intricate structure.

The speargun sequence of *Thunderball* was
filmed on Thunderball Reef. It has numerous
brain and star coral heads. Since it is shallow —
no deeper than 25 feet (eight meters) — and the
tops of the coral heads come to within 10 feet
(three meters) of the surface, it is an excellent
snorkeling area as well.

Another prime wreck is the *Alcora*. This
130-foot (40-meter) ship was confiscated by the
Bahamas government and turned over to diving operators to be sunk and turned into a different kind of undersea treasure. This is a deep
dive, 80 feet (25 meters) to the deck. The boat
sits upright on a sand bottom, surrounded by

the coral formations. Two spotted eagle rays
float by majestically like birds in flight. A sea
turtle swims by. Suddenly, a shadow passes
overhead. Look up, it's there. Your breathing
speeds up, tingles of fear race through your
body as your realize how out of place you are
down here under the sea. It's a hammerhead
shark, perhaps 12 feet (three meters) long.
Fortunately the shark isn't interested in human divers, and it quickly and gracefully
glides off into the depths. Sharks are much
maligned. They rarely molest humans without provocation.

Off the Treasure Cay Beach Hotel, on Great
Abaco, approximately 30 miles (48 km) north
of Marsh Harbour, fine sites include the wreck
of the *San Jacinto*, a 140-foot (42-meter)
Union gunboat that ran aground in 1865 while

low corals. Water is murky at this depth so at
first the diver sees just a huge shadow lurking
below, then the entire hull. The ports are open
so you can swim through two large cargo
holds in the forward and middle portions of
the ship. A light is needed to penetrate the
engine room.

The Abacos face the open Atlantic on one
side and the Little Bahama Bank on the other.
At the northern tip of this chain is Walker's
Cay, a private, 100-acre (40-hectare), one-
resort island. Just off Walker Cay's eastern
shore, a line of coral heads loom upward from
70 feet (21 meters) to just below the surface.
Huge 300-pound (135-kg) jewfish roam under ledges here. Spacious corridors domed by
high-vaulted ceilings wind endlessly inside

in pursuit of a Confederate gun runner.

Near Marsh Harbour, crossroads of the
Abacos Train Wreck is in only 15 to 20 feet
(4.5 to six meters) of water. This recently discovered wreck consists of two mostly intact
locomotives on their sides, huge wheels and
other wreckage. The locomotives were being
shipped on a barge that ran aground. The
wreck of the *Adirondack* is another shallow
wreck in only 10 to 25 feet (three to 7.5
meters) of water. It is mostly rubble, but 12
cannons are still visible.

**A juvenile angel fish (above left) and a spotted
moray eel (above right). The bat fish (right) is a
highly camouflaged creature who could blend in
anywhere if it weren't for her stunning red lips.**

Grand Bahama, the country's second largest resort community, is also home to the 20-year-old UNEXSO (Underwater Explorer's Society), a highly rated scuba facility with superior instruction facilities. There is an 18-foot (5.4-meter) deep training tank for resort courses and scuba instruction, modern rental gear, classroom space and instructors who offer classes in the basics as well as specialities. Theo's Wreck is a 230-foot (69-meter) steel cargo ship deliberately sunk as an artificial reef. It is 110 feet (33 meters) deep, close to the edge of the Grand Bahama Ledge drop-off. The wreck hangs along the edge of a 2,000-foot (600-meter) precipice which provides for some exciting dives.

Into the Abyss: The colossal canyon called the **Tongue of the Ocean** lies just off An-

the wreck of the *Potomac*, run 1952 and now split into two s yards (182 meters) apart with b exposed at low tide. The Barg sunken World War Two Navy l sits upright in 70 feet (21 meters) of water.

At Bimini, a mere 60 miles (100 km) east of Miami, and underwater visibility often reaches as much as 200 feet (60 meters). Along a wall beginning at 120 feet (36 meters), a current of about five knots provides an exciting drift dive amid spectacular scenery including giant tube and basket sponges, black coral, school of giant tuna and amberjack, eagle rays, huge groupers. Another favorite Bimini dive site is the *Sapona*, 300-foot (90-meter) cement-hulled ship which ran aground in the shallows during a hurricane. It sits

dros' eastern shore. It wasn't until 25 years ago that man first viewed this incredible natural wonder. A vertical drop-off borders a broad, steep-sided ocean bowl. Now a dive to the wall is one of the high points of any diver's career. At a drop-off named Over the Wall the projecting ledge juts out at 165 feet (50 meters) where delicate black coral forests reach out in these deep blue depths. The stone ledge drops for 6,000 feet (1,800 meters) into an inky black abyss. Divers seem so very small and insignificant hanging suspended in mid-water and looking down into the drop-off.

Andros has the largest amount of untouched, virgin diving. A magnificent 142-foot (43-meter) wide barrier reef stretches along the length of the island. Sites include

upright in only 15 feet (4.5 meters) and thus makes an excellent snorkeling site. The *Sapona* is home to an amazing number of fish including pufferfish, grunt and snapper, stingrays and sergeant fish.

At the northern end of Eleuthera cluster smaller islands including Spanish Wells and Harbour Island. High on the Spanish Wells dive itinerary is another *Train Wreck* – one of the strangest wrecks in the Bahamas. This stolen train was being transported by the Confederates during the Civil War to be sold to Cuba. Now mostly wheels and axles, it is also a feeding station where handfed fish pose happily for photos.

Fantastic Flight: The Current Cut rates as the wildest scuba experience in the Bahamas. The

narrow pass between the tip of North
Eleuthera and nearby Current Island. At peak
tide the water rushes through at an estimated
seven to 10 knots. Seven knots does not sound
like much, but the drift feels like a sky dive or
roller coaster ride. Extending their arms for
wings, divers soar and glide. Beyond these
sensations is the feeling of being in a giant
aquarium because a diver can see more fish
here in 10 minutes than he might on a dozen
wall dives. Ten minutes of flying and this extraordinary aqua-adventure is over.

The Freighter Wreck is another special dive
near Eleuthera. The Lebonese ship *Arimora*
wrecked in 1971. It is a 260-foot (78-meter)
steel freighter sitting upright on a coral bar
with three quarters of the hull above water.
The wreck is home to a remarkable array of

macro life: shrimp, anemones, arrowcrabs, sea
urchins, crabs as well as schooling gray angelfish, nurse sharks and a giant jewfish.

In the Exumas dive operations serve
George Town, the largest settlement. Sites
are still being discovered. A number of ocean
blue holes are regularly dived. Angelfish Blue
Hole takes its name from the many friendly
angelfish found near the opening. Mystery
Cave opens to a huge horizontal tunnel over
400 feet (120 meters) long beneath Stocking
Island.

Feeding the Sharks: Long Island boasts one
of the Bahamas' more unusual dive sites, the
famous shark reef off Stella Maris Inn. There,
divers have the rare opportunity to watch
sharks feeding in a natural setting. Twice a

week guests watch one of the world's greatest
wildlife shows.

The usual pre-dive excitement is greatly
heightened. Sharks have been much overrated
as vicious creatures of the deep, but still an
element of danger cannot be discounted. Visions of *Jaws* dance through the head. Will
they come? Where will they come from? How
many? Will the whole scene be too fast and
nerve-wracking to photograph?

Down on the reef everything is calm and
quiet. After the divers settle down, divemas-
ters extend a speared fish and the first shark
rushes in for the kill, hitting and severing the
bait. Sharks snatch falling pieces of bait in
mid-water. Another fish is presented and each
approach is bolder. The handouts end, and
after a few more passes the sharks disappear
as they came – into the depths of the sea. The
divers soon realize that they are aliens in this
undersea world and must emerge from watching these fascinating and misunderstood creatures of the deep.

Rum Cay, off Long Island, boasts a fine dive
resort and a number of top sites including vertical walls, shallow reefs, coral caves and pin-
nacles, and more fish feeding experiences.
Grand Canyon is one of several feeding stations, and as soon as the divers enter the water
groupers eagerly flock around looking for
hand-outs. Jewfish Wall, with its vibrant orange basket sponges and purple tube sponges,
is one of several extraordinary wall dives.

It would take months to explore the hundreds of dive sites off the island of San
Salvador, of which 60 are marked and named.
The reefs there, some of the least visited in
the Bahamas, teem with life: flamingo tongues
(with shells the size of a thumb nail), shrimps,
hermit crabs, Christmas tree worms and
seahorses. Larger fish use sections of the reef
as cleaning stations. You can see them settle in
the coral and wait patiently while tiny cleaner
fish go to work on their parasites. The large
groupers can be surprisingly tame and often
don't mind you giving them a friendly chuck
under the chin.

Christopher Coloumbus first made landfall
in the New World on tiny San Salvador, and
divers are still discovering offshore wonders
there and in the rest of the Bahamas. Beneath
the Bahamas' warm, shallow sea is an ever-
changing, living world.

**In a scene as elegant as those in the many James
Bond movies filmed in the Bahamas, divers enjoy
the romance of the deep (left), and the solitude and
mystery of exploring the Bahamas' many underwater wonders (right).**

HOOKED ON FISHING

The sign on the closed shop door which says "Gone Fishing", could well have been invented in the Bahamas, although it is more likely to read "Gone fishnin'." Pronunciation aside, however, there is little doubt that the sentiment is the same and that fishing, in its many and varied forms, is a national pastime of Bahamians.

Picture a typical aficionado as he steals through his darkened home, in search of a midnight snack. The exertions of the previous day's fishing have made him peckish. As he gropes his way into the kitchen he accidentally kicks over a glass-bottom bucket (used in handline fishing) which, in turn, brings down the nearby deepsea fishing rods and a smaller "spinning reel." Startled, he jumps back, tripping over the ice chest and losing balance. Trying to steady himself, he grabs the nearest object, a six-foot spring steel spear, of little use in his predicament, but quite effective in scything the rest of his fishing equipment from the kitchen counter onto the floor. The resulting crash is really quite impressive.

As he lies there without any immediate hope of achieving his original objective, it occurs to him that similar events must befall many of this nation's fishermen, especially those who do not put away their fishing gear before going to bed at night.

The surrounding seas and their incredible bounty have always played a significant part in the life of Bahamians. So much so that in 1670, when Charles II of England granted the Bahamas to the Lord Proprietors, the grant was spelled out to include, "those islands lying in the degrees of twenty and two, to twenty and seven north latitude ... with the fishing of all sorts of fish, whales, sturgeons, and all other royal fishes in the sea, bays, inlets, and rivers within the p'misses, and the fish therein taken, together with the royalty of the sea upon the coasts with in the limit aforesaid."

For the next three hundred years Bahamian history takes on the appearance of a rollercoaster ride with times of great prosperity followed by slumps of almost total despair. Pirates, cotton plantations, wrecking, gunrunning, sisal, sponging, rumrunning and now

Bahamian sponge fishing from Frank Leslie's Illustrated Newspaper of New York, 1872 (left). A Bahamian boat captain must be able to "read" the water's depth by its color (right).

tourism, have brought these islands the good times. But the people always kept their hand in at fishing. As fishermen, they have survived the bad times.

Commercial fishing has seldom been an outstandingly successful business in the Bahamas. Nevertheless, certain historical highlights are worthy of mention.

Sponges and Conch: Perhaps the only time that fishing has been the number-one industry of the Bahamas was during a relatively short period beginning from the close of the 19th Century up to 1940.

These were the days of sponge fishing.

In his 1902 Annual Report to the British Colonial Office, Royal Governor G.T. Carter tells us that 1,319,270 pounds (597,629 kg) of sponges valued at 97,548 pounds sterling were exported from the colony. This represented 48 percent of total exports and employed 265 schooners, 322 sloops and 2,808 open boats. In all 6,200 men, women and boys were employed in the industry, at a time when the entire population of the Bahamas amounted to just slightly over 50,000.

Unfortunately, sponge fishing came to an abrupt halt in 1939 and 1940 when a blight destroyed almost all of the sponges. Attempts to revive the industry in the 1950s were unsuccessful following the introduction of the cheaper mass-produced synthetic sponge. A more recent attempt has proved mildly successful but involves the sale of sponges for tourists to take home as curios.

Today's commercial fishermen catch scale fish year round, mainly to supply local needs - a task which should not be underestimated as each year, the Bahamas receives visitors equal to more than 10 times its own population.

Many of the smaller fishing vessels, especially the traditional Bahamian workboat sloops, actively engage in "conching." Famous for its large and beautiful pink shell, the conch has long been a staple part of the local diet. Its versatility is illustrated by naming only the most popular ways in which it is eaten: raw, in a "salad" or "scorched," cooked in fritters, chowder, "cracked," burgers, soused, conch 'n rice, stewed, steamed etc. Despite its popularity it has never quite made it to the grade of *haute cuisine* although one renowned French chef is said to be working hard to perfect a recipe for "Conch á l'orange."

More importantly, conch has a reputation as an aphrodisiac which, perhaps, accounts for the fact that Bahamian population growth was, until the advent of local television ("not now dearest, I'm watching Dallas"), the second highest in the Western world.

During the spiny lobster season, August 1st to March 31st, many fishermen switch to this more lucrative trade, supplying both local and export markets. In 1984 the Bahamas exported some 2.57 million pounds (1.16 million kg) of lobster, known locally as "crawfish," valued at nearly 17 million dollars.

Oddly enough, it is only since World War Two that the Bahamians have come to realize the value of crawfish. Previously they had been considered well nigh unfit for human consumption and were used primarily as bait for catching other fish. Now, all of a sudden, they have risen to the rarified atmosphere of gourmet's delight. They cost a fortune, and you can't find them when you want to.

Although some of the more organised fishing communities, notably Spanish Wells in North Eleuthera, do very well for themselves, the fishing industry as a whole contributes little to the country's export figures. Nevertheless, its local contribution remains highly significant, both in supplying local needs, and in foreign exchange savings.

For Sport: By outlining the historical background to fishing in the Bahamas, it is easy to understand the deep-rooted love today's Bahamian has for recreational fishing. There are many reasons why Bahamians are so happy to venture forth at the slightest excuse - spear, fishing lines and rods in hand. Obviously the beautiful seas, sunny weather and the abundance of fish are key factors, but the primary factor is geography. Because this nation is made up of long narrow islands, virtually the entire population lives within three miles of the sea - fishing is on everyone's doorstep.

Handline, or "bottom," fishing may seem an odd choice to begin describing Bahamian recreational fishing. Most tourists would tend to think first of "deep sea" or possibly "spear" fishing. Really, the choice is perfectly logical since it is the only native form of recreational fishing which has historical roots in the islands. Other types of recreational fishing de-

scribed below are modern-day introductions relying on motor boats, underwater diving gear and other technical equipment.

Handline fishing grew from the simple necessity of having to catch fish to feed oneself and one's family. It continues to exist as such, particularly in the less populated and more remote Family Islands. To some extent this explains some of its less sporting characteristics, such as the use of 40-pound test line for catching 5-pound (2 kg) fish! It is also the least expensive method of fishing - all you

A Bimini bait and tackle shop. The gear needed for bill fishing is complex, but handline fishing requires only a hook, line and sinker.

need is a hook, line, sinker and bait - which explains its local popularity.

Although handline fishing can be done from the rocks or off dock, the more serious fisherman will often take to his boat. This is usually small with a minimum of rigging, enabling the fisherman to cast his line freely and to "work" the 360 degrees around the boat without obstruction. Having a Bimini top, three radio antennae, a flagpole and a girlfriend between you and the 25 pound hogfish on the other line is a decidedly unhealthy situation. If you don't lose the fish you might lose your girlfriend.

The required tackle is simple. Your line should be as heavy as possible for the fish you intend to catch. Light lines tend to cut your hands, are more difficult to grasp and are more likely to get knotted. You should have two or three sizes of hook ranging from smallish to medium and large-medium. Sinkers are usually nuts, bolts or lead (often made from cutting up old car batteries). You'll also need bait, the most popular being conch and crab (hermit).

And so, with a sunny day, boat, tackle, bait and a rising tide (the best time for fishing), you want to go out and catch some fish. Your first decision is "where?" Unless you can find the fish you will spend the next few hours getting frustrated, bad tempered and burnt to a crisp - with nothing to show for it. You need a "drop" - someplace where there are fish. This is usually learned from local knowledge, aided by a glass-bottomed bucket which enables the fisherman to check a prospective site for the type and number of fish. Often this will be near a small "head" of coral or in a rocky channel. Once a good location has been established the boat is anchored so as to "tail off" into a position from which lines can be cast in or near the targeted site. In order to get the fish into a receptive mood the area is usually "baited up," which involves throwing bits of conch and crab shells plus sand mixed with conch "slop" (the slimy guts of the conch which are no good as bait) into the water around the boat.

The fisherman then unravels 50 to 100 feet (15 to 30 meters) of his line, depending on the depth of the water. The hook is baited with conch or crab etc and then cast towards the "baited up" site. He lets his line run out until the sinker hits bottom. At this point he must quickly take up slack or his bait will be stripped before he feels a thing. The line is then held waiting for a "pick" (nibble). When this happens the fisherman should be able to recognise the type of fish which is having a go at his bait. If he recognises the sharp pick of a turbot (queen triggerfish) or "porgy" he has to be prepared to "strike" quickly. If it is the slow pull of the Nassau grouper or hogfish he must let the line run out before striking.

Once he strikes and hooks a fish he has to pull it quickly, but steadily, to the boat. If any slack gets on the line he will probably lose his fish. If he takes too long, chances are a lurking barracuda will "hit" the line, leaving him with a mangled fish head and hands injured by the line ripping through them.

Fortunately for the beginner, there are so many fish in Bahamian waters that even the least proficient fisherman will usually catch something. It is a fact of life, however, that the best eating fish - grouper, hogfish amd mutton snapper, are the most difficult to catch.

Into the Deeps: In contrast to handline fishing, spearfishing is one of the more recently introduced forms of recreational fishing. Its rapidly increasing popularity comes from several special factors.

First, it is the only type of recreational fishing where the fisherman physically enters the space of his underwater prey.

Second, since SCUBA (self contained under water breathing apparatus) gear is not allowed under Bahamian law in the "capture of any fish or marine product," a spearfisherman needs to be physically fit and an accomplished swimmer.

Third, unlike surface fishermen, he can select the type and size of his prey, limited only by his ability to dive deep, pursue and shoot straight.

Lastly, spearfishing involves certain dangers which, although acceptable to the prudent diver, nonetheless produce moments of great excitement, such as a sudden meeting with an agitated 14-foot (4-meter) hammerhead shark. These moments are accompanied by an overwhelming desire to walk on water. Fortunately, they are mercifully rare and most dangers take the form of a curious barracuda, the more docile nurse shark, moray eels, hidden sting rays, fire corals and jelly fish - not that any of these should be taken lightly!

The spearfisherman's equipment consists of flippers, a mask (which should have a nose piece so that he can "clear" his ears during a dive), a snorkel and a "Hawaiian Sling." The "Hawaiian Sling" is the only type of spear allowed by law and consists of a six- or seven-inch (15 to 18 cm) cylinder of wood with a hole down the middle, onto one end of which is bound a loop of rubber surgical tubing. The spear is between five to six feet long (1.5 to 1.8 meters) and usually made of spring steel so that it won't become bent out of shape (a crooked spear doesn't travel in a straight line). To fire it the spear is fitted through a hole in the wood and the tip inserted into a special fitting in the middle of the loop of surgical tubing. It is then pulled back, aimed and released rather like a crude form of bow and arrow. Unlike the more sophisticated spear gun, the spear of the Hawaiian Sling is unattached and relies on its weight or a good "brain" shot, to bring down its prey.

The effective range of a spear fired in this manner is about 15 feet (4.5 meters), although longer shots are possible. Usually the spearfisherman will try to get within five to 10 feet (one to three meters) of his target. For crawfish, the tip of the spear is often only two or three feet away from its target when fired.

where he should be looking, which will often involve long series of tiring dives as he gets down to look under ledges or into holes. In hunting for crawfish he may only glimpse a few inches of the tip of their whips (antennae) poking from under a rock.

When shooting a fish the best spot to aim for is the brain, a little way up and behind its eye. The advantages of a "brain shot" are considerable. First, it kills the fish outright so you don't have to chase it all over the place and maybe, if it's a larger fish, lose your rather expensive spear. Second, it doesn't have the opportunity to shake out the spear and escape. Third, it doesn't give out distress signals in thrashing about trying to get away, thus attracting unwelcome visitors like sharks, so

An accomplished spearfisherman can usually free dive to a depth of 35 to 45 feet (10 to 13 meters). His ability to stalk prey effectively will also depend on how long he can hold his breath and his ability to dive and swim under water with a minimum of exertion, thus conserving oxygen. He should never smoke or drink before or in between dives, as both these pastimes race the heart beat and impair his ability to stay down.

Most spearfishing is done on reefs or around heads of coral, where the fish hide. Spotting suitable prey is something of an acquired technique amid all the distractions of sea fans, corals, refracted light and hidden shadows. The spearfisherman has to know

that the hunter becomes the hunted. Fourth, there is likely to be less blood in the water and last, but certainly not least, a spear hole in the head does not spoil all that lovely meat on the body of the fish which, after all, is the ultimate reason for going spearfishing in the first place.

Safety is an extremely important aspect of spearfishing but, as with most things, the rules are simple and based on good old common sense. A 50-year-old desk-bound businessman who drinks and smokes excessively, who is unfit and 40 pounds overweight, will probably last 30 minutes before he has a heart attack;

The king of the Gulf Stream billfish, a blue marlin, puts up a valiant fight off Walker's Cay.

it is a strenuous pastime. Nor should anyone, however experienced, dive alone. One should always have a boat close by - preferably within 30 to 40 feet (10 meters) and furthermore, being driven by someone who knows what he or she is doing. Always keep a lookout for large sharks or barracuda and leave the area if you are spotted. Never stick your hand or head into blind holes or caves and, when you do spear something, get it out of the water as quickly as possible.

If anyone finds that "brain shots," lurking barracuda and fish guts are unappealing, they might like to join the growing number of people who substitute a camera for a spear.

Inshore Trolling: "Trolling" is used to describe any form of fishing where a line is towed behind a boat. However, its form varies much depending on location, size of boat, bait and equipment, that it is, perhaps, best described under three separate headings: inshore trolling, deep sea trolling and bill fishing.

Referred to by some locals as "strollin'," inshore trolling is done in shallow water, either close up against a rocky shoreline at high tide, or in amongst shallow coral heads and reef. Although some people are capable of getting carried away with anything, inshore trolling tends to be treated by most as a somewhat lighthearted venture. Very often it will involve putting out a few lines on the trip home from the beach or going out for a couple of hours before sunset for a few beers, a cool breeze and, just maybe, a fish or two.

Usually the inshore trollers' boat will be small, highly maneuverable and of shallow draft. A good knowledge of the area and the ability to "read water" (know how deep it is by its color) are also useful.

The most common tackle consists of a spinning rod, light line (8 to 12 pound test) and an assortment of feathers, spoons and lures. This writer's personal favorite is a small yellow feather readily taken by jack, mackerel, yellowtail snapper and gray snapper. Some fishermen swear by red and white striped feathers, "jellie-bellies," silver spoons, and a host of other lures, silver spoons reputedly being excellent for catching barracuda.

Stalking Big Game: As opposed to the inshore variety, deep sea trolling and bill fishing require a larger boat, fully fledged deep sea fishing rods and tackle, and a fighting chair.

For deep sea fishing, one heads out over the reef where the fish are bigger, if somewhat scarcer. The color of water changes from various shades of turquoise to a deep cobalt blue and the surrounding islands recede to sit low on the horizon. Your attention becomes focused on the boat as she picks up the motion of the waves. Diesel fumes creep over the stern as you watch the lines being baited up: a deep wire line with lure and fish bait, and three shallow with an assortment of feathers, lures, jigs and ballyhoo.

You might begin by trolling along the outside of a reef hoping that a large grouper will take the deep line or for a kingfish, mackerel, wahoo or large jack or one of the others. After forty five minutes nothing has happened and you are giving the rods only an occasional glance. The anticipation wanes, your hat slips over your eyes and you relax comfortably back into your chair soaking up the warm Bahamian sunshine.

An hour later the captain spots a line of seaweed and alters course to check it out for dolphin (not the mammal; the fish is known for its speed, tremendous fight and the brilliant colors which it assumes in the act of dying - it is also, many believe, the best eating of all big game fish).

The deep wire line is reeled in and a shallow feather and fish bait substituted. Success is instant and on the first pass three lines get strikes. The back of the boat is full of people shouting encouragement, pulling in lines, gaffing fish, rebaiting lines, letting them out and pulling them in again. Twenty minutes and twelve fish later, contact with the school of dolphin is lost. The lines go quiet and lunch is served: a welcome respite for aching muscles.

The trolling continues with an occasional strike, checking bait, a couple of fish landed: a small bonito and a barracuda. By mid afternoon everyone is tired but happy and thoughts are of getting back to a warm shower and cool drink. Then you notice the captain studying something through his binoculars - a flock of birds wheeling and diving over an agitated sea - tuna! The boat turns, lines are reeled in, and heavy gear is substituted.

As one approaches, the sight is almost frightening as enormous bluefin tuna engage in a feeding frenzy on the surface of water which literally seems to boil. The captain increases speed and passes ahead of the school - nothing. He turns and heads back. Suddenly a ratchet screams; the rod is bent double. The engines are throttled back. You jump into the fighting chair as a shoulder harness is being strapped on. The boat is dead in the water but the line continues to scream out; it starts to smoke and someone pours water over it; a pause and the rod is jammed into the fighting chair holder, your hands grab ahold. The line screams again and mercifully someone clicks off the ratchet. Almost a half of a mile of line is out before the fish stops. You begin to pull, crank, pull, crank - slowly the fish is coming in. The line scorches out again; ten minutes work is lost in a few seconds. Back, fighting the fish; forward, reeling frantically for every inch of line. After twenty more minutes every muscle aches, your legs are shaking but the big fish is within 50 feet (15 meters); it takes one look at the boat and the line screams out again; this time it goes deep; you pull, crank in line, pull, crank. An hour after the strike you are within 20 feet of success and are exhausted; people on the flybridge can see the shadow of the fish; it's huge, at least 400 pounds (200 kg); you pull, crank; again the line screams and then...slack. The big one gets away...this time.

Big Bills: Bill fishing in the Bahamas involves the pursuit of blue and white marlin, sailfish and swordfish. There are many similarities with deep sea fishing and, in fact, both are often carried on simultaneously, although they are treated separately here.

The main difference between billfish and other deep game sea fish, apart from the obvious fact that one has a "bill" and the other does not, is in the way they catch their prey i.e. smaller fish.

Most large fish simply pursue their prospective dinner, open their mouths and "chomp"! Various methods such as driving schools of small fish up to the surface where they are more easily trapped, the ripping attack of barracuda or the gaping mouthed pounce of grouper, are used; but the result is the same.

To be sure, billfish are also known to employ this form of direct attack (known as "committing suicide"). However, their usual technique is somewhat more refined and involves swimming up alongside their target and then hitting it with their bill. This either stuns or kills their prey outright, which is then swallowed. The time lapse between the "hit" and "swallow" is approximately 5 to 15 seconds.

If billfish hit a bait being trolled behind a boat and it did not stop as expected, they may try to hit it again a few times but, eventually, will probably disappear in a fit of pique, much to the chagrin of the fisherman who will undoubtedly have witnessed the whole episode, have jumped into the fighting chair, had his shoulder harness strapped on, braced his feet on the transom and be clutching his rod in contemplation of how his name will look in the next edition of *Guiness Book of Records*.

Therefore, to create the correct sequence of events, bill fishermen have devised an ingenious, if simple, rig, which allows the bait to act in a manner acceptable to the fish.

First the line is baited up, using various types of fish bait; ballyhoo, small dolphin and mullet are among the favorites. This is let out behind the boat to a distance the fisherman feels is best (usually not as far as with other rigs). The drag is then set and tested. The bait should be running just below the surface of the water, occasionally breaking up to the top.

The line coming from the tip of the rod is then taken and clipped into a glorified sort of clothespeg which is hoisted, rather like a flag, some 25 to 35 feet (10 meters) up a thin antenna-like pole called an "outrigger." The outrigger is then swung out at an angle of about 45 degrees from the side of the boat (this keeps the bait in clear water outside the wake). Finally the fishing reel gear is put into neutral with the ratchet on; everything is set.

The line is now rigged so that it goes back, up and out from the tip of the rod to the clothespeg at the end of the outrigger, and then trails off, slightly to one side, behind the boat.

In theory it works as follows: first the bill fish sees the bait and comes up to take a look. From his position on the raised flying bridge the captain should spot what's happening and shout down a warning to the fishermen, "bill fish!" Meanwhile, if the fish is satisfied with the bait he hits it with his bill. The jolt causes the line to snap out of the clothespeg at the end of the outrigger, usually like a pistol shot. This causes slack in the line which, in turn, causes the bait to stop dead in the water. Simultaneously the captain drops back on the throttles. By now line is running slowly off the fishing reel, the ratchet buzzing gently. The rod is taken quickly from the gunwale holder and placed in the fighting chair holder. The fisherman grasps the rod and braces his feet against the transom. On a count of 10 from the snap of the outrigger, the captain throttles up and simultaneously the brake (drag) is thrown on the fishing reel. This maneuver is designed to "set" the hook and is followed by one or two things; either some agricultural phrases to the effect that the fish didn't take the bait or, an explosive scream as up to half a ton of angry, untamed muscle rips hundreds of yards of line off your fishing reel in a matter of seconds. The fight is on.

For the conclusion of this tale, you might read Ernest Hemingway's *Islands in the Stream*. Hemingway, an avid deep sea fisherman, based much of the book on his experiences on the island of Bimini, often regarded as the deep sea fishing capital of the Bahamas.

Bill fishing is one of the most exciting and glamorous types of fishing, but it creates an all too common scene: in the late afternoon a "sports" fishing boat comes in, full of people laughing, bragging and drinking. They tie up to the fish dock and begin unloading half a dozen bill fish. These are hoisted up with ropes around their tails and hung from a metal cross bar. Pictures are taken of the fishermen and their catch. Someone says, "let's go to the bar," and off they go leaving the fish behind.

As darkness begins to fall a passerby asks a Bahamian lad what is to become of these magnificent animals. He replies "De fishermen dem don' wan dese no more. We does chop dem and trow dem back fo' de sharks."

or salt water, that any angler could ever hope to catch." And, by all accounts, there are more bonefish in the Bahamas than anywhere else in the world.

To be sure, the world record is temporarily held by Brian W. Batchelor who caught a 19-pounder in Zululand, South Africa. However, Bahamian commercial fishermen quite frequently net specimens in excess of this weight and it is surely only a matter of time before one is brought in on rod and reel.

The bonefish's feeding habits are such that they move in schools onto shallow sandbanks with a rising tide, and off again as the tide goes down. In all fairness to prospective bonefishermen, this is one of only two predictable things which this fish does; the other being

If a sports fisherman wishes to have a fish mounted by a taxidermist as a trophy, or if he intends for it to be eaten (the sword fish is Malta's national dish), then fair enough. Otherwise, whenever possible, all catches should be tagged and released.

The Gray Fox: The bonefish (in Latin, *abula vulpes*, or gray fox) has been described many times in many ways but never better than by one seasoned and widely experienced fisherman who said (with deep emotion), "He is the gamest fish of any size or type, in either fresh

At the end of the battle, the prize blue marlin is hauled aboard. These fish are caught all year round, but most commonly in June and July.

that, once hooked, it will give you, ounce for ounce, the toughest fight of any fish you have ever had the privilege to have on the other end of your line.

Bonefishing comprises two quite distinct elements. First of all, it is necessary to find ("stalk") the fish and, since his likely whereabouts tend to vary enormously, depending on tide, wind direction, water temperature and weather, you will almost certainly need to employ a local guide.

The bonefish spook very easily and any sound, such as something banging in a boat or someone splashing through the water, will likely set them off like a flock of birds. They also have very keen eyesight and have even been known to take off because of the shadow of a bird passing overhead. Almost instinctively, many fishermen will crouch as the fish get close. It is, therefore, virtually impossible to cast your line amongst them as the splash will probably result in the entire school taking off like scalded cats. The technique employed is more one of ambush, where you locate the fish, work out in which direction they are moving, and try to cast some 20 to 30 feet (six to 10 meters) ahead of them.

Bonefishing is usually done in very shallow water (nine to 30 inches or 23 to 76 centimeters), either wading or operating from a flat-bottomed, shallow draft skiff. Because the water is so shallow it is often easy to spot the bottom being stirred up as the fish rummage through the sand and mud for small crabs and other crustaceans. Alternatively, in extremely shallow water one will often see their caudal (tail) fins breaking the surface ("tailing") as they angle down to feed with their "bottoms in the air."

Although many fishermen are very enthusiastic about trying to find schools of tailing bonefish, it is a fact that they are harder to catch in very shallow water than in water which is a couple of feet deep.

Wet fly fishing is occasionally employed when going after bonefish or, more often, a weighted jig with feather. But the most usual tackle is a spinning rod with as much line as it will carry of between four to 10 pound test. The common bait is crab, but also popular are small squid, shrimp, crawfish and conch.

Once you have cast your line it is a matter of waiting patiently as the fish work back and forth across the bottom, towards your bait, you hope. Once there the fisherman has to play by instinct. A tweak on the line; has the fish taken the bait, or is he sitting there watching it to see if you give the game away by striking too soon? Sometimes he'll pick up the bait and swim straight towards you, chewing it off before you can reel in the slack.

If you do manage to strike and hook your fish, the result is explosive! The first run is lightning fast and long.

More often the first run will take 300 to 500 feet (100 to 150 meters) of line, followed by the frantic reeling of the fisherman before the second run which, although usually shorter than the first, will probably result in an additional net loss of line. There then follows a series of frantic reelings, and powerful runs as fisherman and fish fight to gain the upper hand. But the Gray Fox has only just begun; if he spots anything in the water that he can wrap the

line around, he will make a bee line for it. Mangrove roots, a solitary sea fan (the only one within a mile), a channel marker pole, even the propeller of your boat; if he reaches his objective you can kiss him goodbye.

If the fisherman survives all this and brings the fish to within 100 feet (30 meters) or so, its frantic tactic will usually involve running rapid circles back and forth with short bursts aimed at trying to pass under the boat. The scene can be quite interesting as the fisherman pirouettes around with everybody ducking frantically to avoid the slashing line.

This writer has tried for a middle ground of accepted norms (such as they are), on the premise that not much would be gained by describing such techniques as spearfishing by being towed on a rope behind a boat (although this is widely practiced) or handline fishing for bonefish and running hooked fish down in the mangroves (not widely practiced).

It has been said that out of 10 bites a good average would be to hook three and land one, but once that "one" is in the net, the triumphant fisherman can only sit back and reflect in respectful wonder at the tremendous battle which this little fish has just given him.

Sharkfishing and More: Of course there are many less popular types of fishing in the Bahamas. Specialized areas of the sport such as sharkfishing, fishing the "drop off," spinning, night fishing or the use of downriggers as in swordfishing, would all need lengthy and, in some cases, highly technical descriptions which there is not space to include here. However, with the possible exception of swordfishing, the visitor is not likely to come across these types of fishing.

Doubtless many local fishermen will find fault in the foregoing descriptions of fishing techniques, tackle, bait etc. This is to be expected! Bahamian sportsfishing is approached in a highly individualistic manner; virtually every Bahamian fisherman has his own bag of tricks, knows more than any other Bahamian fisherman and he "ain't gonna tell he secrets to no one, no suh"!

Perhaps the most important thing about sportsfishing in the Bahamas is that there are plenty of fish, they come in a variety of shapes and sizes, and they bite.

If you have never fished in the Bahamas why not give it a try? Who knows, you might get hooked!

Weighed, photographed and admired, the marlin fulfills its promise as the centerpiece of a big game fishing weekend.

257

OBEAH, SUPERSTITION AND FOLKLORE

People of all races and cultures have three fundamental things in common: the family; religion; and folklore. Human beings also distinguish between religion, medicine and superstition. With the advent of travel, immigration, the mass media and almost instant communication, it is difficult at times to keep these distinctions clear.

The Bahamas is no different from many other countries or cultures in that throughout its history it has adopted and integrated many aspects of superstition and folklore into a dominant occult — a supernatural system called Obeah. Obeah is not unique to the Bahamas. Throughout the Caribbean, especially the English-speaking Caribbean, Obeah and similar practices are found. Haiti has the religion of Voodoo; Trinidad has Shango; Cuba has Santeria. In fact, wherever African slaves were transported and settled, African religious belief, healing and superstition naturally went with them, and especially in countries that are predominantly African in racial configuration, these practices still exist. Black Americans, and even some American whites (especially in the Southern states) have similar belief systems to those found in the Caribbean. Many unexplained "mysteries," supernatural happenings and illnesses are ascribed to the influence of being "hexed," "fixed," "hagged," "obeahed" or "placed under a curse or spell"!

A few years ago, a Bahamian musician, then resident in New York, suddenly burst on the international and Bahamian scene with songs all Bahamians could identify with. His name: Tony McKay — a Cat Island-born Bahamian who called himself "Exuma, the Obeah man." *Kifaru Magazine* of Freeport said of him: "Everything is a bit mysterious about Exuma, from his outfits to his music, his paintings, his poems, his life. 'Exuma is one,' he has written. 'Exuma is three. One, two, three, they all can see.' Also, 'His time is short, his time is long. Exuma ain't right and Exuma ain't wrong.' Also, 'Exuma took his wooden hand and scorched his mark across the land.'

Around the same time, Obeah had reached its height on the comeback road in the Bahamas, and Exuma's rhythms and songs not only highlighted a practice that was embedded into every Bahamian's psyche, but also provided a meaningful departure point as people

A tree in Nassau hung with bottles is an exaggerated version of an Obeah practice that occurs throughout the Bahamas.

searched for cultural expressions of African beliefs that had relevance to a newly independent Bahamas.

Good and Evil: Bahamian Obeah is the phenomenon of the supernatural. It renders evil or good; makes dreams come true; influences individuals either for their demise or holds them in another's power. Its practice can cause one to become rich or poor. It can cause an illness (either physical or mental) or can cure any physical or mental problem. It can cause *death*!

Obeah is a type of spiritualism, surrounded by many tales of unexplained phenomena and replete with superstitions that generate a plethora of articles (fetishes), bush medicines, "signs" and specific directions as to what one might do to solve a certain problem. Obeah, then, in its present context, appears to be the bastard child of African religion and superstition, Judaeo-Christian beliefs and interpretations and European superstitions. There are also elements of Black Magic, White Magic, Satanism (with its demons) and Witchcraft.

One can also assume that Obeah probably originated from an African religion that had elaborate ceremonies with "priests," "saints," "special days," etc., but Obeah, in its present day form, is *not* a cult or religion. There are no priests, collective rituals, gods or saints. It does not resemble the type of ceremony that is found in Voodoo (Haiti), Shango (in Cuba and Trinidad) or other types of African religion that can still be found in parts of South America with large populations of African origin and descent, such as Brazil.

The interaction with the Obeah man or woman and society is on a one-to-one basis. An Obeah practitioner may chant or sing or "go into a trance" to give an impression, gain some special power, or to set the right mood, but there are no meetings, dancing, drum playing or collective singing. Although some ministers of religion may practice what closely resembles "Obeah" in the form of "White Magic," there are no "priests" or "ministers of Obeah." Theoretically, most Christian revivalist leaders are not involved in the practice of Obeah, and Obeah Men and Women are, supposedly, evil persons who engage in magic without having church groups. Nevertheless, the temptation for revivalist leaders to try their hand at Obeah is strong because of the requests made by followers, and, of course, there is a profit!

African Origins: The origin of Obeah and the word itself has never been carefully researched in the Bahamas, nor is there any comprehensive historical or current literature on the topic, except for Dr. Timothy McCartney's book, *Ten, Ten the Bible Ten — Obeah in The Bahamas*. Without exception, however, authors agree that Obeah was originally practiced by people of African heritage.

L.B. Powles, a circuit justice, writing about the Bahamas in 1888, reported that "the people here are very superstitious and what is called 'Obeahism' is very common among them. I have never been able to find out exactly what the 'Obeah-men' are supposed to do, further than that they are species of African magicians, who, for a trifling, will bewitch your enemies and charm your friends, so that any one stealing from them will by punished by supernatural agency without the intervention of the policeman or the magistrate."

In 1905, J.B. Shattuck observed that "at some of the islands we found hanging to various trees, fantastically draped bottles and sticks, which, we were informed, were charms to frighten away thieves and evil spirits. It is believed by the negroes that if anyone but the rightful owners should eat the fruit from a tree on which this spell has been placed, he will swell up and burst."

But in the Bahamas, the clearly defined categories of supernatural practices which one finds in Africa — religion, medicine and superstition — are not found. Many Obeah men and women possess all the attributes of religion, superstition and medicine. With regard to witchcraft and medicine, Bahamian practitioners appear to follow the traditions of Yoruba beliefs.

Obeah practitioners were uniquely African and, later, people of African descent. It is believed that in the Bahamas those Africans who were freed on arrival in the Bahamas, who were never in slavery, and were never exposed to the influence of Christianity, were the principal carriers and practitioners of these beliefs. Though Obeah originated in Africa and may have had roots in some African religion or cult, it developed into an individual practice. It was essentially a type of sorcery which largely involved harming others at the request of clients by the use of charms, shadow catching, and poisons. The Obeah professional performed Obeah practices and was paid by his clients. Many European superstitions and practices (e.g. white magic) were incorporated into Obeah. Eventually, healing by bush medicines was also practiced.

The islands of Cat Island and Andros have strong historical Obeah roots and the most powerful and renowned of the Obeah practitioners lived on these islands. Obeah beliefs are also strong in the Exuma Cays, Acklins, Mayaguana, South Eleuthera and Crooked Island. Each island has its Obeah center. On Cat Island it's the Bight; on San Salvador it's Breezy Hill; on Andros it's North Andros; and in New Providence it's Fox Hill.

Most of the older Bahamian practitioners are Bahamian-born, but there is an increasing number of Haitians, Haitian-Bahamians, Jamaicans and a few other nationalities who have quite lucrative practices.

There appears to be a remarkable belief in Obeah among *all* West Indian Negroes, but the magical practices of a neighboring or distant island are always more powerful than one's own. Hence Bahamians believe that Haitian voodoo is more powerful than Bahamian Obeah. The very high influx of Haitan immigrants to the Bahamas, with their different language and reputation for the supernatural, have added to the dimensions of superstition in the Bahamas. A common Bahamian rumor is that a few prominent Bahamians who have died can be seen roaming the mountains of Haiti as zombies! Anytime there is an election, it is rumored that many politicians pay a visit to Haiti to ensure success at the polls.

Many Bahamian Obeah men and women were apprenticed to older wise men or women, and some learned the art from their parents, or they were "born" with their special gifts and these "gifts" were recognized at an early age. Some received their "power" during adulthood with a "vision" or, while "in a trance" were instructed into their art. The more professional of these Obeah practitioners have studied in Haiti, Jamaica and Harlem, New York.

Pa Beah, Uncle Boy: The claims of Obeah practitioners are legion, and people that have profited from these ministrations often attest to the "powers" of these people. Two Obeah men, now deceased, were greatly renowned.

Zaccharias Adderley had the reputation of being a very powerful Obeah man. He was affectionately known as "Pa Beah," ("Beah" naturally being a derivative of Obeah) and was the "king" of Obeah on New Providence Island. He lived in Fox Hill, was a farmer and started practicing Obeah in his spare time as a hobby — a hobby which was much more lucrative than farming the land!

He once told someone, "If people are stupid to gimme money, I ain't too stupid to take it."

According to legend, Pa Beah could fix his field so that if anyone went in to steal his cassava, they wouldn't be able to find their way out of the field until he arrived to catch them. One day, someone foolishly stole his groceries and a friend said to him, "My Lord, how yer ginna manage this week fer food?"

"Don't worry yer head 'bout me, yer betta worry 'bout the fella who take ma food. He'll soon bring ma food back or else!"

Pa Beah then took a doll, measured it against a candle and cut the candle to the length of the doll and stuck pins in the doll and the candle, the same distance apart in each. All the time he was doing this, he was calling the names of known pilferers in the area. He then, dramatically, lit the candle and said: "When the candle burns down to the first pin, the thief will have a bad, bad pain." That evening, Pa Beah's groceries were left on his doorstep!

"Uncle Boy" was the reputed "king" of Obeah on Cat Island. The nephew of "Uncle Boy" lives in Nassau and has told stories which have been authenticated with Cat Islanders, including a religious leader, who knew Uncle Boy.

Uncle Boy had a coconut farm which was the pride of Cat Island. He worked hard, was a shy retiring man, and lived in the middle of his farm. He had few visitors and was a man who kept very few friends. He was well read, and had quite a library — some of these books (many on the occult) are, at present, in the possession of Uncle Boy's nephew. It appears that someone was constantly stealing Uncle Boy's prime coconuts. Fed up, he posted the following notice:

"To whom it may be concerned: Whoever been in my white land and poached my coconuts for the purpose of shipping, come to see me immediately. You could be carried down and would be carried down if you don't come see me. In the future, be more careful!"

No one turned up to answer Uncle Boy's notice. A short time afterwards, a man in the village started to swell up. No amount of medication or treatment could help him. He soon died, as a result of this "strange" illness. It was found out afterwards that it was this man who stole Uncle Boy's coconuts.

Other Obeah practitioners use primarily bush medicine and white magic. One such practitioner is a 75-year-old woman who lives in Nassau. Her father, born in Cat Island, was a well-known herbalist. She was taught by him, at an early age, to distinguish between different "bushes and barks" and the effects of these on the human body and mind.

This lady lives in an unpretentious house in the heart of the "Over-the-Hill" district. There is a little shop that actually adjoins her home, and this is stocked with groceries, primarily the basic Bahamian needs of rice, grits, flour, assorted canned goods, jars of Mortimer brand candies, bubble gum, chicklets and the proverbial kerosene oil dispenser. There is also a small refrigerator with cold sodas and malt tonic and other bottles of her own "tonics" and "medicine." Behind her counter are about three rows of "sets," — photographs, articles of clothing and other memorabilia belonging to her clients or clients' relations, enemies, etc. on whom a "fix" is to be directed. In the back room of the shop are all kinds of local bushes, barks and bottles of all sizes filled with liquid barks and herbs.

She attributes her power to God and uses, white magic exclusively. She has stated that she never utilized her "gift" to harm anybody. She says she will remove the harm from a client if he or she had an "evil fix," but although she knows how to harm (or "carry down," in Obeah terminology) someone, she never does it. Although she is a known Obeah woman, she claims that it is not really Obeah, but the power God has given her (though she doesn't object to being called an Obeah woman). She relies, very heavily, on the Bible, and claims that the 109, 110 and 111th Psalms are the most powerful in the Bible. She also warns not to "fool around" with "calling the Spirit!"

"Even though I can do it," she explains, "dat's very dangerous, and it must be done with someone who knows what they're doing, 'cause it can ruin you for life. Don' mess wid dat at all — dat's de devil and evil forces — de devil is powerful too — don' mess wid dat!" So the following Obeah practices are described with that warning!

Fixing: Fixing a person is the most common method of Obeah practice in the Bahamas. This entails placing a spell, placing a "set" or "hagging" (whether it is an individual, house, property or object). Being fixed must be distinguished from a curse directed through use of the Bible. Also, "putting mouth on ya" is a type of curse, but does not necessarily have to originate from any Biblical implication. There are subtle differences between a fix and a curse.

If you are fixed you can be "cleared" or "cured" by an Obeah practitioner or even a medical doctor or other type of professional. But if you are cursed, only the individual who gave the curse can clear or remove the curse. Unfortunately, if the one who gives the curse dies, then no one can clear you — you've had it!

One can be fixed either by black magic or white magic. In black magic, not only is the Devil used, but all the "demons" or "imps" can be called upon, or those personalities from the Bible who were against God or died as a result of defying God. *Seven Steps to Power, Black Guard, Seven Keys to Power,* and *Master Key* are the principal books used in Bahamian black magic practice.

White magic entails using the name of Jesus, the Bible and/or verses from the Bible, forms of prayer, prayer objects (e.g. handkerchiefs, scarves, underclothing) and religious symbols.

The psalms are particularly valuable. "I gon read the Psalms to you" or "God don't like ugly" are common Bahamian threats.

White magic is, evidently, more powerful than black magic. For example, a combination of a fix and a curse, put on by black magic, can be cleared (cured) by white magic. If the individual who is cursed by white magic goes to the curser and asks forgiveness, then the curse will revert to the curser.

The following is an example of how white magic can be used to cure alcoholism: pay the Obeah man a prescribed sum of money; the Obeah person will read Psalms 109 and 110 and place the money on the Psalms in the Bible, then close the Bible on the money (no coins are used for this particular fix!); the Obeah person will pray that the spirit of drunkeness will be taken away; the patient will be "cleared" of his problem. (What a pity this has not been found to be effective!)

Calling the Spirit: From time immemorial, man has tried to find means of communicating with the dead and the spirit world. Necromancy, the art of "calling the dead," is universal and goes back to earliest antiquity. "Calling the Spirit" is a ritualistic form of Obeah practice used to obtain knowledge that can be used either for good or evil.

Belief in the spirit world and ancestor worship are strong components of African belief, and, although there is no evidence in Bahamian literature which suggests that Bahamian slaves ever practiced any ancestral cult worship, the belief in ghosts or spirits was, and still is, widespread.

The common word in the Bahamas for any form of ghost or spirit is "sperrid." Sperrids may be found anywhere, but in Bahamian tradition, they like to reside in the very large silk cotton trees that abound in the Bahamas. This belief probably came directly from Africa, as many African tribes venerate the cotton tree as the dwelling place of powerful spirits of the dead.

Bahamian sperrids get up to all kinds of mischief — they haunt houses, hag people, influence human habits (good or evil) or scare the hell out of you!

Bahamian sperrids appear to wander around "willy nilly," but only the Obeah practitioner can "call," "control" and utilize the sperrids to effect good or evil deeds.

The Bahamian believes that to protect oneself from a sperrid, all one has to say is "Ten, Ten the Bible Ten." And if you want to actually see a sperrid, you have only to remove some "bibby" (a local name for mucus) from a dog's eye and put it in your eyes, and you will have the gift of seeing sperrids. Horses also see sperrids, so their "bibby" will help you also.

Working Witch: The term "working witch" is based on the tradition that an individual can buy or hire a witch to do his bidding. Working witch is also a term for working Obeah, a term used mostly on Cat Island.

Anyone could buy or hire a witch, but it was very expensive. Some Cat Islanders would go to South America to work and save their money. They would return home, then go to Haiti (presumably the only island where one could obtain a witch) to get their witch.

The most popular witches were animals like the snake, rat and rabbit. A snake witch was extremely expensive, so much so that the owner of a snake witch would sell it or will it to another person. The "snake-witch" was a short, thick snake and was always distinguishable by the ribbon tied around its neck. This snake could swim for long distances, get on a ship or plane to "fix" people in distant lands if need be. It also had the power to go inside people — eating their insides so that eventually the "fixed" individual would have a high fever, start to have convulsions, then waste away and die.

Many pregnant women who became fixed with a snake would lose their babies, or the snake would go inside them, eat the foetus and then, nine months after, would be born in place of the baby. There are very many Obeah stories that attest to women being pregnant and then giving birth to snakes. Many reputable people, including Bahamian midwives, would "swear on the Bible" that they have seen snakes come out of women.

Rat witches were notorious for the havoc they waged on agricultural fields and barns. Today in the Bahamas, the old timers still threaten to "work witch on ya."

Bush Medicine: The widespread use of bushes, barks and herbs for healing extends back to the prehistory of the entire world. Medicine from the earth or bush medicine is still a very important part of Bahamian life and is utilized by all ethnic types. Most Bahamian herbalists have nothing to do with Obeah and use local bushes and barks strictly for preventive and healing purposes, sexual potency and longevity. Poultices and salves are used, as well as other food products such as lard, olive oil, kerosene, salt, port, onion and garlic. An excellent guide to local healing plants is *Bush Medicine in the Bahamas* by Leslie Higgs.

Though herbalists are not necessarily Obeah practitioners, the majority of Obeah men and women use bush medicine as part of their practice; in fact, the more effective practitioners rely very heavily on their knowledge of this art.

Songs and Stories: Old stories, music, rhythms, and Obeah stories have always been integral parts of the Bahamian way of life. In *New World Groups: Bahamians* (1944), Dorothy Ford wrote that "the myths contributed greatly to the music and lyrics were improvised for the purpose of morale-building. Ad-libbing or 'rigging,' as the old Bahamians termed it, went on for hours at a time and supplied fun for all concerned. Morals controlled the songs of necessity: the children could not be dispatched anywhere (all members of the family were within shouting distance and facilities were close at hand) so they were in on every move the adults made. As children were not aware of anything implied in the songs, the composers were as adept as Doane in disguising the real meaning of words, so when we sung in imitation of them, 'Mama look up in daddy's face all night long,' it never entered our guileless minds that mama and daddy were doing anything else but sitting down facing each other, talking all night. The image of adults sitting up, talking all night, was a familiar one; the other action was not."

Religious beliefs, references to heaven, hell, sperrids, angels and the Devil abound in the stories and songs of Bahamians.

In trying to understand Bahamian folklore, one must go back to the source and examine the Bahamians' ancestors (Africans) who were uprooted from their societies and placed in a new cultural setting. Added to this was the Euro-American influence that molded the African through religious missionary zeal, and both clerical and secular education. There were gradual displacements of African names, beliefs, superstitions, foods, festivals and holidays.

Surely the expression of the Bahamian-African's cultural traditions was discouraged. To begin with, the majority of "house slaves" were Christianized and, emulating their masters, looked upon African cultural expression as pagan. The minority "field slaves" were not tribally strong enough to find common grounds for expression. Except for the islands of Cat Island, Exuma and Andros, where the retention of African practices was strongest, the majority of Afro-Bahamians followed strongly Euro-American cultural traditions.

It is significant, though, that through research Bahamians are realizing the importance of the "remoteness" of the Family Islands. Slaves and free Africans who were concentrated in isolated pockets in these islands maintained their culture — the expression of which, today, is represented in an almost unchanged art form. Free from the Euro-American cultural infusions that invaded New Providence and Eleuthera, for example, Negroes on these islands never developed cultural expressions like those of slaves in the U.S. on southern plantations.

Robert Curry wrote in *Bahamian Lore: Folk Tales and Songs* (Paris, 1930) that "Many of the Bahamian stories will be found to have a marked similarity with those of the Negroes in the southern states of America. It is indeed not always easy to distinguish the story of Bahamian origin from one which has been imported." Evidence of these stories are the Brer Bookie and Brer Rabbie stories that are of the animal-trickster-hero folk type. The "chiccharnies" of Andros Island are favorite, mysterious three-legged animals that resemble the "leprechauns" of Ireland. They supposedly live in the silk cotton trees and get up to all sorts of mischief. The chiccharnie has become a favorite tourist ornament, as replicas and memorabilia are made up in clay, glass and other media, along with various stories surrounding them.

The most important Obeah folk tale, however, (other than the millions of sperrid or ghost tales), is the legend of Sammy Swain. This legend has been popularized by the brilliant Bahamian pianist composer Clement Bethel, who set it to music and dance. It was performed in 1985 before the Queen of England.

Spirituals: Folk songs of the Bahamas were initially religious, linked to slavery and freedom, as evidenced by many spirituals. These spirituals were brought to the Bahamas by the slaves coming with their masters from the U.S. plantations. The Bahamian spiritual, however, has added features that Clement Bethel describes as the "rhyming spirituals." He believes that it is a Bahamian adaptation, with traditional lyrics, but with rhyming, exchange of voices and "call and answer" techniques that are unique to the Bahamas.

Many spirituals (mostly traditional) told about death: "Swing low, sweet chariot, Coming forth to carry me home." Sometimes they were expressions of the feeling of God in their bodies: "Every time I feel the spirit, Moving in my heart, I will pray." More secular songs, however, were working songs, linked to fishing, sponging, farming: "Watermelon is spoiling on the vine..." There were also songs that were very much like the calypso songs, composed extemporaneously to cite some local event of scandal, politics, superstition, love, sex and marriage: "There's a brown girl in the ring, and she looks like a sugar in the plum..."; or "Love, love alone, cause King Edward to leave the throne"; or "Obeah don' work on me."

Festivals, Feasts: There were generally four annual holidays during slavery: Christmas, Boxing Day, New Year's Day and Easter. Both master and slaves participated in these festivals. After slavery was abolished, Fox Hill Day, when only those of African descent celebrated, and

August Monday (Emancipation Day) were added to the people's festivals, though Fox Hill Day was not a public holiday.

Emancipation Day was a great holiday for the Bahamian. As recounted in *A Relic of Slavery:* "Everyone ditched work and headed for Fox Hill by whatever means of transportation he could muster. For the majority, this meant walking: therefore, the trip from Grant's Town, Bain Town and Conta Butta (African settlements on New Providence Island) started early in the morning along the winding footpath of what is now Wulff and Bernard Road. The weeks of preparation by the various tribes resulted in a day of high-strung festivities: dances, quadrilles, concerts and jumping-dance. The entire community moved round as a whole, going from one church to lodge hall to the next, thus allowing for everybody to see everyone else's performance prepared for the day."

There was no retention of any African festivals as such in the Bahamas. No yam festival or river (or water) festivals were commemorated. The Bahamas never enjoyed such outstanding harvests of yams as to occasion the celebrating of them. Harvests of sponges, pineapples, tomatoes and conch have been sung about, and Bahamians have improvised words and music as they suited the current events.

Harvest time was celebrated as a religious festival of thanksgiving by the white population (mostly Americans) and was not a public holiday. It was also incorporated into the church services of the majority black Christian denominations on a seasonal basis. This was not unusual since the major denominations for blacks in the Bahamas were started by free American blacks who had been converted to Christianity.

Junkanoo: By far, the biggest pre- and post-slavery celebration was Christmas, when Bahamians had an almost free rein to "do their thing." The activities centered around Junkanoo, an African-influenced festival. This persists even today.

The preparation of food and the preparation of the Junkanoo festival with the making of costumes became a joint family-neighbor venture. Unlike Carnival in other West Indian countries, and countries with a strong Lenten tradition, when the biggest celebrations precede Lent, Bahamian Carnival (or Junkanoo) is celebrated during the Christmas season with official parades on Boxing Day and New Year's Day.

The original Junkanoo — said to be a corruption of the name John Canoe (reputedly an African king) or *Gensinconnu,* meaning individual with masks — is the strongest remaining African tradition.

A number of Bahamians appear to have come from the Yoruba tribe, and early Junkanoo garb resembles constumes worn by members of the Yoruba Egungun cult. The Yoruba, like most African tribes, worship their ancestors. This worship is based on the belief that the spirit of a human being never dies.

Egungun is a secret society of masqueraders headed by a hereditary chief called "Alagba." An Egun mask usually represents the spirit of a particular person, and it is always the priest of the Ifa oracle who will decide which spirit must receive special attention. Many of these masks consist of colored cloth and leather, covering the whole body of the dancer, who looks out through a closely knitted net. Some actually wear masks over the face, while others wear a carving on top of the head.

The original Bahamian Junkanoo dancers wore costumes of cloth or frilled paper. Another local adaptation was the use of sponges on a type of cloth netting worn over the body. Many of the "masks" were really paintings on the facial skin itself, and the depiction of the Obeah man was usually a man dressed in white with a white mask or white paint on his face, jester-like. There were also stilt dancers, street dancers, clowns and acrobatic dancers. These Junkanoo dancers were accompanied by the goombay drums (goat skin stretched over a wooden frame and heated to obtain the maximum sound), whistles and another Bahamian adaptation, the cowbell.

Junkanoo music, played on goat skin drums, cowbells, bugles, horns, whistles and conch shells is deeply rooted in Bahamian culture. It is played not only at Christmas and New Years but on many occasions that call for celebration. The Junkanoo beat rang out when the Progressive Liberal Party (PLP) won the elections in 1967, at Independence in 1973, and to honor Sidney Poitier, a native Bahamian, on a return visit to his country.

Since the 1920s, Junkanoo has been gradually commercialized, but what it has lost in sheer spontaneity may well be made up for by the wide exposure and by the fact that it has become perhaps the most popular Bahamian institution. Many Bahamians belong to one of the Junkanoo groups that compete for prizes for the best costumes in Nassau's Boxing Day and New Year's Day parades.

Though Junkanoo is found in Jamaica and other of the smaller English-speaking Caribbean islands, the Bahamas has retained Junkanoo in its most elaborate fashion — a fashion that is uniquely Bahamian.

Drums, masks and tall hats are enduring Junkanoo motifs (right). Following page, Junkanoo "Vibrations" by Bahamian artist R. Brent Malone.

TRAVEL TIPS

GETTING THERE

BY AIR

Close to a dozen major airlines make stops in Nassau or Freeport and several charter services carry passengers from Florida to the Family Islands. With over a million visitors flying into Nassau and Freeport every year, the Bahamas air travel market is competitive and it pays to shop around.

Bahamasair, the national carrier, serves Nassau and Freeport from Miami, Dallas, Newark, Orlando, Tampa, Washington D.C., and is the major air link to the Family Islands. Trans World Airlines has flights to both cities from New York and St. Louis. Delta flies from Atlanta, Fort Lauderdale, Dallas and Denver to Nassau; Delta's affiliate, Comair, has a popular route between Fort Lauderdale and Freeport and connections to cities in the Midwest. USAir flies direct to Nassau from Fort Lauderdale, West Palm Beach, Baltimore or Charlotte. Midway specializes in service from Chicago; Braniff flights run between Orlando and Nassau.

Air Canada flights originating in Montreal serve Nassau and Freeport; Toronto flights land in Nassau.

British Airways connects Nassau with London, Montego Bay and Kingston, Jamaica.

Chalk's International is a commuter airline with scheduled service from downtown Miami or Fort Lauderdale to Paradise Island and Bimini, and charter service to Cat Cay.

Air Canada, 327-8411 (Nassau), 352-7266 (Freeport)

Bahamasair, 327-8511/9 (Nassau), 352-8341 (Freeport)

Braniff, 800-272-6433

British Airways, 322-8600 (Nassau)

Chalk's International, 363-2845 (Paradise Island)

Comair, 800-354-9822

Delta, 322-1911 (Nassau), for Freeport call 800-354-9822

Eastern, 327-7392 (Nassau)

Midway, 800-621-5700

Pan American, 327-7992 (Nassau), 352-7406 (Freeport)

Trans World Airlines, 327-6660 (Nassau)

USAir, 800-423-7714

BY SEA

Travelers who prefer the leisurely life aboard ship and the shorter stay ashore can choose among the many cruise lines serving the Bahamas. Most ships dock in Nassau, but quite a few also stop at Freeport. Some, such as the *Star Princess* and *Nordic Prince*, continue through a round of Caribbean ports. Holland America Lines and Norwegian Caribbean Lines also visit Great Stirrup Cay in the Family Islands. Cruises on Premier ships can include visits to four Family Islands.

Admiral Cruises, (*Emerald Seas*) 800-327-0271

Carnival Cruise Lines, (*Carnivale, Mardi Gras, Jubilee, Fantasy*) 800-327-9501

Chandris Cruise Lines, (*Galileo, Crown Del Mar*) 800-223-0848

Crown Cruise Lines, (*Viking Princess*) 800-841-7447

Dolphin Cruise Lines, (*Dolphin*) 800-222-1003

Holland America, (*Westerdam*) 800-426-0327

Norwegian Caribbean Lines, (*Sunward, Seaward, Norway*) 800-327-7030

Premier Cruise Lines, (*Oceanic, Royale, Atlantik, Majectic*) 800-327-7113

Princess Cruises, (*Star Princess*) 800-421-0522

Seascape, (*Scandinavian Sky, Scandinavian Sun*) 800-432-0900

Royal Caribbean Cruise Lines, (*Nordic Prince*) 800-327-6700

In the Bahamas, two steamship agencies that handle cruise bookings are:

R. H. Curry, 322-8681/7 (Nassau), Telex: 20-155
United Shipping, 322-1330/3 (Nassau), 352-9315 (Freeport), Telex: NS. 160

The Bahamas' close proximity to the United States makes it a popular destination for yachts. Sailors who don't have their own vessels can rent one from the numerous bareboat yacht charter companies on the Florida coast.

TRAVEL ESSENTIALS

VISAS AND PASSPORTS

United States citizens do not need a passport or visa to enter the country if their stay is limited to eight months or less. A birth certificate, naturalization card, voter registration card, military identification or driver's licence with photograph will do. However, carrying a passport definitely smooths the way through checkpoints, especially on re-entry into the United States. U.S. Immigration requires proof of U.S. citizenship such as an original or certified birth certificate (no photocopies). Voter cards and driver's licences are supporting documents, but not proof in themselves.

Citizens of Canada and the United Kingdom do not need passports for visits of up to three weeks. But passports are required for entry to, and departure from, the U.K. No visas are required from citizens of British Commonwealth countries.

Citizens of the following countries must have passports and visas to enter the Bahamas for any purpose: Dominican Republic (except in transit), Haiti, South Africa, Spain and all Communist countries. To check entry requirements, write to the Immigration Department, P.O. Box N-831, Nassau.

ON ARRIVAL

If you fly to the Bahamas, you'll be asked to fill out an immigration form on the plane. Save the duplicate. You will need it for departure. All travelers must have a return or continuing ticket upon entry.

If you sail to the Bahamas in a yacht or arrive in a private plane, you must clear with customs and immigration at an official port of entry. Boats must fly a yellow quarantine flag and only the captain is permitted ashore until the vessel has been cleared. The excellent *Yachtsman's Guide to the Bahamas*, published annually, lists ports of entry and procedures for boaters.

ON DEPARTURE

If you are flying from Nassau, arrive at the airport at least two hours before your flight is scheduled to leave. In contrast to the usually relaxed and efficient arrival process, long lines and cramped quarters for departure check-in can add a sour note to an otherwise perfect visit, if you are not prepared.

On leaving the Bahamas, you'll be required to pay a $7 departure tax. Children under three years old are exempt. You will also be asked to surrender the copy of the Immigration Card you filled out on arrival.

Visitors leaving Nassau and Freeport for most destinations in the United States clear U.S. Customs prior to departure. No further customs formalities are required on arrival in the U.S. Canadian and European passengers clear customs at their destinations.

CUSTOMS

In the Bahamas, customs officials have made it easy. Only an oral declaration is required. All bags are subject to inspection and cleared luggage receives a sticker.

Bahamian law allows visitors to bring in personal belongings, one quart of liquor, 50 cigars or 200 cigarettes, one quart (.9 liters) of wine and small gifts worth $100 or less. There are no restrictions on the amount of foreign currency you can bring in.

Prohibited items include firearms, unless you have a Bahamian gun licence, animals, unless you have a permit from the Ministry of Agriculture, Trade and Industry; and of course, marijuana or narcotics of any kind.

U.S. Customs regulations allow each returning resident to take home purchases totaling $400 without paying duty, provided the resident has been out of the country at least 48 hours and has not claimed the exemption within the past 30 days. Family members living in the same household can pool their exemptions. Only one customs declaration form per couple or family traveling together is required. If you think you might exceed the limit, consider mailing home some gifts. You can send an unlimited number of gifts worth up to $50 each, as long as one person doesn't receive more than $50 worth in one day. However, these gifts may not include cigars, cigarettes, liquor or perfume. For more information, call U.S. Customs at Nassau International Airport (327-7126), or write for the booklet, *Know Before You Go*, from the U.S. Customs Service, Washington D.C. 20229.

Returning residents of Canada who have been out of the country over 48 hours may bring back CAD $100 worth of merchandise without paying duty. The merchandise must accompany the resident, and the exemption, claimed in writing, may be taken no more than once per quarter. Canadians who have been abroad more than seven days may bring home duty-free goods worth up to $300 once each calendar year. These goods may be shipped separately, but must be declared when the traveler reaches Canada. Canadians are eligible to take *both* the $100 and $300 exemptions on separate trips, but the two cannot be combined. The $100 or $300 duty-free total may include up to 200 cigarettes, 50 cigars, 2 pounds (.8 kg) of tobacco for residents over 16, 40 ounces of wine or liquor, or 24 cans of beer, if you meet the legal age limits of the province where you arrive.

The total exemption for residents returning to the United Kingdom from outside the EEC is £32. This may include nine fluid ounces (225 grams) of toilet water, two fluid ounces of perfume (50 grams), and for persons over 17, 1/2 pound (250 grams) of tobacco, or 200 cigarettes, or 100 cigarillos or 50 cigars. If you live outside Europe, double the tobacco limits. Duty-free alcohol is a liter of spirits or two liters of sparkling wine, plus two liters of still table wine.

HEALTH

A yellow fever vaccination certificate is required from travelers over one year of age who arrive in the Bahamas from an infected area, or within seven days of leaving one of the following countries:

Africa: Burkina Faso, Gambia, Ghana, Nigeria, Sudan, Zaire
America: Bolivia, Brazil, Colombia, Peru

Few precautions are necessary for a trip to the Bahamas. Tap water in Nassau and Freeport is pure and tropical diseases were wiped out long ago. The biggest hazard may be the sun. At the beach, be sure to apply a strong sunscreen, avoid direct noonday rays, and build up exposure gradually – no matter what your skin color.

ADMISSION OF ANIMALS

No animals may be brought into the Bahamas without an Import Permit from the **Ministry of Agriculture, Trade and Industry** (Box N-3028, Nassau; 322-1277/9). To obtain a permit, you must apply in writing to the Ministry and pay a $10 processing fee. Dogs and cats require a Rabies Vaccination Certificate. A Veterinary Health Certificate must also be issued by a licenced vet within 24 hours of the time you leave for the Bahamas. A licenced Bahamian veterinarian must examine the dog or cat within 24 hours of its arrival.

RESERVATIONS

The Bahamas Reservation Service (800) 327-0787 will make reservations at hotels and inns throughout the Bahamas. In the slower summer season, advance reservations are not always necessary, though you may not get your first choice in accommodations. Staff at the Information Booths at Nassau and Freeport International airports will be glad to assist if you arrive without a reservation.

WHAT TO WEAR

Lightweight casual clothes are the most popular dress in the Bahamas. During the day, you will probably wear a swim suit, shorts or slacks. In the evening there are more occasions to dress up. In the winter peak season, dress is more formal. Long skirts, cocktail dresses, and dressy pantsuits are acceptable for women. A wrap or sweater may come in handy too, when winter ocean breezes push temperatures into the 50s(°F/10°C). In the summer, temperatures are higher, prices are lower, and dress is more casual. Fewer restaurants require men to wear jackets at that time of year, but it is still advisable to bring one. An umbrella comes in handy in summer for the brief, rainy season showers that sometimes fall in the afternoon.

Bathing suits are permitted only on the beach or around the pool. In town, skimpy clothing looks out of place.

MONEY MATTERS

Bahamian bills come in the same denominations as U.S. dollars. Coins come in 1, 5, 10, 15, 25 and 50-cent pieces. Special $1, $2, and $5 coins are less common. Collectors will want to take home the Bahamian dime with its scalloped edges and the 15-cent piece shaped like a square. The B$, or Bahamian dollar, is held equivalent to the U.S. dollar, and both currencies are accepted throughout the country. If you've brought currency other than US$, note that banks handle currency exchange in the Bahamas. All branches, including those at airports and ship terminals, operate only during regular banking hours: 9.30 a.m. to 3 p.m., Monday through Thursday, and 9.30 a.m. to 5 p.m., on Friday. Some hotels will change limited amounts of foreign currency at more convenient hours. But they also charge a high commission.

If you plan to visit the Family Islands, consider changing your money before you arrive. On some islands, banks are open only a few days a week and then only for a few hours.

Credit cards are accepted at most large stores, restaurants and resorts in Nassau and Freeport, but somewhat less often in the Family Islands. There you should come prepared to pay with cash or traveler's checks. The better known international brands of traveler's checks are accepted throughout the islands.

TIPPING

A 15 percent tip is standard but make sure you don't pay twice. Many resorts and restaurants automatically add it to the bill.

GETTING ACQUAINTED

GOVERNMENT AND ECONOMY

A British imperial outpost for over 300 years, the Bahamas became a sovereign state in 1973. The nation retains the British monarch as its official head of state, represented by the Governor General. But a bicameral parliament and a prime minister govern the country. The current prime minister, Sir Lynden O. Pindling, has been returned to office consistently since independence.

Bahamians enjoy one of the highest standards of living in the Americas. Tourism is the leading industry, providing close to two-thirds of the nation's revenue, and employing roughly three-quarters of the population. International banking is the second biggest industry. The country's economic and political stability, as well as its many tax breaks, attract foreign investment from all over the world.

GEOGRAPHY AND POPULATION

Over 700 islands make up the Bahamas. The archipelago begins 100 miles (180 km) off the eastern coast of Florida and stretches southeast for 500 miles (900 km) to the mouth of the Caribbean Sea. Just over 30 of the islands are inhabited and 20 are well developed for tourism.

New Providence, one of the smallest of the populated islands, claims 65 percent of the population, mainly in the capital city of Nassau. Grand Bahama, one of the larger islands, is home to another 15 percent of the population. Freeport is the largest city there. The remaining Bahamians are spread through the Family Islands, with the largest concentrations in Eleuthera, Andros, the Abacos and Long Island.

The population is made up of 85 percent Blacks, 12 percent Whites, and 3 percent Asians and Hispanics.

TIME ZONES

Like the eastern United States, clocks in the Bahamas are set to Eastern Standard Time, switching to Eastern Daylight Savings Time for the first Sunday in April to the last Sunday in October.

CLIMATE

Bahamian weather is mild year round, with only a 12 degree average difference between the warmest and coolest months. Winter (mid-December through mid-April) boasts average temperatures of 70-80°F (21-26°C). The sun shines nearly every day and there is very little rain. Summer stretches from mid-April to mid-December, and temperatures rise to about 80-90°F (26-32°C). Humidity also increases (the yearly average is 75-80%), and short tropical showers fall occasionally. Mid-summer visitors from the U.S. may well find Bahamian temperatures and refreshing breezes a relief from the heat at home.

Like its neighbors in the Caribbean and Southern U.S., the Bahamas lies in the hurricane zone. These powerful tropical storms can strike anytime from June to November, but August, September and October are high-risk months. But history shows that the storms strike land only once every nine years.

WEIGHTS AND MEASURES

The Bahamas uses non-metric weights and measures: ounces and pounds, quarts and gallons, inches and miles. Given below are some standard equivalents of metric units:

1 inch = 2.54 centimeters
1 foot = 0.305 meters
1 mile = 1.609 kilometers
1 square mile = 2.69 square kilometers
1 gallon = 3.785 liters
1 ounce = 28.35 grams
1 pound = 0.454 kilograms

ELECTRICITY

110 volts/60 cycle alternating current—the North American standard. You will need a transformer to use European appliances.

BUSINESS HOURS

Most businesses operate from 9 a.m. to 5 p.m., Monday through Friday, though some open and close up to an hour later. Banking hours in Nassau are 9.30 a.m. to 3 p.m., Monday through Thursday, 9.30 a.m. to 5 p.m. on Fridays.

Freeport banking hours are 9 a.m. to 1 p.m., Monday through Thursday; 9 a.m. to 1 p.m. and 3 p.m. to 5 p.m. on Fridays. Banks in the Family Islands are open fewer hours. Check with your innkeeper for further information.

HOLIDAYS

Holidays when businesses close are:

New Year's Day - January 1
Good Friday
Easter Monday
Whit Monday - eighth Monday after Easter
Labour Day - first Friday in June
Independence Day - July 10
Emancipation Day - first Monday in August
Discovery Day - October 12
Christmas Day - December 25
Boxing Day - December 26

FESTIVALS

Junkanoo is an African derived celebration creolized into the most spirited and lighthearted holiday in the Bahamas. In Nassau on Boxing Day and New Year's, Bahamians take to the streets in colorful crepe paper costumes and masks. Thousands parade along Bay Street in a dancelike motion called "rushin" to the beat of cowbells, goatskin drums and clackers. The Boxing Day parade begins at 4 a.m., and is the culmination of months of preparation.

Many Bahamians belong to Junkanoo groups sponsored by local businesses, pooling their talents to create the costumes. Amid secrecy and keen competition, groups choose the themes that their costumes will illustrate – for example, the Valley Boys' "Just Say No to Drugs", the Fox Hill Congos' "Bahamian History", or the 1989 winning Saxons' "Let the World Know the Bahamas is Our Pride and Joy". Lively scrap gangs join the parade with impromptu costumes, horns, bells and whistles. Some of the Bahamas' most prominent citizens are seen ringing in the New Year in a scrap gang.

The **Goombay Summer Festival** is simply a three-month long excuse to have a good time. Parades, cookouts and street fairs, performances by Nassau's famed police band, sports competitions and fashion shows are all part of the fun which lasts from June 1 to August 30.

There are also several neighborhood festivals: **Pond Hill Festival Week** (Easter Week), **Fox Hill Festival**, and **Over The Hill Festival Week**. During these special weeks of celebration there are concerts, storytelling, indigenous (rake and scrape) music, exhibitions of artifacts and photographs, and demonstrations in handicrafts such as cooking local specialities, sewing and plaiting.

In a somewhat different vein, the **National Arts Festival**, sponsored by the Ministry of Education, in the early spring, showcases talent in music, drama, and poetry. It is open to all school-aged children, with a section for adult entrants too.

RELIGIOUS SERVICES

Christian churches predominate in the Bahamas. There are also Ba'hai, Jewish, and Moslem congregations. Visitors are welcome at most religious services, but do dress appropriately. For a more personal introduction to religious services, join the Bahamas' People-to-People program (see "Orientation" below) which introduces visitors to Bahamians with similar interests.

COMMUNICATIONS

MEDIA

There are two national daily newspapers, appearing Monday through Saturday: the *Nassau Guardian* in the morning, *The Tribune* – usually critical of the incumbent government – in the afternoon. Readily available in Nassau and Freeport, their arrival in the Family Islands usually keeps pace with the slow moving mail boats. The *Freeport News* is a regional newspaper published Monday through Friday. Foreign papers including the *New York Times, Wall Street Journal, The Times*, and *Daily Telegraph,* are available at hotels and newsstands in Nassau and Freeport one day after publication.

An excellent Bahamian magazine, though not available on newsstands is *Goombay,* the in-flight monthly of Bahamasair. *Goombay* covers developments in tourism and the nation at large. The Island Shop, on Nassau's Bay Street, boasts the biggest selection of books by and about Bahamians. Newsstands in the larger cities and towns carry a large array of foreign magazines.

The country's three major radio stations, **ZNS 1**, **2** and **3**, and its only television station, **ZNS Channel 13**, are owned and operated by the government. They are financed, however, by advertising. Two talk shows – "Perspective", hosted by Ed Bethel on Monday nights, and "Reaction", with Debby Bartlett on Wednesdays – allow visiting viewers to sample Bahamian opinions on a range of issues.

Satellite dishes are the wave of the future in the Bahamas. Many Bahamians receive the full range of U.S. television programs via a backyard dish, even on the remotest of Family Islands.

POSTAL SERVICES

Only *Bahamian stamps* are valid for items mailed in the Bahamas. In Nassau and Freeport, Post Office hours are 8.30 a.m. to 5.50 p.m., Monday through Friday, and 8.30 a.m. to 12.30 p.m. on Saturday. Family Island post offices are open fewer hours. Check at your hotel or inn.

OVERSEAS AIRMAIL RATES TO:

Canada, the West Indies and the U.S.: 45 cents per half ounce;
South America, Europe and the U.K.: 50 cents per half ounce;
Asia, Africa, Australia, the Pacific and Indian Oceans: 60 cents per half ounce.
Postage for airmail postcards to all destinations is 40 cents.

Beautiful Bahamian stamps deserve more attention than a passing lick. The General Post Office on East Hill Street at the top of Parliament Hill in Nassau has a Philatelic Bureau (323-7814/5) that worth visiting.

Mail from the Family Islands moves slowly. Speed mail services for delivery to postal boxes and International High Speed Mail are available. For more information, call the main Post Office (322-3344).

TELEPHONE AND TELEX

In the Bahamas, the telecommunications system (**BaTelCo**, 323-4911) is a government enterprise, except on Grand Bahama, where the private Grand Bahama Telephone Company is in charge. Direct dialing is available to many of the islands from North America, Europe, the United Kingdom and Japan. Long distance calls from some Family Islands still require operator assistance.

The area code for the Bahamas is 809.

Calls from public pay phones cost 25 cents.

Fully automated telex service is available at the Centralised Telephone Office on East Street, Nassau International Airport, and in Freeport at BaTelCo's office on Pioneer Way, and the Freeport International Airport.

Telex and international facsimile (FAX) subscribers are listed in the Bahamas telephone directory.

EMERGENCIES

SECURITY AND CRIME

Don't be fooled by the laid-back atmosphere and seemingly crime-free streets of the Bahamas. Visitors to New Providence, Grand Bahama and Paradise Island should take some precautions they would in any other cosmopolitan area. Watch out for your wallet and don't leave valuables unattended in your room or at the beach. Avoid deserted streets after dark and keep car doors locked. A late evening stroll might be pleasant, but don't do it alone.

The Family Islands are generally very safe. Still, it's wise to look after your valuables wherever you go.

In New Providence and Freeport, you can get help by calling the **Fire and Police** emergency number, **919**.

MEDICAL SERVICES

A large number of physicians practise in Nassau and Freeport, where the major hospitals are located: **Princess Margaret Hospital** (322-2861) on Shirley Street and **Doctor's Hospital** (322-8411), Centreville and Shirley Street, Nassau; **Rand Memorial Hospital** (352-6735) East Atlantic Drive, Freeport. Call an **Ambulance** at **322-2221** (New Providence) or **352-2689** (Freeport).

If accident or illness strikes in the Family Islands, you'll probably be flown to Princess Margaret Hospital, or possibly Miami. Air Ambulance Associates (305-776-6800) and National Air Ambulance (305-525-5538 or 800-327-3710), based in Fort Lauderdale, Florida, offer emergency transportation in medically equipped aircraft to hospitals in the United States or the Bahamas. Less urgent problems can be taken care of at one of the 50 clinics which serve the Family Islands. In addition to the nurses, many have staff doctors and visiting dentists.

If an emergency occurs at sea, call Bahamas Air Sea Rescue Association – **BASRA**, tel. 322-3877, emergency frequencies VHF 16, single sideband 2182 kHz and AM2738 kHz – or the **Coast Guard** (2182 SB).

GETTING AROUND

ORIENTATION

Over three million people visit the Bahamas annually, making it one of the most popular island vacation spots. To help these travelers, **The Bahamas Ministry of Tourism** and its many branches provide an endless amount of information on accommodations, restaurants, sightseeing and other pastimes. For travelers interested in specialized sightseeing, the Ministry issues the Bahamahost roster, a list of tour guides who have passed a special training course.

Through its highly successful cultural exchange program, **People-to-People**, the Ministry can also arrange for you to meet socially with Bahamian citizens who share your interests or occupation. Ideally, to participate, you should return a simple form to the Ministry of Tourism (P.O. Box N-3701, Nassau) three weeks prior to your visit. Forms are available from the Ministry and its branches. But if you are already in the Bahamas, it's not necessarily too late; call or drop by one of the Information Booths, located at the airport and Rawson Square in Nassau or the International Bazaar in Freeport, for more information.

TOURIST OFFICES

Bahamas

Ministry of Tourism Headquarters, Market Plaza, Bay Street, Nassau
322-7500/1/2/3/4

Ministry of Tourism, Freeport
352-8044/5

Information Booths
Nassau International Airport, 327-6806/6782
Rawson Square, Bay Street, 326-9772/9781
Nassau/Paradise Island Promotion Board, Hotel House, West Bay Street, 322-8383/2/3/4
Freeport International Airport
Freeport Harbour Cruiseship Port
International Bazaar, West Sunrise Highway, 352-8044
Grand Bahama Promotion Board, International Bazaar, 352-7848

Canada

Montreal: 1225 Phillips Square, Montreal, Quebec H3B3G1,
(514) 861-6797
Toronto: 121 Bloor Street East, Suite 1101, Toronto, Ontario M4W3M5
(416) 968-2999

England

London: 10 Chesterfield Street, London, W1X8AH
(01) 629-5238

France

Paris: 9 Boulevard de la Madeleine, 75001 Paris
(1) 42-61-61-30

Japan

Tokyo: Togun Takanawa Bldg. Room 203, 20-3, Takanawa 4 Chome, Minato-ku, Tokyo Japan 108
03-447-6411

West Germany

Frankfurt am Main: 6000 Frankfurt am Main, Postrasse 2-4 (049) 069 25 20 29
41-41-3648

United States

Atlanta: 2957 Clairmont Road, Suite 150, Atlanta, Georgia 30345

(404) 633-1793

Boston: 1027 Statler Office Building, Boston, Massachusetts 02116

(617) 426-3144

Chicago: 875 North Michigan Avenue, Suite 1816, Chicago, Illinois 60611

(312) 787-8203

Dallas: World Trade Center, Suite 186, 2050 Stemmons Freeway, P.O. Box 581408, Dallas, Texas 75258-1408

(214) 742-1886

Detroit: 26400 Lahser Road, Suite 309, Southfield, Michigan 48034

(313) 357-2940

Houston: 5177 Richmond Avenue, Houston, Texas 77056

(713) 626-1566

Los Angeles: 3450 Wilshire Blvd., Suite 208, Los Angeles, California 90010

(213) 385-0033

Miami: 255 Alhambra Circle, Suite 425, Coral Gables, Florida 33134

(305) 442-4860

New York: 150 East 52nd Street, 28th Floor North, New York, New York 10022

(212) 758-2777

Charlotte: 1000 Independence Tower, 4801 East Independence Blvd., Charlotte, North Carolina 28212

(704) 532-1290

Philadelphia: Lafayette Building, 437 Chestnut Street, Suite 212 Philadelphia, Pennsylvania 19106

(215) 925-0871

San Francisco: 44 Montgomery Center, Suite 503, San Francisco, California 94104

(415) 398-5502

St. Louis: 555 N. New Ballas, Suite 310, St. Louis, Missouri 63141

(314) 569-7777

Washington D.C.: 1730 Rhode Island Avenue, N.W., Washington, D.C. 20036

(202) 659-9135

MAPS

In addition to high quality atlas and fold-up maps, small maps are included in most tourist literature. Not all brochure maps are entirely accurate. For example, some of the more stylised maps represent the manmade islands, Silver Cay (home of Coral World marine park) and Arawak Cay

as if they were floating free from each other and the north shore of New Providence. However, these cays are linked by road to each other and the larger island; both are accessible by car.

FROM THE AIRPORT

Unless your tour package includes airport transfers, you will probably take a taxi from the airport. On New Providence, fares run approximately $9 to Cable Beach, $15 to Nassau and $18 to Paradise Island. Count on around $6 to hotels in downtown Freeport. In the Family Islands, distances between airports and accommodations vary, and taxi fares in between can be quite expensive. It's wise to check on transportation to and from the airport when making hotel reservations.

WATER TRANSPORTATION

For spectacular scenery and some local color, try traveling between Nassau and the Family Islands by mailboat. In addition to the mail, cargo on these battered diesel-powered boats often include cases of rum, mattresses, oil drums and provisions. All the boats are a far cry from any luxury liner– you share the same food and shelter as the crew–but some do boast comfortable, basic accommodations and good Bahamian cooking. They also give visitors a chance to get to know Family Islanders who are on their way home from the city. When boarding, note the location of the life rafts. More than one of these boats has run into trouble in a storm.

A number of boats leave Nassau on Tuesday, returning later in the week; the days for weekly departure and return depend on the destination. Trips can take anywhere from four hours to all day, also depending on destination. One-way fares average about $30. First class passengers get a bunk bed and (usually) clean sheets; second class passengers sit on the deck.

The Ministry of Tourism provides information about rates and travel times, but for the most current information, inquire personally at the harbormaster's office at Potter's Cay Dock, next to the bridge to Paradise Island.

DOMESTIC AIR TRAVEL

Bahamasair, the national airline, flies to 19 destinations around the country, and offers package rates for stays of three nights or more in the Family Islands. Daily service runs from Nassau to Great Abaco, Andros, Eleuthera and Exuma. There are flights two or three times a week to the less populated islands. British Hawker-Sidley twin engine planes are used for domestic trips. Since almost all flights to the Family Islands originate in Nassau, would-be island hoppers must generally fly back to the capital before soaring on to the next destination. Although these prop planes do come under criticism for delays and changed schedules, Bahamasair is the most economical way to travel between Nassau and the Family Islands.

Another option is Chalk International Airline's seaplanes, flying between Miami, Paradise Island and Bimini and, by charter only, to Cat Cay. An excellent safety record and meticulous adherence to schedules make Chalk's the first choice of many. Chalk's also flies to Fort Lauderdale.

A bit more costly, but more convenient for island hopping, are the charter services operating from Nassau and Freeport. Round trip fees fall in the $500 to $700 range for a plane seating four to six persons.

Some hotels in the Family Islands fly guests to and from Nassau. Check with your hotel for prices and details on this service.

Bahamasair Reservations

United States, (800) 722-4262
Nassau, 327-8511
Freeport, 352-8341
Eleuthera, 332-2196

Chalk's International Airlines

Miami, (305) 871-1192/84
Broward County, (305) 947-1308
United States (except Florida), (800) 327-2521
Florida Toll Free, (800) 432-8807
Nassau, 363-2845/6
Bimini, 347-2024

Nassau Charters

Bahamasair Charter Service, 327-8223
Condorair, 327-6625
Trans Island Airways, 327-8329
Pinder's Charter Service, 327-7320
Reliable Air Service, 327-7335/6

Freeport Charters

Helda Charters, 352-8832
Lucaya Air Service, 352-8885

PUBLIC TRANSPORTATION

Taxis: In the Bahamas, taxi rates are set by the government. The first one-fourth mile costs $2 and each additional quarter mile, 30 cents. Beyond two passengers, there is an additional $2 charge for each extra rider. Most taxis have meters – though the meter may not be readily visible from the passenger seat. Unfortunately, a few drivers take advantage of this, so ask the fare before setting out, and look at the meter before paying. Taxis can also be hired on an hourly basis for sightseeing. Rates range from $12 to $20, depending on the size of the vehicle. There is an additional charge for waiting.

On the Family Islands, taxi tours are a good way to sightsee, and can be arranged by your inn or resort. Usually several drivers are on hand at the airport when flights arrive.

Bus: Also known as the *jitney*, in New Providence privately owned buses serve tourist and residential areas. The fare ranges from 50 to 75 cents. In Freeport, regular bus service is available, and a special red, double decker bus makes stops at all hotels and sightseeing attractions. On Paradise Island, buses circle the island every 20 to 30 minutes.

PRIVATE TRANSPORTATION

Car Rentals: Nassau, Freeport and Paradise Island are served by the major car rental companies such as Hertz, Avis, National and others. Typical rates (subject to change, of course) run from about $60 to $70 per day, depending on the model, and $350 to $415 weekly. On the Family Islands, smaller concerns – sometimes the local filling station or an individual with an extra car – handle rentals. Some Family Island hotels also rent cars to guests.

Motor Scooters rent for about $35 for a full day, $20 for a half day, plus $5 insurance and a deposit. Bicycles rent for $10 per day, plus a $10 deposit.

Caution: Whatever you drive, remember: **drive on the left**.

WHERE TO STAY

Accommodations in the Bahamas range in size from intimate inns and seaside cottages to huge resort and casino complexes; in locale, from Nassau's cosmopolitan atmosphere to the most secluded corners of the Family Islands. Accommodations orient to particular kinds of activities. Relaxation on the beach is the mainstay of most hotels. But if you favor scuba diving, golf or game fishing, you may prefer one of the specialty hostelries scattered through the islands.

On the whole, the Bahamas is not an inexpensive destination. But prices are lower during Goombay Summer and the autumn Discovery Season from September through November. Moderate prices begin at about $65 per night for a single room and run up to roughly $90; inexpensive rates are slightly lower, and there is no shortage of first class accommodations at the other end of the scale.

NASSAU AND CABLE BEACH

Best Western British Colonial Beach Resort, Bay and Marlborough streets, 322-3301, for room reservations only, 322-3311. Expensive.

Carnival's Crystal Palace Resort and Casino, P.O. Box N-8306, Cable Beach, 327-6200, U.S. and Canada 800-722-2248. Luxury.

Casuarinas, P.O. Box N-4016, Cable Beach, 327-7921/2. Moderate.

Coral World Hotel, Silver Cay, P. O. Box N-7797, Nassau, 328-1036. Expensive.

Divi Bahamas Beach Resort and Country Club, South Ocean Village, P.O. Box N-8191, 326-4391/2/3/4. Expensive.

Dolphin Hotel, West Bay Street, P.O. Box N-3236, 322-8666. Moderate.

Grand Central Hotel, Charlotte Street, P.O. Box N-4084, Nassau, 322-8356/7/8. Moderate.

Graycliff Hotel, West Hill Street, P.O. Box N-10246, Nassau, 322-2796. Expensive.

Le Meridien Royal Bahamian Hotel, P.O. Box 10422, Cable Beach, 327-6400. Expensive.

Lighthouse Beach Hotel, West Bay Street, P.O. Box N-195, Nassau, 322-4474. Moderate.

Nassau Beach Hotel, P.O. Box N-7756, Cable Beach, 327-7711. Expensive.

Ocean Spray Hotel, West Bay Street, P.O. Box N-3035, Nassau, 322-8032. Inexpensive.

Wyndham Ambassador Beach Hotel, P.O. Box N-3026, Cable Beach, 327-8231. Expensive.

PARADISE ISLAND

Harbour Cove Inn, P.O. Box SS-6249, 363-2561. Expensive.

Ocean Club, P.O. Box N-4777, Nassau, 363-2501. Expensive.

Paradise Island Resort and Casino, P.O. Box SS-6333, 363-2000/3000. Expensive.

The Sheraton Grand Hotel, P.O. Box SS-6307, 363-2998.

GRAND BAHAMA

Atlantik Beach Hotel, Royal Palm Way, P.O. Box F-531, Freeport, 373-1444. Moderate.

Bahamas Princess Resort and Casino, The Mall at Sunrise, Freeport, 352-6721, U.S. and Canada 800-223-1818. Expensive.

Castaways Resort, The Mall, P.O. Box F-2629, Freeport, 352-6682. Inexpensive.

Holiday Inn Lucaya Beach Resort, Royal Palm Way, P.O. Box F-2496, Lucaya, 373-1333. Expensive.

Lucayan Beach Resort and Casino, Royal Palm Way, Lucaya, 373-7777, U.S. and Canada 800-772-1227. Expensive.

Lucayan Marina Hotel, Midshipman

Road, P. O. Box 2505, Lucaya, 373-8888, U.S. and Canada 800-772-1227. Moderate.

The Windward Palms Hotel, The Mall, P.O. Box F-2549, Freeport, 352-6782. Moderate.

Xanadu Beach and Marina Resort, Sunken Treasure Drive, Freeport, 352-6782, U.S. and Canada 800-222-3788. Luxury.

THE ABACOS

Abaco Inn, Hope Town, 367-2666. Moderate.

Elbow Cay Beach Inn, Hope Town, 367-2748. Moderate.

Hope Town Harbour Lodge, Hope Town, 367-2277, U.S. and Canada 800-626-5690. Moderate.

Conch Inn, Marsh Harbour, 367-2800. Moderate.

Great Abaco Beach Hotel, Marsh Harbour, 367-2207. Expensive.

Treasure Cay Beach Hotel and Villas, Treasure Cay, 367-2847. Luxury.

Green Turtle Club, Green Turtle Cay, 367-2572. Expensive.

ANDROS

Las Palmas, Driggs Hill, 329-4661. Moderate.

Andros Beach Hotel and Scuba Club, Nicholl's Town, 329-2552. Moderate.

Conch Sound Beach Resort, Conch Sound, 329-2341. Expensive.

Chickcharnie Hotel, Fresh Creek, 3368-2025. Inexpensive.

Small Hope Bay Lodge, c/o P.O. Box 21667, Fort Lauderdale, Florida, 305-463-9130 or 800-223-6961. Luxury.

Nottages Cottages Resort and Fishing Camp, Fresh Creek, 329-4293

BERRY ISLANDS

Chub Cay Club, P.O. Box 661067, Miami Springs, Florida 33266, 305-445-7830. Moderate.

BIMINI

Bimini Blue Water, Ltd., P.O. Box 627, Alice Town, 347-2166. Moderate.

Sea Crest Hotel, P.O. Box 654, Alice Town, 347-2071. Moderate.

Bimini Big Game Fishing Club, P.O. Box 699, Alice Town, 347-23391/3. Expensive.

Brown's Hotel, P.O. Box 601, Alice Town, 347-2227. Inexpensive.

Compleat Angler Hotel, P.O. Box 601, Alice Town, 347-2122. Moderate.

CAT ISLAND

Bridge Inn, New Bight, 354-5013. Moderate.

Fernandez Bay Village, P.O. Box 2126, Fort Lauderdale, Florida 33303, 305-764-6945. Moderate.

The Hawksnest Club and Marina, c/o 847 N. Andrews Street, Fort Lauderdale, Florida 33311, 305-523-2406.

CROOKED ISLAND

Pittstown Point Landings, Landrall Point, 336-2507. Rates on request.

Crooked Island Beach Inn, Colonial Hill, 336-2096. Inexpensive.

ELEUTHERA

Pineapple Cove Club, Gregory Town, 332-0142. Expensive.

Coral Sands Hotel, Harbour Island, 333-2350. Expensive.

Ramora Bay Club, Harbour Island, 333-2324, Fort Lauderdale, Florida 305-760-4535, U.S. and Canada 800-327-8286. Moderate to expensive.

Valentine's Yacht Club and Inn, Harbour Island, 333-2080. Moderate to expensive.

Spanish Wells Beach Resorts, Spanish Wells, 333-4371. Moderate.

Spanish Wells Yacht Haven, Spanish Wells, 333-4328. Moderate.

Cotton Bay Beach and Golf Resort, Rock Sound, 334-2101/3, U.S. and Canada 800-223-1588. Luxury.

Edwina's Place, Rock Sound, 334-2094. Moderate.

Ethel's Cottages, Rock Sound, 334-4233. Inexpensive.

Windermere Island Club, Windermere Island, 332-2538, New York 212-839-2538. Luxury.

Winding Bay Beach Resort, Rock Sound, 334-2020, U.S. and Canada 800-223-1588. Luxury.

EXUMA

Hotel Peace and Plenty, George Town, 336-2551/2 or call in U.S. and Canada 800-327-0787, Miami 443-3821. Moderate.

Hotel Pieces of Eight, George Town, 336-2600. Moderate.

Two Turtles Inn, George Town, 336-2545. Inexpensive.

Out Island Inn Village, P.O. Box 49, 336-2171. Expensive.

INAGUA

Ford's Inagua Inn, Matthew Town, Phone: Matthew Town 277. Inexpensive.

Main House, Matthew Town, Phone: Matthew Town 267. Inexpensive.

LONG ISLAND

Stella Maris Inn, P.O. Box SM-105, 336-2106, Florida 305-467-0466. Moderate.

Thompson Bay Inn, P.O. Box 30123, Phone: Stella Maris Operator. Inexpensive.

SAN SALVADOR

Riding Rock Inn, San Salvador, 332-2631. Moderate.

Ocean View Villas, Cockburn Town; call Cockburn Town operator. Inexpensive.

The **Bahamas Reservation Service** (9 a.m. to 5 p.m., U.S. and Canada 800-327-0787, Miami 443-3821) will help you make arrangements. This is especially recommended for travelers to the Family Islands where mail is slow and telephone service occasionally spotty.

The Bahamas also has a good selection of rental villas, apartments, and self-catering flats: an alternative for groups, families, business travelers and visitors planning longer stays. A few sources are:

Bahamas Home Rentals, 230 Lawrence Avenue, Pittsburgh, Pennsylvania, U.S.A. 15238, 412-828-1048

Bay View Village, P.O. Box SS-6308, Paradise Island, 363-2555

Cable Beach Manor, P. O. Box N-8333, Cable Beach, 327-7785

Dillet's Guest House and Apartments, P. O. Box N-204, Nassau, 327-7743, 325-1133

Henrea Carlette Apartment Hotel, P. O. Box N-4227, Cable Beach, 327-7801

The Orchard Apartment Hotel, Village Road P.O. Box N-1514, Nassau, 393-1297 or 393-1306.

Camping is not permitted in the Bahamas.

FOOD DIGEST

If you are staying in Nassau or Freeport, the cuisine of the Bahamas may at first seem largely American spiced with a touch of the tropics. Most hotels and resorts serve a variety of continental food, and many have thematic restaurants specializing in Italian, Chinese and French cuisine. But the real delight is Bahamian home-cooking. Goombay Summer visitors to Nassau can begin a tasting tour when locals stir up their favorite dishes in booths along Bay Street on Wednesday evenings. Throughout the islands there are restaurants and take-out stands serving Bahamian specialities. Usually these are family businesses with ingredients bought fresh at local markets.

Traditional Bahamian fare is tasty, sometimes spicy and filling. Seafood favorites include turtle steaks, crawfish, the delicious clawless Bahamian lobster, grouper– a tender white fish, and conch (pronounced conk), – a shellfish that is reputedly an aphrodisiac. Conch salad, conch chowder, and cracked conch, which is strips of conch meat deep fried, are all popular. Bahamian chefs also have a flair with curried chicken and mutton. Souse, slow boiled and spiced pig's head, feet, or sheep's tongue, is traditionally served with hot johnny cake, which is rather like light, sweet cornbread. The ubiquitous side dish is peas and rice; the "peas" are pigeon peas, not green ones, that look and taste a lot like lentils. For a delicious dessert, ask for guava duff.

NASSAU

Albrion's, at Casuarinas in Cable Beach, 327-7921. Bahamian specialties. Breakfast, lunch and dinner is served. Dinner reservations suggested.

Buena Vista, Delancy Street, 322-2811. Continental. Dinner from 7 p.m. Reservations advised.

Coco's Cafe, West Bay Street, 323-8778. Breakfast plus seafood, pasta, burgers. Hours: 7.30 a.m. to 11 p.m.

Da Vinci, Bay Street just west of British Colonial Hotel, 322-2748. Italian and French. Dinner served from 7 p.m. to 11 p.m. Reservations preferred.

Del Prado, Bay Street, 325-0324 or 325-1121. French and Continental. Dinner 6 p.m. to 11 p.m. Reservations suggested.

Graycliff, West Hill Street, 322-2796. Continental. Dinner 7 p.m. to 10.30 p.m. Reservations requested.

Ivory Coast Seafood and Steak Restaurant, top floor of the **Harbour Club**, East Bay Street, 393-3771 or 395-5393. Open until 11 p.m.

Lum's, Bay Street, 322-3119. Hot dogs steamed in beer and other specialties.

The New Bahamian Kitchen, one block off Bay Street at the corner of Market Street and Trinity Place, 325-0702. Bahamian cooking, peas and rice, turtle steak and conch. Open 8 a.m. to midnight.

Peanuts Taylor's Drumbeat Supper Club, West Bay Street, 322-4233. Seafood, steaks and two All Bahamian Revue shows nightly. Seaside Cafe opens 11 a.m. to 2 a.m., dinner served from 7 p.m. Reservations suggested.

Prince George Cafe, upstairs at Prince George Plaza on Bay Street, 322-5854. Bahamian breakfasts, salads, sandwiches, gyros. Open 8 a.m. to 6 p.m.

Roselawn Cafe, Bank Lane, off Bay Street, 325-1018. Italian and Continental. 11.30 a.m. to 2.30 p.m., 6.30 p.m. to 10 p.m., specialties from 10 p.m. onward. Dinner reservations suggested.

Swank's Pizza, three locations: Paradise Island Shopping Center, 363-2765/3152; Cable Beach Shopping Center, 327-8749/7495; corner of Village and Bernard roads, 393-4000/1. Delivery service.

Tony Roma's A Place for Ribs, two locations: West Bay Street across from Saunders Beach, 325-2020/6502; East Bay Street across from Paradise Island Bridge, 323-2077/393-1956.

CABLE BEACH

Carnival's Cable Beach Riviera Tower, 327-6000. Restaurants include: **The King Conch Cafe**, tropical casual; **Pirates Inn**, all-you-can-eat buffet; **Regency Room**, French; **The Riviera**, Continental.

Carnival's Crystal Palace Resort and Casino, 327-6200. Restaurants are: **Sole Mare**, Italian; **Oriental Palace**, Chinese; **Le Grille**, steaks.

Frilsham House, next door to Nassau Beach Hotel, 327-7639. French. Dinner seatings every half hour from 6.30 p.m. to 9.30 p.m. Reservations.

Kentucky Fried Chicken, Cable Beach Shopping Center, 327-7495 or 327-8749. Open daily from 10 a.m. to 11.45 p.m.

PARADISE ISLAND

Calypso Cruises, left after crossing bridge, 363-3577. Lunchtime and dinner cruises. Reservations taken between 9 a.m. and 5 p.m.

Paradise Island Resort and Casino, 363-3000. Restaurants include **Bahamian Club**, Continental and American; **The Boathouse**, steaks and prime rib; **Cafe Martinique**, gourmet; **The Coyaba**, Polynesian and Chinese; **Seagrapes**, Bahamian and American buffet; **Villa d'Este**, Italian.

Paradise Pavilion, Paradise Hotel, 363-2541. Steaks, ribs, seafood. Breakfast 8 to 10.30 a.m., lunch 11 a.m. to 5 p.m., dinner served from 6 p.m.

The Rotisserie, Sheraton Grand Hotel, 363-2011. Specialties include grilled beef, fresh game, seafood and poultry. Dinner 6.30 p.m. to 10 p.m.

GRAND BAHAMA

The Crown, Princess Casino, Freeport, 352-7811. International gourmet dining.

Ruby Swiss Restaurant, West Sunrise Highway, Freeport, 352-8507. Gourmet breakfast, lunch and dinner; Swiss specialties.

Island Lobster House, on the Mall, Freeport, 352-9429. Live music and stuffed lobster.

Guanahani's, at the Princess Country Club, Freeport, 356-6721. Inclusive prix-fixe international menu.

Mai Tai, Princess Emerald Golf Course, Freeport, 352-7637. Szechuan and Polynesian specialties.

Cafe Michel, International Bazaar, Freeport, 352-2191. French.

Cafe Valencia, International Bazaar, Freeport, 352-9521. Ribs, lamb and seafood specialties.

Les Oursins, Lucayan Beach Hotel, Lucaya, 373-7777. Continental. Dinner only.

The Stoned Crab, Taino Beach, Lucaya, 373-1442. Fresh seafood and steaks.

Lucayan Lobster and Steak House, Midshipman Road, Lucaya, 373-5101.

Buccaneer Club, Deadman's Reef, Eight Mile Rock, 348-3794. Bahamian and Continental. Open from December through April.

Freddie's, Hunter's just outside Freeport, 352-3250. Bahamian specialties.

THE ABACOS

Conch Inn Restaurant, Marsh Harbor, 367-2800. Seafood.

Great Abaco Beach Hotel, Marsh Harbor, 367-2158. Seafood and Continental.

Abaco Inn, Elbow Cay, 366-0133. Seafood.

Betty & Alphonso's Sea View Restaurant and Bar, Green Turtle Cay, 365-4111. Seafood.

Green Turtle Yacht Club, Green Turtle Cay, 367-2572. American and Bahamian.

ANDROS

Chickcharnie Hotel, Fresh Creek, 368-2025/6. Seafood.

Small Hope Bay Lodge, Andros Town, 328-2014. Seafood and American beef.

BIMINI

Anchorage Restaurant and Bar, Alice Town, 347-2166. Seafood.

Bimini Big Game Fishing Club, 347-2391. Seafood.

Red Lion Pub, North Bimini, 347-2259.

ELEUTHERA

Cotton Bay Club, Rock Sound, 334-2101. Seafood and steaks.

Winding Bay Club, Rock Sound, 334-2020. Seafood and American fare.

Edwina's Place, Rock Sound, 334-2094. Seafood.

Ramora Bay Club, Harbour Island, 333-2324. Bahamian food with a French touch.

EXUMA

Kermit's Lounge, George Town Airport, 336-2002.

Peace and Plenty, George Town, 336-2551. Seafood.

Hotel Pieces of Eight, George Town, 336-2600. Seafood.

LONG ISLAND

Stella Maris Inn, 336-2106. Bahamian, Continental and American.

Thompson Bay Inn, Salt Pond; call Stella Maris operator. Bahamian.

DRINKING NOTES

The Bahamas have contributed their share to the world's exotic cocktails with specialties like the *Bahama Mama*: rum, orange juice and crème de cacao; and the *Goombay Smash*: coconut rum, Galliano, pineapple juice, sugar and a dash of lemon. You'll also find plenty of tropical classics like *Banana Daiquiris, Pinã Coladas and Planter's Punch*.

Drink prices in restaurants and bars run high because of the duty on all imported liquor. But in liquor stores imported liquor can be a bargain. The best buy, of course, is rum distilled in the Bahamas, including all Bacardi products, coconut rum from Grand Bahama and Eleuthera's pineapple rum.

There are also international and local soft

drinks in abundance. *Goombay Punch* is a super-sweet soda with a hint of pineapple; *Malta* and *Mauby* have a bittersweet treacle taste. Finally, there's water. It is faintly salty tasting throughout the Bahamas, so you may prefer the bottled water sold in most restaurants and grocery stores.

The legal drinking age in the Bahamas is 18 years.

THINGS TO DO

With sun and sea as common denominators, each island in the Bahamas has its own set of possibilities. Away from the cities in the Family Islands sightseeing is more or less built into the landscape, both natural and manmade. In town activities tend to be more structured.

COUNTRY

The Bahamas are home to a number of exotic birds, plants and rare animal species. Often these require a good bit of persistence and luck to view first hand. Once found throughout the islands, iguanas still inhabit secluded islands and cays. Living separately on their islands, they have evolved dozens of forms, including iguanas on Andros that grow to be over five feet (1.5 meters) long. The hutia may be Bahamas' only unique mammal. Once widespread, it can now be seen only on East Plana Cay. The most spectacular of the Bahamas' birds is the flamingo, whose nesting ground is protected in Inagua National Park.

Funded entirely by private donations and memberships, **The Bahamas National Trust** administers many sites designated for the protection of wildlife. These include **Black Sound Cay Park**, **Exuma Cays Land and Sea Park**, **Inagua National Park**, **Pelican Cays Land and Sea Park**, **Peterson Cay Park**, **Conception Island**

Park and **Lucayan National Park**. Park wardens protect land and sea life in the parks, and provide information. For more information on visiting the parks, write to the Trust (P.O. Box N-4105, Nassau, The Bahamas) or call 809-393-1317.

CITY

Some attractions in the Nassau and Freeport areas are:

NASSAU

Ardastra Gardens and Zoo, Chippingham Road off West Bay Street. Tropical plants, animals and the marching flamingoes; 323-5806.

Botanic Gardens, Chippingham Road off West Bay Street; 323-5975.

Calypso Getaway Cruise, left side of Paradise Island Bridge. Sail to an island lagoon with water sports and dining; 363-3577. Reservations.

Coral World, Silver Cay off West Bay Street. Marine observatory, aquarium, restaurant, snack bar and shops; 328-1036.

Hartley's Undersea Walk, Nassau Yacht Haven, East Bay Street. Cruise on a boat culminates in a walk on the sea floor; 393-8234 or 393-7569. Reservations required.

Nautilus, Deveaux Street Dock. Glassbottom boat; 325-2871 or 325-2876. Reservations requested.

The Retreat, Village Road. Headquarters of the Bahamas National Trust with an 11-acre tropical garden; 323-1317 or 323-2848.

FREEPORT

Garden of the Groves. Botanical garden with many rare species, plus a small museum of Bahamian history; 373-2422. Closed Wednesday.

Mermaid Kitty, Port Lucaya. Glass bottom boat to reefs and sea gardens; 373-5880/5891/5892.

Rand Memorial Nature Center, Settler's Way East. Trails and guided tours through a 100-acre (40-hectare) park; 352-5438. Closed Saturday.

SIGHTSEEING TOURS

In Nassau and Freeport, there are dozens of bus tours of historic sites, tropical gardens and nature areas, shopping districts and the nightclub circuit. Most large hotels have a tour desk, or you can call one of the agencies below. Fares range from about $12 to $45 for a tour including nightspots. If you'd rather walk, take advantage of the free **Goombay Guided Walking Tours** offered all year round. Walks begin at the Rawson Square Information Booth in Nassau.

Some tour companies are:

NASSAU

Happy Tours, 323-5818
Playtours, 322-2931
Majestic Tours, 322-2606
Bahamas Taxi Unions, 323-4555

FREEPORT

Executive Tours, 352-8858
Grand Bahama Tours Ltd., 352-7234
Greenline Tours, 352-3465
Sun Island Tours, 352-4811

CULTURE PLUS

THEATRE, DANCE AND MUSIC

The lively arts are thriving in the Bahamas with its fertile mixture of international and regional culture. Check newspaper entertainment sections, especially during the winter, when the benefit and concert season is in full swing. The recently refurbished **Dundas Centre for the Performing Arts** on Mackey Street is the venue for many performances in Nassau; call 322-2728 for information. In Freeport, the **Regency Theatre** (352-5535) is a hub of artistic activity, and the group, Friends of the Arts, sponsors

guest performers from abroad. The Nassau Players, Bahamas School of Theatre, Grand Bahama Players, the Dundas Repertory Company and Freeport Players Guild are a few of the better known theatrical groups. James Catalyn and Friends is an excellent professional company which regularly performs in Bahamian dialect, a recently revived art form. Amateur dance groups include the New Breed Dancers, Nassau Civic Ballet and National School of Dance. Popular local choral ensembles include the Diocesan Chorale, Lucayan Chorale, Chamber Singers and Nassau Operatic Society.

ART

Art Exhibitions are also hosted by various galleries including the Temple, Marlborough Antiques, Nassan Glass, Lyford Gallery and are displayed in the foyer of the Main Post Office. The Archive Department holds an annual exhibit at the Post Office during February.

CINEMAS

Bahamian cinemas show mostly American-made movies, but video players are the main form of movie consumption. Film buffs will be interested to know that the Bahamas has been the set for many feature films, including the James Bond thrillers *Never Say Never Again* and *Thunderball*. More recently, *Jaws the Revenge*, *Cocoon II*, *Shoot to Kill*, *The Abyss*, *Blood Relations* and *Deadly Spy Games* have all had their share of Bahamian scenery.

NIGHTLIFE

Casinos, bars and nightclubs line the shores of Nassau, Paradise Island and Freeport, and some stay open all night. In Nassau, popular attractions include Las Vegas style revues at the **Palace Dinner**

Theatre in Carnival's Crystal Palace Resort and Casino and **Le Cabaret Theatre** in the Paradise Island Resort and Casino. Both clubs present singers, comedians, magicians, acrobats and animal acts. Another hit is the so-called "native shows" featuring local Bahamian talent and some very un-Bahamian acts like fire-eating. To see a master bongo drummer and native revue, visit Peanuts Taylor's Drum Beat Club on West Bay Street. Paradise Island Resort and Casino's **Tradewinds Calypso Show Lounge** has a musical revue, limbo and fire dancers, and a Wednesday night Junkanoo Festival (by advance ticket purchase only).

For dancing, try **Pastiche Disco** in the Paradise Island Casino; **Le Paon**, also on Paradise Island at the Sheraton Grand Hotel; on Cable Beach in the **Out Island Bar** at the Nassau Beach Hotel; and the **Junkanoo Lounge** at Carnival's Crystal Palace. Then there are the casinos themselves: vast, sparkling and seductive on Cable Beach and Paradise Island.

In Freeport, the main attraction is the **Princess Casino**, a huge Moorish palace, with an extravagant French cancan revue at the **Casino Royale Theatre**. In nearby Lucaya, the scene of much recent development, the Lucayan Beach Hotel and Casino's **Flamingo Showcase Theatre** presents a Las Vegas style spectacular and big-name 50s and 60s musical groups in its "Little Darlin" Rock n' Roll Review. Freeport/Lucaya also has its share of native shows: The Holiday Inn's **Bahamian Showcase** on Monday, Wednesday and Saturday, and **The Yellow Bird Show Club** at the Castaways Resort, are two of the better ones. For dancing, there are the **Sultan's Tent Disco** at the Bahamas Princess Tower and **New Electric City Disco** on East Atlantic Drive.

Nightlife on the Family Islands is decidedly tamer: a quiet drink at the hotel bar or perhaps some after dinner dancing on the terrace. If you want more action, ask where the locals go.

SHOPPING

With no sales tax and low tariffs, the Bahamas can be a bargain hunter's delight. Merchants can afford to sell imported goods at prices 20 to 50 percent lower than those in the United States, but not all pass along the savings. Compare the prices of goods at home before you go.

Bay Street in Nassau offers the biggest and best selection of shops. For fine china, crystal and figurines, visit **Treasure Traders**, **Little Switzerland** and **Bernards**. The **Nassau Shop** carries Irish linens and jewelry, with a good bookstore upstairs. The largest selection of French perfumes are at **Lighbourne's**, the **Perfume Shop** and the **Perfume Bar**. Several stores, like **Greenfire Emeralds**, feature fine gems. Look for handcrafted conch and coral jewelry, at the **Treasure Box** and **Johnson Brothers**. For Bahamian batik fashions, visit **Mademoiselle**, especially the **Androsia Boutique**. Finally, there is the open-air straw market selling handwoven goods. Bargain here, but not at other Bay Street establishments.

On Paradise Island, **Bird Cage Walk** is the place to shop. But many of the stores are smaller than the Nassau stores, with similar stock. This is true of the Cable Beach hotel shops as well.

In the Freeport area, the **International Bazaar** and **Port Lucaya Marketplace** dominate the shopping scene. The Bazaar is a 10-acre (four-hectare) arcade. Over 70 shops carry tourist items from about 25 countries, as well as crystal, porcelain and antiques. Several Nassau stores also have branches here. A showcase for Bahamian entrepeneurs, Port Lucaya Marketplace is newer, with a mixture of small thematic shops and entertainment reminiscent of Boston's Faneuil Hall.

In the Family Islands you can find gifts at roadside stands throughout the islands selling straw goods.

SPORTS

The key fact to remember about sports in the Bahamas is the toll free phone number of the **Bahamas Sports Information Center**, (800) 32-SPORT. They offer guidance and a useful calendar of events.

SPECTATOR

Baseball may be the most popular team sport among Bahamians. But cricket and rugby also have loyal followings. On New Providence, the Queen Elizabeth Sports Center (323-5163) is the major complex, with a stadium and track and field arena. In January, auto racing fans gravitate to the Grand Bahama Vintage Grand Prix. April and May is the season for fly-ins, air shows and aviation races. Sailing regattas checker the calendar from January through October in the waters off Exuma, New Providence, Long Island, Cat Island, the Abacos and Eleuthera. And throughout the year, runners take to the streets in numerous road races and triathalons. At this point the lines between spectator and participant sports begin to blur; a visitor can be running in the track for one event and cheering on the sidelines for another.

PARTICIPANT

Not surprisingly, watersports opportunities abound. The larger hotels offer wind surfing and snorkeling. Many islands have a fleet of charter boats for deep sea fishing, and bareboat yacht rental facilities. Dive operations are everywhere. Despite the pre-eminence of water sports, golf and tennis buffs and even equestrians will find plenty to do in the Bahamas.

Sailors can consult the current edition of the *Yachtman's Guide to the Bahamas* for an up-to-date review of marinas and suppliers.

Some **golf and country clubs** are:

Ambassador Beach Golf Club, Cable Beach, 327-8231
Bahamas Princess Country Club, Freeport, 352-6721
Cotton Bay Beach and Golf Resort, Eleuthera, 334-6161
Divi Bahamas Beach Resort and Country Club, New Providence, 362-4391
Lucayan Golf and Country Club, Grand Bahama, 373-1066
Paradise Island Golf Club, Paradise Island, 363-3925
Treasure Cay Golf Club, Abaco, 367-2570

Some **dive operations** are:

NEW PROVIDENCE

Bahama Divers Ltd., 326-5644
Coral Harbour Divers, 326-4171, 800-241-6573
New Providence Divers, Ltd., 326-4391, ext 269, 414-251-8283
Dive Dive Dive, 362-1401
Smuggler's Rest Resort, 326-1143
Sun Divers, Ltd., 322-3301

GRAND BAHAMA

Deep Water Cay Club, 305-684-3958
Underwater Explorers Society (UN-EXCO), 373-1244, 800-992-3484
West End Diving Center, 373-1244

ABACO

Brendal's Dive Shop, 367-2572
Island Marine Dive Shop, 367-2014
Dive Abaco, Ltd., 367-2014
Treasure Cay Divers, 305-763-5665 (call collect)
Walker's Cay Dive Shop, 800-223-6961, 305-522-1469

ANDROS

Small Hope Bay Lodge, 368-2014, 800-223-6961, 305-463-9130
Andros Undersea Adventures, 800-327-8150, 305-763-2188

BERRY ISLANDS

Chub Cay Undersea Adventures, 800-327-8150, 305-763-2188

BIMINI

Bimini Undersea Adventures, 800-327-8150, 305-763-2188

CAT ISLAND

Hawk's Nest Club, 800-426-4222, 904-368-2500

ELEUTHERA

Cotton Bay Club, 334-2101, 800-843-2297
Spanish Wells Dive Centre, 332-2645, 800-327-5118

EXUMA

Exuma Aquatics, 336-2600
Exuma Divers, 336-2030

LONG ISLAND

Stella Maris Inn, 336-210

RUM CAY

Rum Cay Club, 305-467-8355 (call collect)

SAN SALVADOR

Island Water Sports, 800-272-1492, 305-761-1492

SPECIAL INFORMATION

DOING BUSINESS

The Bahamas' stable government, strict bank secrecy laws, tax breaks and special government incentives make it attractive to investors from all over the world. Foreign investment is a leading industry, second only to tourism in revenues. In the Bahamas, there are no income, sales, witholding, cor-poration, capital gains, estate or inheritance taxes. The Industries Encouragement Act offers complete exemption from duties and taxes on equipment, raw material, and earnings. The Hotel Encouragement Act and the Agricultural Manufacturers Act also give generous packages of exemptions. Established in 1981, the **Bahamas Agricultural and Industrial Corporation** provides information about investment opportunities and acts as a link between investors and the government.

CHILDREN

Most hotels offer substantial discounts for children, and often children under 12 receive free accommodation in their parents' room. If you are traveling with children, you may find that an apartment or villa complex with cooking facilities is more convenient than a hotel. Some complexes offer lessons in watersports and other activities that children will enjoy. Most hotels and resorts will find a baby-sitter for you if you request one in advance.

FURTHER READING

HISTORY, POLITICS AND PEOPLE

Albury, Hazel I., *Man-O-War, My Island Home*. Holly Press, 1977.

Albury, Paul, *Paradise Island Story*. London: Macmillan Caribbean, 1984.

Albury, Paul, *The Story of the Bahamas*. London: Macmillan Caribbean, 1975.

Barratt, P. J. H., *Grand Bahama*. London: Macmillan Caribbean, 1972.

Bloch, Michael, *The Duke of Windsor's War*. New York: Coward McCann, 1983.

Cartwright, Donald and Saunders, Gail, *Historic Nassau*. London: Macmillan Caribbean, 1979.

Cash, Philip et al, *The Making of the Bahamas: A History for Schools*. London: Collins, 1978.

Craton, Michael, *A History of the Bahamas*. London: Collins, 1962.

Dodge, Steve, *Abaco: The History of an Out Island and its Cays*. Decatur, Illinois: White Sound Press, 1983.

Dupuch, Sir Etienne, *A Salute to Friend and Foe*. Nassau: The Tribune, 1982.

Dupuch, Sir Etienne, *The Tribune Story*. London: Ernest Benn, Ltd.

Eneas, Cleveland W., *Bain Town*. Nassau, 1976.

Hughes, Collin A., *Race and Politics in the Bahamas*. New York: St. Martin's Press, 1981.

Johnston, Randolf W., *Artist on His Island, A Story of Self Reliance*. Park Ridge, New Jersey: Noyes Press.

Malcolm, H., *Historical Documents Relating to the Bahamas Islands*. Gordon Press, 1976.

McCartney, Timothy O., *Neurosis in the Sun*. Nassau: Executive Ideas of the Bahamas, 1971.

Pye, Michael, *The King Over the Water*. London: Hutchinson, 1981.

Riley, Sandra, *Homeward Bound: A History of the Islands to 1850*. Miami: Island Research, 1983.

Russell, S., *Nassau Historic Buildings*. Bahamas National Trust.

Saunders, Gail, *Bahamian Loyalists and Their Slaves*. London: Macmillan Caribbean, 1983.

Saunders, Gail, *Slavery in the Bahamas, 1648-1838*. Nassau, 1985.

Symonette, Michael A., *Discovery of a Nation*. Nassau: Bahamas International Publishing Co.

Thompson, Anthony, *An Economic History of the Bahamas*. Nassau: Commonwealth Publishers, Ltd., 1978.

Williams, Mackey, *A History, A Memoir*. Nassau: Williams Publishing Co., 1984.

Young, Everild, *Eleuthera: The Island Called Freedom*. London: Regency Press, 1966.

Zink, David, *The Stones of Atlantis*. Englewood Cliffs, New Jersey: Prentice Hall, 1978.

NATURAL HISTORY

Brudenell-Bruce, P. G. C., *The Birds of New Providence and the Bahama Islands*. London: Collins, 1975.

Campbell, David G., *The Ephemeral Islands: A Natural History of the Bahamas*. London: Macmillan Education, 1978.

Carstarphen, Dee, *The Conch Book, All You Ever Wanted to Know About the Queen Conch from Gestation to Gastronomy*. Pen & Ink Press, 1982.

Catesby, Mark, *Natural History of Carolina, Florida and the Bahama Islands*. Johnson Reproductions.

Correll, Drs. Donovan and Helen, *Flora of the Bahama Archipelago, including the Turks and Caicos Islands*. Monticello, New York: Lubrecht & Cramer, 1983.

Greenberg, Idaz, *Guide to Corals and Fishes*. Miami: Seahawk Press.

Hannau, Hans, *Tropical Flowers of the Bahamas*. Miami.

Hardie, Lawrence A. *A Sedimentation of the Modern Carbonate Tidal Flats of Northwest Andros Island, Bahamas*. Baltimore: John Hopkins University Studies in Geology, 1977.

Lennox, G. W. and Seddon, S. A., *Flowers of the Caribbean: The Bahamas and Bermuda*. London: Macmillan Caribbean, 1980.

Lennox, G. W. and Seddon, S. A., *Trees of the Caribbean: The Bahamas and Bermuda*. London: Macmillan Caribbean, 1980.

Patterson, Jack and Stevenson, George, *Native Trees of the Bahamas*. Hope Town, Abaco, Bahamas.

Wiedenmeyer, Felix, *Shallow Water Sponges of the Western Bahamas*. Stuttgart, West Germany: Birkhauser Verlage.

PHOTOGRAPHY

Hannau, Hans W., *The Caribbean Islands in Full Color*. New York: Doubleday, 1972.

Hannau, Hans W., *Islands of the Bahamas in Full Color*. New York, 1971.

SPORTS

Cohen, Shlomo, *Bahamas Diver's Guide*. Tel Aviv: Seapen Books, 1977.

Smith, Frank K., *Flying in the Bahamas: The Weekend Pilot's Guide*. TAB Books, 1983.

Wilensky, Julius M., *Cruising Guide to the Abacos and the Northern Bahamas*. Wescott Cove, 1980.

Yachtsman's Guide to the Bahamas.

Miami: Tropic Isle Publishers, Inc. Updated annually.

FOOD

Mendelson, Marie and Sawyer, Marguerite, *Gourmet Bahamian Cooking*. Green Turtle Cay, Abaco, Bahamas, 1985.

St. Andrew's School Committee, *It's Cookin' in the Bahamas*. Nassau, 1983.

Williams, Cindy, *Bahamian Cookery*. Boynton Beach, Florida: Star Publishing Co., 1976.

LANGUAGE

Holm, John A. and Shilling, Alison W., *The Dictionary of Bahamian English*. New York: Lexik House, 1982.

RELIGION & FOLKLORE

Crawley, Daniel J., *I Could Talk Old-Story Good: Creativity in Bahamian Folklore*. Berkeley: University of California Press, 1966.

Eneas, W., *Let the Church Roll On: A Collection of Speech and Writings*. Nassau.

Higgs, Leslie, *Bush Medicine in the Bahamas*. Nassau: Bahamas Nassau Guardian, 1969.

McCartney, Timothy O., *Ten Ten the Bible Ten*. Nassau.

FICTION & POETRY

Bagley, Desmond, *Bahama Crisis*. London: Collins, 1980.

College of the Bahamas, *Bahamian Anthology*. London: Macmillan Caribbean, 1983.

Culmer, Jack, ed., *A Book of Bahamian Verse*. Gordon Press, 1977.

Hemingway, Ernest, *Islands in the Stream*. New York: Charles Scribner & Sons.

Johnstone, Wilhelmina Kemp, *Bahamian Jottings: Poems and Prose*. Nassau: Bruce Publishing Co., 1973.

Norton, Andre, *The Opal Eyed Fan*. New York, 1977.

Ryan, Dennis, *Bahamas: In a White Coming On*. Ardmore, Pennsylvania: Dorrance & Co., 1981.

GENERAL

Bahamas Business Guide. Nassau: Commonwealth Publications, 1979.

Bahamas Handbook and Businessman's Annual. Nassau: Etienne Dupuch, Jr. Publications. Updated annually.

Bregenzer, John, *Tryin' to make It: Adapting to the Bahamas*. Washington, D.C.: University Press of America, 1982.

Evans, F. C. and Young, N., *The Bahamas*. New York: Cambridge University Press, 1977.

Hunte, George, *The Bahamas*. London, 1975.

Ives, Charles, *The Isles of Summer: Or Nassau and the Bahamas*. Elliots Books, reprint of 1880 edition.

Kline, H., *Bahama Islands*. New York: Charles Scribner & Sons.

Northcroft, G. J., *Sketches of Summerland: Nassau and the Bahama Islands*. Gordon Press, 1976.

Robinson, Bill, *South to the Caribbean*. New York: W.W. Norton & Co., 1982.

Saunders, Gail, *The Bahamas: A Family of Islands*. London: Macmillan Caribbean.

Saunders, Gail, and Cartwright, D., *Historic Nassau*. London: Macmillan Caribbean.

Schoepf, Johann D., *Travels in the Confederation, 1783-1784*. Ben Franklin, 1968. Reprint of 1911 edition.

Secondary School Atlas for the Commonwealth of the Bahamas. Ministry of Education, Bahamas. Kingston, Jamaica: Kingston Publishers.

USEFUL ADDRESSES

EMBASSIES & CONSULATES

A few of the represented governments are:

Canada: Honorary Consul Donald G. Joss, Out Island Traders Building, Nassau,

393-2123 (office hours), 393-2124 (after hours)

France: Honorary Consul Irene Hoyningen-Huene, P.O. Box 11132, Nassau, 326-5061

Germany: Honorary Consul Ernst Brokmeier, P.O. Box N-3035, Nassau, 323-2156 (business), 325-1230 (residence)

Haiti: The Haitian Embassy, 7th Terrace and West Avenue, Nassau, 326-0325, 326-0931

Israel: The Honorable Ralph D. Seligman, Lyford Cay, P.O. Box N-7776, Nassau, 362-4421, 323-7276

Japan: Honorary Consul Basil Sands, P. O. Box N-4665, Nassau, 322-8560 (office), 324-2391 (residence)

Norway, Denmark: Honorary Consul Berlin W. Key, P.O. Box N-4005, Nassau, 322-1340 (office), 322-2359 (residence)

Sweden: Honorary Consul Anders Wiberg, P.O. Box N-8333, Nassau, 327-7944, 327-7785

United Kingdom: British High Commission, Bitco Building, East Street, Nassau, 325-7471 (emergency only, after hours, 323-4286)

United States of America Embassy: Queen Street, P.O. Box N-8197, 322-1181.

Art/Photo Credits

Ping Amranand	Cover, 3, 5, 6/7, 8/9, 10/11, 12/13, 14, 29, 50/51, 52/53, 54/55, 56, 59R, 60, 61, 62L, 63, 65, 66/67, 68, 73, 74, 78-79, 80/81, 82, 86/87, 88, 90/91, 96L, 96R, 97, 98, 99, 100, 101L, 101R, 102, 103, 104, 105, 106, 107, 108, 110, 111, 112, 113, 114, 115, 116, 117, 118, 120, 122, 123, 124, 125, 126/127, 128/129, 130, 132, 133, 135, 136, 137, 138L, 139, 140, 141, 142, 143, 146, 147, 150/151, 152/153, 154/ 155, 156, 157, 158/159, 160, 161, 162, 163, 164, 165L, 165R, 166, 167, 170/171, 174, 175R, 176, 177, 179, 180, 181, 182/ 183, 184, 186, 187R, 188, 189, 190, 191, 192, 193, 194/195, 206, 207, 208, 209, 210, 211, 212, 213, 214L, 215, 216, 217, 218, 219, 224/225, 229, 241, 249, 250, 258
Tony Arruza	236/237, 252, 255, 257
Moira Attrill	231
Roderick Attrill	230, 232
Bahamas Historical Society	25, 26, 28, 31, 36
Bahamas News Bureau	22, 27, 46, 47, 49, 265
Balmain Antiques	16/17, 18, 20, 21, 23, 32, 33, 34, 35, 37, 92/93, 226, 248
Maxine Cass	24, 43, 168, 169
Department of Archives, Nassau	39, 40/41, 214R
Fernandez Bay Village Resort	196
Stephen Frink	72, 75, 119, 138R, 148, 242, 243, 244L, 244R, 245, 246, 247
Donald Gerace	204
Courtesy of Graham Groves	145
Bob Krist	62R, 202L, 202R, 203, 220, 221, 228, 233
Courtesy of the artist, R. Brent Malone	266/267
Nassau Public Library	70
Susan Pierres	48, 59L, 172, 178
Kathy Pursel	197, 199, 201, 222, 223
The Tribune, Nassau	42, 44, 45
Tony Stone Worldwide	76/77, 121, 149, 234/235, 238/239, 240
Stanley Toogood	38, 71
Sara Whittier	198
Deborah Williams	205

INDEX

C

D

E

T

B
C
D
E
F
G
H
I
J
a
b
c
d
e
f
g
h
j
k
l